MANAGEMENT, WORK AND ORGANISATIONS

Series editors:
Gibson Burrell, The Management Centre, University of Leicester
Mick Marchington, Manchester Business School
Paul Thompson, Department of Human Resource Management,
University of Strathclyde

This series of new textbooks covers the areas of human resource management, employee relations, organisational behaviour and related business and management fields. Each text has been specially commissioned to be written by leading experts in a clear and accessible way. The books contain serious and challenging material, take an analytical rather than prescriptive approach and are particularly suitable for use by students with no prior specialist knowledge.

The series is relevant for many business and management courses, including MBA and post-experience courses, specialist masters and postgraduate diplomas, professional courses and final-year undergraduate courses. These texts have become essential reading at business and management schools worldwide.

Published

Peter Boxall and John Purcell
STRATEGY AND HUMAN RESOURCE MANAGEMENT

Paul Blyton and Peter Turnbull
THE DYNAMICS OF EMPLOYEE RELATIONS (3rd edn)

Irena Grugulis
SKILLS, TRAINING AND HUMAN RESOURCE DEVELOPMENT

Karen Legge
HUMAN RESOURCE MANAGEMENT: anniversary edition

Hugh Scullion and Margaret Linehan
INTERNATIONAL HUMAN RESOURCE MANAGEMENT

Damien Hodgson and Svetlana Cicmil
MAKING PROJECTS CRITICAL

Sharon C. Bolton
EMOTION MANAGEMENT IN THE WORKPLACE

Keith Grint
LEADERSHIP

Jill Rubery and Damian Grimshaw
THE ORGANISATION OF EMPLOYMENT

Marek Korczynski
HUMAN RESOURCE MANAGEMENT IN SERVICE WORK

J. Martin Corbett
CRITICAL CASES IN ORGANISATIONAL BEHAVIOUR

Helen Rainbird (ed.)
TRAINING IN THE WORKPLACE

Harry Scarbrough (ed.)
THE MANAGEMENT OF EXPERTISE

Diana Winstanley and Jean Woodall (eds)
ETHICAL ISSUES IN CONTEMPORARY HUMAN RESOURCE MANAGEMENT

Adrian Wilkinson, Mick Marchington, Tom Redman and Ed Snape
MANAGING WITH TOTAL QUALITY MANAGEMENT

D0218180

For more information on titles in the Series please go to www.palgrave.com/business/mwo

Invitation to authors

The Series Editors welcome proposals for new books within the Management, Work and Organisations Series. These should be sent to Paul Thompson (p.thompson@strath.ac.uk) at the Dept of HRM, Strathclyde Business School, University of Strathclyde, 50 Richmond St, Glasgow G1 1XT

Series Standing Order

If you would like to receive future titles in this series as they are published, you can make use of our standing order facility. To place a standing order please contact your bookseller or, in case of difficulty, write to us at the address below with your name and address and the name of the series. Please state with which title you wish to begin your standing order.

Customer Services Department, Macmillan Distribution Ltd
Houndmills, Basingstoke, Hampshire RG21 6XS, England

Praise for *Skills, Training and Human Resource Development*

'The skills debate has raged for many years throughout the world. As governments have seemingly accepted the view that education and training policy has to produce the skills that will grow modern economies, a powerful critique of the role of skills and of these policies has emerged. This is the book we have been waiting for that finally pulls together the disparate threads of this critique into a coherent and integrated whole. Professor Grugulis has written a masterly and very lucid account of the role of skills and the changing nature of work in 21st century society. This is a book that deserves to be widely read by scholars, students and policy makers everywhere. This book will be a classic.' – **Professor Andy Smith**, *Head, School of Commerce, Charles Sturt University, Australia*

'At last, an HRD textbook that moves beyond the bland, standardised "best practice" prescriptions and locates skill within the complex contexts of work organisation, job design and employment relations. Grugulis makes a compelling case for seeing HRD and skill information as one component within wider organisational and competitive strategies.' – **Professor Ewart Keep**, *Deputy Director, ESRC Centre on Skills, Knowledge and Organisational Performance, School of Social Sciences, University of Cardiff, UK*

'Irena Grugulis skilfully examines studies of HR development and addresses new issues including knowledge work, emotional/aesthetic labour and the rise of soft skills. A most stimulating text. Highly recommended.' – **Dr Stephen Bach**, *Reader in Employment Relations and Management, King's College London, UK*

'[Grugulis's text] is an impressively rich exploration of the nature of skill, the changing contexts of learning and knowledge at work and the management of people in contemporary organisational contexts. It was a pleasure to read, and it is good to see the various debates and arguments that are often largely developed in various journals brought together into a book form.' – **Claire Valentin**, *Higher and Community Education, The Moray House School of Education, The University of Edinburgh, UK*

'. . . one of the most innovative and exciting texts in human resource management for a long time. A book that will make a major impact.' – **John Hassard**, *Professor of Organisational Analysis, Manchester Business School, UK*

'An excellent and well-written book full of rich insights and examples. A stimulating "must read".' – **Professor Adrian Wilkinson**, *Department of Industrial Relations, Griffith Business School, Queensland, Australia*

Skills, Training and Human Resource Development

A Critical Text

Irena Grugulis

First published 2007 by
PALGRAVE MACMILLAN
Houndmills, Basingstoke, Hampshire RG21 6XS and
175 Fifth Avenue, New York, N.Y. 10010
Companies and representatives throughout the world

PALGRAVE MACMILLAN is the global academic imprint of the Palgrave
Macmillan division of St. Martin's Press, LLC and of Palgrave Macmillan Ltd.
Macmillan® is a registered trademark in the United States, United Kingdom
and other countries. Palgrave is a registered trademark in the European
Union and other countries.

ISBN-13: 978–1–4039–4802–1
ISBN 10: 1–4039–4802–X

This book is printed on paper suitable for recycling and
made from fully managed and sustained forest sources.

A catalogue record for this book is available from the British Library.

A catalog record for this book is available from the Library of Congress.

10   9   8   7   6   5   4   3   2   1
16   15   14   13   12   11   10   09   08   07

Printed in China

To mum, dad, Lin, Shaun and Daniel with love

Contents

Preface

Skills, training and human resource development are key aspects of economic life. They feature heavily in organisational rhetoric (investing in people; people are our greatest asset) and form an important part of governmental aims and targets (the knowledge society). Few people, of whatever political persuasion, doubt the genuine benefits that investing in these areas can bring. Yet the accounts which do nothing but heap praise on training (and there are many of these) do the area a disservice conflating, as they do, the good that *some* developmental activities accomplish with the achievements of *all*. In practice, development is phenomenally varied in structure, content and impact. It can succeed in preparing a person for skilful, creative and autonomous work, increase their earning potential and improve their status in society. It can also confine them to horizontal moves between a series of ill-paid and alienating jobs.

This book, by drawing on some of the excellent empirical studies on skills and training which have been conducted over the last few years, aims to provide a fuller picture of such activities, exploring the regimented and tedious aspects of organisational life as well as the knowledge intensive ones. It also seeks to shift the focus beyond the narrow confines of the training department, course or module, to the nature of skill, work, organisations and societies. This is vitally important if we are to appreciate the nature of the skill in work. After all, firms are not entities designed with the sole aim of supporting the development of their workers. They exist to produce a product or provide a service, to make a profit or fulfil a social need. To do this they may devise strategies or focus on particular markets. Developmental activities for employees will be prioritised or neglected accordingly. Equally, the labour that firms recruit will have varying experiences of education, work and development, so national systems of education, sectoral legacies of vocational training and qualifications, the existence of tertiary bodies to support development and the

ix

relations that exist within and between firms will influence which skills are developed and the way they are put into practice.

Essentially, in order to understand skill we need to understand both work and the context (organisationally, sectorally, nationally) that that work is situated in. What this text seeks to do is provide an account of skills and work in practice. Its focus is always on skills (or the lack of them) in the workplace but in the process it also seeks to integrate the realities of workplace life. These include differences of interest between employers and employees, the disadvantages in the 'labour queue' that can accrue from gender and race, the impact (both positive and negative) that integrating and controlling emotions has and the hopes and prospects held out for knowledge workers in a knowledge society. It aims to be critical in the sense of subjecting these (and other) activities and initiatives to analytical scrutiny, but not to condemn; to observe the differences that exist between rhetoric and reality and to consider how such incongruities affect those subjected to them. I hope it will prove a useful teaching resource. Having already tried out most of the ideas, controversies and cases on my own students I found their responses both stimulating and helpful (and several may recognise their comments, criticisms and discussions in this, the latest version of the material). Thanks are also due to those researchers whose work I have so freely quoted. The writers whose surveys probe the details of employment, who immerse themselves in organisational life and whose theoretical pieces help to explain the complexities of the social world. This area is such a rapidly changing one no work can pretend to be a final word. My hope for this book is that it stimulates further, constructive and critical, debate.

IRENA GRUGULIS

1

Human resource development

Here is a modern myth about work. Contemporary workplaces are peopled by high performing, highly committed individuals, bound together into a common cause by a corporate mission enshrined within a strong organisational culture. Workplaces themselves have been 'transformed' by new technologies, new forms of organisation and a new generation of management thinking that stresses flexibility, quality, teamwork and empowerment. The workers in these establishments are motivated by ambition and a sense of purpose. (Noon and Blyton 1997:1)

'[T]raining', according to Joan Payne, in her 1991 book, *Women, Training and the Skills Shortage*, '. . . is the opposite of sin – everybody is for it.' Governments of all political persuasions, trade unions, employers and their representative bodies, professional associations and employees, if they agree over nothing else, can be reasonably sure of consensus when considering the importance of training, learning and skills. Such harmony is impressive and to a certain extent it is legitimate. Acquiring skills and knowledge can turn round organisations and transform lives. Their possession and effective deployment can provide the basis for both national and organisational competitiveness (Department for Education and Skills/DTI/HM Treasury/Department for Work and Pensions 2003), helping firms to increase productivity and 'value added' (Keep and Mayhew 2001; DfES 2004a; DfES 2004b).

The expertise employees possess is a key element of economic competitiveness (Del Bono and Mayhew 2001; Streeck 1992). When high-quality goods and services are provided, when innovations are introduced or when products are customised it is often the skills of employees that make the difference: developing new products (Attewell 1992), adding value to existing ones (Mason *et al.* 1996); controlling complex processes (Arthur 1999) or providing higher-quality services (Finegold *et al.* 2000).

Given this, training and development may safeguard productivity as well as supporting it, insulating firms from skills shortages by preparing employees for current and future jobs. To a certain extent training and recruitment are mutually substitutable (Keep 1989). When a firm needs skills it may either develop them internally (by training existing staff) or advertise for new workers who possess the required expertise. When jobs can be filled internally, firms are less dependent on the outside labour market and do not run the risk of recruits not being available (or not being available at the price the organisation wishes to pay). Such security is welcome. According to Hillage *et al.* (2002) 8 per cent of employers in England have skill-shortage vacancies and 23 per cent report internal skills gaps (in which not all employees are fully proficient at the work that they do). The problems reported as a result of these gaps include difficulties with customer service, delays developing new products, increases in operating costs, problems introducing new working practices, difficulties with quality standards, the withdrawal of products or services and loss of business (pp. 48, 84).

Within firms skills may affect the way workers are managed; employee development is a key human resource practice and has been described as the 'litmus test' of human resource management (Keep 1989; Felstead and Ashton 2000). When employees' skills are developed, other 'soft' human resource practices such as employee involvement and performance-based pay are both appropriate and more likely to be effective since they encourage and reward staff for using their skills. In the absence of training, in organisations that do not develop individual skills nor encourage individual contributions, such practices are less relevant (Keep and Mayhew 1996).

Skills may also benefit employees. For trade unions and professional associations, training enhances members' expertise, facilitating negotiations for pay and status. Unsurprisingly perhaps these bodies have been among the most enthusiastic supporters of training and accreditation (Keep 1994; Heyes and

Stuart 1998; Rainbird 1990). There are individual benefits too, and people can gain knowledge that is intrinsically valuable as well as portable credentials to facilitate progress in the labour market. Earnings will be higher, periods of unemployment are both less likely and less lengthy, work is likely to be more interesting and, given this higher pay, higher status and better prospects, job satisfaction is also likely to be higher (Dearden *et al.* 2000; Rose 2005).

In addition to these substantive factors, training and development also serves an important and very positive symbolic function. Everything a firm does sends messages (of one kind or another) to its employees (Purcell 1979). Organisations that spend money on raising skills are, quite literally, investing in their workers. Employees who participate in firm-sponsored training are more likely to say they have better career prospects and intend to stay with their employer than those who do not (Heyes and Stuart 1996) – a finding that raises interesting questions on current discussions about 'employability' as a substitute for employment security.

The realities of training

Small wonder then that consensus exists in this area, that governments, employers and individual workers report favourable attitudes towards training and development and exhort everyone involved to ever higher levels of activity (Skills Task Force 1999; CEML 2002; DfES 2004a; DfES 2004b). Given these positive attitudes, and given the tangible benefits to be gained we might expect to see extensive training and development. Yet, in Britain at least, participation lags far behind support. It is not that employers and employees are not aware of the advantages of training and development. They are. They simply choose not to engage in it (Matlay 1998). Some firms and sectors do do a great deal of training and development and do it extremely well but others are much less active. The *National Employers Skills Survey* (IFF 2004), which attempts to put figures on the amount industry sectors spend per employee, brings out these differences. It ranks Computing and Related as the highest-spending sector at £668 per employee per annum, but this impressive figure is more than double the £324 spent by Professional Services, the next most generous funder of developmental activities. Of the 27 sectors collated, only 10 spent more than £200 per worker and Textiles and Clothing spent a miserly £81 (pp. 144–5). Such figures need to be treated with caution since British firms are not required to keep records of the monies spent on training and development and estimates are notoriously inaccurate (Coopers and Lybrand Associates 1985; Keep *et al.* 2002).

It seems likely that these figures err on the side of generosity and that participation is lower than suggested here (surveys of training and development tend to overstate activity for a number of reasons, including the very simple fact that firms which do not train and develop staff tend not to respond to surveys about training and development). According to the Labour Force Survey, which covers a wide range of work-related issues and attempts to represent the whole labour force, 16.2 per cent of workers in Britain received either on- or off-the-job training in 2005 (Labour Force Survey 2005). This is a substantial improvement on the 7 per cent recorded in spring 1985; however, while participation rates have nearly doubled overall spend has not, and much of the reported increase can be attributed to the same amount of effort being spread rather more thinly, funding more and shorter courses (Finegold 1991; Ashton and Felstead 1995; Spilsbury 2001). Clearly, duration is not a proxy for quality, but it is unlikely that fundamental changes to the skills base can be achieved when programmes are short.

The experience of training is also unevenly distributed. While 14 per cent of managers and 25 per cent of professionals receive training, participation rates for process, plant and machine operatives are only 6.5 per cent (Cully *et al.* 1999). This suggests that, as in the USA, access to training is polarised with workers who are already highly educated having greater opportunities for further participation (Rubery and Grimshaw 2003). There is also evidence in

---

Box 1.2

Expansive and restrictive approaches to training and development
Systemic approaches to training and development can also be observed *within* firms. One manufacturer of bathroom showers, described by Fuller and Unwin (2004), took an *expansive* approach to development. It had a long-established apprenticeship programme and many ex-apprentices had progressed to senior management. Apprentices were rotated around different departments to gain wider knowledge of the business and improve their skills. They also attended college on day release, working towards knowledge-based qualifications which would give them access to higher education, went on residential courses designed to foster team-working and were involved with local charities through the company's apprenticeship association. Contrast this with the *restrictive* environment of a small steel-polishing company where apprentices had been reluctantly taken on only when managers were unable to recruit qualified staff. After less than a year, the two apprentices who had learned on the job had gained all the skills necessary for their work. There was no system of job rotation and formal training was limited to ten half-day courses on steel industry awareness (the sum total of the apprentices' outside involvement) and an NVQ.

Taken from Fuller and Unwin (2004b).

Britain of a division between the *types* of training offered, with developmental training concentrated on those who are already highly educated while narrow and restrictive programmes are targeted at those disadvantaged in the labour market (Young 2001; Grugulis 2003).

Reinforcing this, the two types of training most commonly funded by employers are health and safety and induction, a factor that may explain why temporary workers are more likely to receive training than their permanent colleagues (20 per cent as opposed to 15 per cent; DfES 2003:63). Heyes and Gray (2003), in their survey of SMEs after the introduction of the national minimum wage, found that training spend had risen, but that this was because employers were hiring younger (and cheaper) workers rather than upskilling existing staff. Clearly it is important that workplaces are healthy and safe places to be and that new recruits receive adequate induction. However it is highly unlikely that such forms of training will affect productivity, product quality or individual career development.

Reasons *not* to train and develop

Even given this proviso, such a low level of activity seems, at best, irrational. If employers, employees and the state all benefit from training and development then it would seem to be in their interest to fund it and to ensure that when one party fails to provide high-quality training the others make up for this omission. Yet this behaviour may not be quite as unreasonable as it first appears. Training and development does not occur in a vacuum, rather it is one aspect of an organisation's activities and exists to support the others. As Keep and Mayhew (1999) argue, training is a third-order issue, following on from decisions about competitiveness, product specification and job design (see also Wensley 1999). For organisations that choose to compete on the basis of quality, highly skilled workers are essential; for ones that compete on cost, they are an unjustifiable extravagance – and large sections of the British economy still compete on cost (Finegold and Soskice 1988; Bach and Sisson 2000; Bach 2005). The second reason, related to the first, is that many jobs are designed to be tightly controlled, with employee discretion (and with it skill) taken away. One employer, interviewed by Dench *et al.* (1999), said that their ideal worker had two arms and two legs. When this is what jobs demand, it is difficult to see how training will help.

Then too, most job growth seems to be concentrated in areas which have had little history of training and development. Small and medium-sized enterprises (SMEs) are an 'engine' of job creation and a great deal of official effort has been put into supporting activity here and encouraging entrepreneurship. Admittedly much of this job growth can be accounted for by 'churn', since

SMEs are also likely to go bankrupt or make staff redundant, but still SMEs do account for a growing proportion of people in employment (Dundon *et al.* 2001; Noon and Blyton 2002). In terms of training and development this is not good news since SMEs are significantly less likely to train staff than large firms or public sector organisations (Matlay 1998; Cully *et al.* 1999).

There has also been a massive structural change over the last half-century, shifting employment in most of the developed world away from manufacturing and towards services. In the United States, McDonald's now boasts more employees than US Steel (Macdonald and Sirianni 1996), while in Britain 79 per cent of jobs are located in the service sector (National Statistics 2005:22). In 1967, 38 per cent of people in work (some 8.591 million) were employed in manufacturing in Britain (Employment and Productivity Gazette 1968). By 2005 numbers working in this sector had more than halved, to 3.5 million (National Statistics 2005). Service work includes many of the most highly skilled and knowledgeable workers such as medics, teachers and IT professionals but it also covers care workers, security staff and personal services, who are far more numerous and whose numbers are rising far faster than those of the 'knowledge workers'. Manufacturing jobs tended to be full-time, unionised, undertaken by men and often well paid. Service sector work tends to be part-time, non-unionised, poorly paid and done by women or young people. Few have access to the sort of skills development and career ladders that will enable them to progress and many of the jobs are designed to limit the skills used.

This need not be the case. McGauran's (2000; 2001) research into retail work in France and Ireland shows how French employers expect their workers to be experts in the products sold and French customers request advice on products and product care when shopping. However, it is not clear that this skilled variant of shop work influences behaviour elsewhere. Rather, pressure for hyperflexibility, described by Gadrey (2000:26) as 'tantamount to a personnel strategy based on zero competence', zero qualifications, zero training and zero career, means that retail work is dominated by poorly paid part-time workers and the flexibility demanded of them is availability for shift work at short notice. In Germany, this is threatening long established traditions of training and qualifications as employers avoid training employees, since this would make them expensive to hire, and rely instead on large numbers of low-paid staff supported by small numbers of highly skilled 'anchor' workers (Kirsch *et al.* 2000).

Training and performance

It seems that, from the evidence above, *not* developing staff is an entirely rational response to certain labour market conditions or strategic choices. Firms compete on cost, jobs are designed to demand few or no skills and job growth is concentrated in sectors that tend not to train or in firms that cannot afford to do so. Yet despite this, one of the most commonly repeated management truisms is that there is a link between training and performance, that productivity, profits and quality can all be boosted by increasing training or by focusing on the right training. Such a link certainly makes intuitive sense. After all, well-trained experienced workers will outperform novices, and at a national level Britain's lack of vocational preparation is consistently cited as one of the main reasons for its underperformance. Manufacturing productivity in the US is 81 per cent higher than in the UK, in Germany is 59 per cent higher and in Sweden 72 per cent (Nolan and Slater 2003).

However, within firms proof is much harder to gather. Employers certainly believe in the links between training, performance and profitability (Coopers and Lybrand Associates 1985; DTZ Pieda Consulting 1999) and many surveys on the connections between various employment practices and performance cite training and development as a key activity (see, for example Huselid 1995; Huselid and Becker 1996; Ichniowski et al. 1997). Few of these studies, though, measure the same practices or define productivity or performance in the same ways (Grugulis and Stoyanova 2005) and, even when the same aspects of employment are surveyed, there is a great deal of difference between the ways individual organisations implement practices (Bacon 1999).

To make this issue more confusing, organisations may use training as a means to escape from an economic downturn – increasing spending when profit levels are low – or deploy it symbolically, to motivate and reward. From the perspective of encouraging training and development, both of these approaches are welcome; but they do cause problems for academics attempting to establish links between an organisation's training activities and its performance. Then too, official measures of training success such as increases in employment (a factor of key interest to governments) may be less welcomed by individual organisations whose managers are more concerned with the impact practices have on profitability and share price (for a fuller discussion of these issues see Keep et al. 2002).

What is training and development?

Yet crucially, what most of these accounts neglect is the fact that the words 'training' and 'development' cover a multitude of sins. Three years of professional examinations and guided practice for an accountancy qualification count, but so too do the quizzes and team games organised by the call centre team leaders in Kinnie et al.'s (2000) study. Courses leading to qualifications in management, plumbing, electrical engineering and design count; but so does basic induction, in which the new recruit is shown their desk and the coffee machine; and so does a workshop on health and safety.

Training and development may pass on information on organisational events, it may introduce workers to new workplaces, products or practices and it may provide a source of entertainment that distracts from monotonous routines. It may also build employee skills or increase organisational capacity. But not all forms of development have all these objectives, which themselves are far from uniform – not least because there may be a great deal of difference between training that boosts employees' skills and that which develops organisational capacity. Two examples may help to illustrate this. Becoming a doctor requires many years of dedicated study. Prospective medics are required to enrol on an accredited university course, provision is limited and competition for places fierce. While on these courses student doctors have no income and may be expected to pay high fees. The education and professional training they gain during their degrees provides them with a sound knowledge of medicine and this is supplemented by several years of guided work experience during which individuals may choose to specialise in particular branches of the subject, a choice that may require further study. Once qualified, doctors enjoy high earnings and high status. At the other end of the skills spectrum is the training provided for call centre workers. In some call centres, if a customer service representative lets their voice drop during a telephone conversation and this is noted by their supervisor, they may be sent to a half-day workshop to learn how to keep their voice tone and tempo even (Callaghan and Thompson 2002). The training is short and the lessons it teaches may be useful for the call centre but they confer little advantage on the individual worker who gains no pay, no status and no skills.

Training can be developmental. It can equip workers with skills that give them power in the labour market, improve their career prospects and add considerably to their lifetime earnings. But none of these results are inevitable and it would be naïve to assume that all forms of training take us one step closer to a knowledge based economy. Different types of training advantage different parties to the employment relationship (see, for example Payne 1991;

Box 1.3

[A]ccreditation for clerical training is not transferable: it is not developmental, does not accumulate, and does not assist individuals in progressing either through clerical occupations or into other occupational areas.

Metropolitan Toronto Clerical Workers' Labour Appointment Committee, cited in de Wolff and Hynes (2003:35).

Peck 1993; Mole 1996; Keep 1999; Mole 2004). Advantage may be shared, as in professional qualifications, or it may be unequal, as for the call centre worker.

Such a conclusion may be self-evident but it rarely enters discussions of human resource development, which tend to adopt a *unitarist* perspective on the employment relationship. This view assumes that that the interests of managers and workers are identical (Fox 1966). Those who hold it may describe the workplace as a team, with managers as coaches and lower-ranking employees as players. However, such a consensus is often assumed to exist because workers will agree with and adopt management's views, rather than management agreeing with workers' views. A *pluralist* frame of reference, by contrast, assumes that the workplace has a 'babel of different voices' (Cully *et al.* 1999), that people who work together may agree over some things but not all, and that while the interests of managers and workers may coincide they may also differ. In the unitarist frame of reference conflict is pathological, in the pluralist one it is inevitable.

The implications of this for training and development are significant. When a unitarist perspective is adopted, any developmental process that benefits the firm must also benefit the employee. So the unfortunate call centre workers being taught to control their voices are assumed to be gaining from this process because their interests are the same as those of the call centre. From a pluralist frame of reference their complaints, misbehaviour and resistance are legitimate, because their interests differ from those of their employer (Ackroyd and Thompson 1999; Callaghan and Thompson 2002; Korczynski 2002).

Clearly the description of these two frames of reference are simplifications. Most workers when asked say that they are on the same side as managers and overt conflict is rare. But interests do not entirely coincide, and it may be extremely difficult to secure agreement over what constitutes 'a fair day's work for a fair day's pay'. Employees may seek good terms and conditions, pleasant work colleagues, interesting work and good prospects for promotion. Employers may seek to maximise profits, produce more or better goods, enter new markets or reduce costs. There is a partial, rather than a complete, coincidence of interest (for a more detailed discussion of unitarism and pluralism see Edwards 2003:10–13).

Just as the interests of employers and employees may differ so the power relations in work are unequal, and Tesco or Wal-Mart or Aldi have far greater power than any Ms Smith, Mr Jones or Herr Fischer who work for them. When an employee signs an employment contract they allow an employer to give them orders. Moreover the consequences of not gaining paid employment are far more severe for an individual, who may be deprived of income, a source of identity and status and access to social networks, than they are for an employer, who may suffer inconvenience because a post has remained unfilled (Allen 1997; Brown 1997). However, while power relations are unequal this exchange is not one-way. An employer is not guaranteed that a job will be done simply because they hire someone to do it and they certainly are not guaranteed that it will be done well. Even when an employee has the necessary skills, competence or capacity to perform a task they may choose not to do so, and most management systems are divided between attempts to secure workers' commitment so that they are motivated to act and processes for controlling work so that employees can be restrained from undesirable activity and compelled to follow procedures.

Nor is it accurate to depict the workplace as an area where antagonism is inevitable. Conflict may be a natural part of the employment relationship, but so is cooperation (Edwards 2001). Most workers say that even if they were financially secure and did not need to earn money they would continue to work (Noon and Blyton 2002). While studies of workplaces show how often employees approach their tasks with enthusiasm, gaining identity from occupation (Kidder 1981; Casey 1995), taking pride in doing tasks well (Burawoy 1979) and resenting being given too little work as much as being given too much (Edwards, Collinson and Rees 1998). The workplace is a contested terrain in which activities and structures are not neutral and may create both advantage and disadvantage for those who work with them (Edwards 1979) but it is also the site of cooperation and enthusiasm.

Human resource development and developing resourceful humans

This understanding of the nature of work has implications for human resource development. Rigorous studies of human resource management have always been careful to locate their findings in accounts of the workplace as a whole. Human resource management involves empowerment, ethics, diversity, downsizing, team-working, discipline, the nature of 'good' and 'bad' jobs, performance management and customer service, among many other topics (Legge 1995; Redman and Wilkinson 2001; Bach 2005). It includes the work of the personnel or the human resource function (Buyens and De Vos 2001) but it is by no means limited to that. This is not to detract from the work of human resource professionals. Rather it is an acknowledgement that, given the list of areas of interest, confining attention to one specialist unit in the organisation would do little to help analysis.

Yet while human resource management requires the study of the individual, the whole of the organisation and the various national systems each is located in, human resource development's purview is often confined to the human resource development department. Not only does considering courses and qualifications in isolation tell us little about the development of resource-ful humans; it also (ironically) makes it extremely difficult to judge the value of the very activities observed. The most talented chef in the world could be put to work in McDonald's and would be so constrained by the regulations that their burgers would be indistinguishable from those of their colleagues. The most inspirational training programme, when accompanied by news of redundancies or wage cuts (unfortunate coincidences of timing which do happen in reality; see, for example, Keenoy and Anthony 1992; Grugulis and Wilkinson 2002), is unlikely to prove effective. The training function is impor-tant, as the personnel function is, but we cannot understand the way skills are developed or people are motivated to action by restricting our attention to their activities.

Accordingly, what this book seeks to do is to focus on the development of resourceful humans. It acknowledges the fact that organisations may seek to exploit as much as they empower; that the skills and expertise of individual workers may be the central pillar of organisational strategies, but may also be its unwitting beneficiaries or its collateral damage; and that the existence of some well-treated highly skilled workers in an organisation does not guaran-tee that all enjoy such terms and conditions. Each individual chapter engages with the ideas and structures underlying human resource development and makes extensive use of research to provide a picture of current practice.

Structure of the book

Chapter 2 provides a detailed discussion of one of the most fundamental ideas underlying human resource development, namely skill. Skill can be part of a person, part of a job or part of the social setting. Changes to any of these, such as the introduction of new technology or work reorganisation, can impact on what skills are developed and demanded (often in unpredictable ways). Moreover, because judging and accrediting skill is a social as well as a techni-cal process it is vulnerable to the prejudices and preconceptions of any social interaction. An assessment of an individual's skill may depend on their status in the labour market. So skills possessed by women may not be rated as highly as those possessed by white men.

Chapter 3 explores the ways different national systems of vocational educa-tion and training (VET) and employment affect both the skills developed and the ways these can be exercised. It describes the differences between volun-tarist and regulated systems and provides some detail about the way factors such as employment security and cooperative industrial relations contribute to skills development. In particular it contrasts the experience of VET in regu-lated economies with that in ones where actions are voluntary and the 'hidden hand of the market' is deemed to set required activity levels before going on to discuss the way labour market innovations can shape both the supply of skills, and the demand for them.

Chapter 4 deals with the British experience of vocational education and training in more detail. Britain is, at least notionally, a voluntarist economy but an awareness of the importance of skills, together with a repeated lack of employer activities, has resulted in extensive state intervention and subsidy. This chapter considers the impact of education, NVQs and Investors in People and the prospects for future activities.

The supply and demand for skills is also affected by the changing nature of work, particularly the shift from manufacturing to service-based employment. This has implications for the way nations compete and the nature of economies but it also directly affects the work people do, how they are expected to do it and the way work is controlled. Traditionally, when tangible goods are being produced, management's efforts and energies are directed towards that production. They may regulate the quality and speed and safety of work (see, for example Roy 1958; Beynon 1975; Burawoy 1979; Pollert 1981), but little emphasis is put on the way workers feel. In the service sector, where customers visit restaurants for attentive service as well as good food, the process of being served is as much a part of the sale as the product or service being purchased, so this 'shadow side' of employment (Edwards 1995) starts to attract management attention. It affects the way work is controlled and the way workers are expected to feel.

As a result, the skills employers demand also change, as does the definition of skill itself, an issue dealt with in Chapter 5. In the 1950s accounts of skill focused on technical know-how, manual dexterity and spatial awareness. By the 1970s personal attributes and qualities such as loyalty, punctuality or communication started to appear under the label 'skills'. Today these traits dominate skill lists. Many are not new – after all, employers have long demanded loyalty from those they hire – but calling them skills has some very worrying implications. Chapter 5 queries the extent to which such qualities are skills or are generic and draws out the extent to which the search for these qualities is overshadowed by the pursuit of 'whiteness, maleness and middle classness' (Ainley 1994:80).

Many of the prejudices observed in valuing these new soft skills simply mirror the way women and ethnic minorities with technical skills are treated. But there is also a significant difference. The acquisition of technical skills confers labour market power on the individual worker. The possession of skills helps in the search for work and adds to earnings. Soft skills are rather more precarious, significantly more difficult to transfer and confer value only to the extent that they are acknowledged and admired by employers. The implications for those who possess them are worrying.

Chapter 6 continues to look at these changing workplace demands as it deals with the way that work incorporates emotions and aesthetics – how workers feel and the way they look. Significantly, when emotions are part of the work-effort bargain, when they are directed, controlled and limited by others, they may become more of a pain than a pleasure. Workers still can and do enjoy genuine emotional interactions with customers, they still can and do resist or ignore managerial prescriptions about work, but when work involves expressing emotions, such expression often becomes a chore and workers may find it difficult later to deal with emotions that are not bought and sold.

Organisations may also seek to manage their cultures, controlling, dictating or guiding what employees believe so that they can secure loyalty and commitment. Such an approach certainly resolves the traditional control–commitment dilemma, but by designing a different type of control system rather by offering freedom from control. Managing culture can go hand in hand with a considerable degree of job autonomy and this affective commitment is a long established way of securing loyalty from managerial and professional workers whose work is by its nature hard to control (see for example Barnard 1962; Dalton 1966; Watson 1994). Chapter 7 reviews the successes and failures of managing culture and, most importantly, the reasons behind them. It explores empowerment programmes and the troubling and elusive link between controlling culture and firm performance.

Chapter 8 takes another section of the workforce, namely leaders and managers, considers what they do (and which aspects of that work are specifically leader-like or managerial) and draws out the lessons for management and leadership development. This is a key occupational group. They control resources and influence organisational decisions. But they are also extremely diverse and this diversity has implications for their development.

Chapter 9 deals with knowledge management. This is an area that has attracted a considerable amount of interest, with commentators claiming that there has been a fundamental shift in the economy and most work is now knowledge work. This chapter explores both the myths and the realities. It draws on detailed accounts of knowledge intensive workplaces such as R&D departments, consultancies and advertising agencies, where expertise gives competitive edge and where management practices are self-consciously different and designed to foster the creativity of the prima donnas. But it also distinguishes between such exclusive knowledge-intensive firms and 'knowledgeability in work' where customer service staff, clerks and call centre workers know a great deal about the work they do but where tasks are constrained and discretion is limited.

Finally, Chapter 10 considers the future for human resource development. It asks whether we are moving towards knowledge economies in which knowledge will replace capital as a key element in production (Trist 1974) or whether the skill levels in work are steadily being eroded as tasks are fragmented and controls tightened (Braverman 1974). It finds reasons for optimism, several paradoxes, some continuities and some (not unexpected) problems.

This book attempts to hold a mirror up to practice. It does not seek to portray the workplace as an inevitable site of exploitation where the only relationship possible between employee and employer is mutual antagonism. But nor does it automatically subscribe to the optimistic portrayals which suggest that things can only get better – especially since the evidence suggests that enlightened self-interest has proved particularly ineffective at improving workplace terms and conditions (Thompson 2003). Its aim, fundamentally, is to inform both the theory and practice of human resource development. Training courses, organisational strategies, individual choices and national employment systems should all have as one of their objectives increasing skill levels. For this aim to be achieved all parties to the employment relationship need to be aware of any conflicts of interest as well as any shared hopes.

2

Skills at work

'I've actually got the convenor saying to me, "we've got to watch this multi-skill thing, because it's too interesting for them."' (Managing Director, GKN Hardy Spicer, cited in Hendry, 1993:92)

[S]killed work is work done by skilled men. (Oliver and Turton 1982:196)

The importance of skill is difficult to overstate. Workforce skills play a key role in both quality and productivity levels, and they provide a meritocratic means of deciding pay rates or relative status; also when certified by qualifications, skills give employees labour market power and allow employees and employers to find one another. Yet still, skill is an elusive concept that comes, as Keep (2001:1) wryly notes, with what bomb disposal experts describe as 'anti-handling devices'. The qualifications so valued in recruitment are proxies for skill, rather than skills themselves, and their value stems from the knowledge, know-how or dexterity they are assumed to certify. They are comparatively easy to measure, but give only the loosest indication of which skills are actually used in the workplace.

Nor is there a simple equation between the possession, exercise and valuation of skill (Attewell 1990; though see also Spenner 1990). Work undertaken predominantly by women is routinely ranked below that undertaken by men, even when it is objectively more complex (Phillips and Taylor 1986). And the range of factors that contribute to skill, such as abilities, qualifications, formal training, job design and social status (Gallie 1991; Francis and Penn 1994), are both resistant to measurement and subject to change as workplaces adopt new technologies, change their personnel practices or adjust product specifications. But the fact that skill is a moving target does not make it any less important. Indeed, it is difficult to see how skill levels can be raised, strengthened or developed if we have only a partial understanding of what skills are

15

and none at all of the way the various parts of the system interact. Accordingly, this chapter explores the nature of skill and the way it is put into practice in the workplace.

The most helpful starting point for this discussion is Cockburn's (1983) tripartite definition. Skill may be possessed by individuals, through qualifications, experience, expertise or attributes. It is built into jobs, the successful completion of which may demand autonomy, decision-making, technical know-how or responsibility. And it produces, and is itself the product of, status (p. 113):

> There is the skill that resides in the man himself, accumulated over time, each new experience adding something to a total ability. There is the skill demanded by the job – which may or may not match the skill in the worker. And there is the political definition of skill: that which a group of workers or a trade union can successfully defend against the challenge of employers and of other groups of workers.

In practice this means that skill is part of a complex social system, and skilled and expert work the product of the way different parts of this system relate to one another (Littler 1982; Vallas 1990). Few of these elements are static: firms may adapt their strategies, individuals can gain expertise and the status of groups and occupations may change over time. To add to the complexity, while these interrelationships all influence the skills that are deployed and the way they are developed, they do not dictate them, and highly skilled workers may be found in organisations where strategies concentrate on cost-cutting, just as low-skilled and tightly regulated employees are hired to work in technologically sophisticated workplaces.

Skill in the individual

Labour is not a homogeneous category. In the majority of jobs, the skills individual employees can exercise, their knowledge of the firm, its processes, products and services, its clients and the market it serves can and do make a difference. Productivity, quality and service levels all depend on the work people do and the way they do it. Individual workers can acquire skills in a range of ways. They can enrol on training courses, participate in formal apprenticeships and gain expertise through experience on the job or in the formal education system.

Traditionally Britain has been a low-skills economy where both education and vocational education and training catered for small sections of the population. In 1975, 62 per cent of young people left the education system at the age of 16, the first moment they could legally do so (Keep and Rainbird

2000:179). The majority of these young people held no formal qualifications and once in the workplace, in marked contrast to Germany or the Netherlands, there was no extensive system of vocational education and training that could remedy any educational deficits. However, over the last three decades a combination of factors (including high youth unemployment, benefit changes and the introduction of criterion-referenced rather than norm-referenced qualifications) has resulted in a dramatic increase in educational participation. By 2003, 72 per cent of 16 year olds were in full time education with a further 15 per cent undertaking some form of training (DfES 2004a). University participation also increased. In 1970–1 there were 414,000 full-time undergraduate students in Britain. By 2000–1 this figure had risen to 1.1 million, some 38 per cent of the age cohort, figures more than matched by the increase in part-time and postgraduate students (Elias and Purcell 2003; Purcell and Elias 2004). These are welcome developments, but many problems remain. While participation levels are high and the number of people with qualifications is increasing there are still some 21 million adults who have not reached level 3 or equivalent (intermediate qualifications, roughly equivalent to A-levels), and around 7 million have poor literacy and numeracy skills (Felstead *et al.* 2002:25).

This dramatic shift in the supply of educated young people has the potential to significantly upskill work and materially benefit the workers themselves. Qualifications can help employer and employee to find each other, provide access to more interesting work, reduce both the likelihood and duration of unemployment and add considerably to lifetime earnings. Gary Becker's (1964) *Human Capital Theory* argues that, just as investment in plant or equipment can produce productivity gains so, for an individual, investment in skills (through education, qualifications and training) will add to earnings. There is evidence for this. Men with A levels earn 17 per cent more than their colleagues with GCSEs or O levels and those with a first degree earn a further 28 per cent (the figures for women are 19 per cent and 25 per cent respectively). A professional qualification can add 35 per cent to a man's lifetime earnings and 41 per cent to a woman's (Dearden *et al.* 2000, cited in Machin and Vignoles 2001:8).

But the incentives for individuals to invest in their own development are neither so positive nor so straightforward as Becker suggests. The returns accrue from the fact there is a market for particular skills, and markets distinguish on the basis of the price a purchaser is willing to pay, rather than the skill levels involved. So language qualifications in German, English, Latin, Sanskrit, Latvian, Welsh, Chinese or Hindi are likely to produce very different returns for reasons unrelated to linguistic complexity (Noon and Blyton 2002, 1997). Then too, markets are the product of societies and may reflect prejudices in their pricing. Women consistently earn less than men, even when more highly qualified and even after the influence of sector, working hours and child-rearing are controlled for (Steinberg 1990). As Purcell and Elias's (2004) study demonstrates, this holds true even for recent graduates, almost none of whom had children and despite the fact that many were likely to be working for employers committed to equal opportunities. In the first year after graduation women earned 11 per cent less than men, after three and a half years this had risen to 15 per cent and seven years after graduation the gap stretched to 18 per cent (p. 9).

It is also naïve to assume that workers are simply mechanistic aggregations of skill. After all, hiring employees does not guarantee that their knowledge and expertise will be used in the workplace (Block 1990:75):

> It is not actual human beings that are an input into the production process, but one of their characteristics – their capacity to do work. But this is an inherently paradoxical strategy since the individual's capacity to do work is not innate; it is socially created and sustained.

Motivation, willingness to deploy skills and opportunities to do so are all crucial in practice yet all are missing from this model.

Nor do all qualifications carry positive returns. Some certificates add considerably to an individual's earning power but others, particularly low-level vocational qualifications, produce zero or negative returns (Bennett *et al.* 1992; Machin and Vignoles 2001). Some of these differentials stem from the quality of the qualifications themselves (Grugulis 2003). But they also come from the fact that qualifications are used as a signalling device, to mark out those who are most able. When employers seek the top percentile, improving education can be an individual solution (in that it can move one person up the rankings) but not a collective one because when more people gain qualifications employers simply seek other ways of identifying the 'top' students (Crouch *et al.* 1999). Under these circumstances, qualifications aimed at students and workers who are already high achievers will generally show greater returns, regardless of substantive content, than those targeted at disadvantaged groups.

Finally, human capital theory targets only the supply of skills and it is by no means certain that an increasing supply stimulates appropriate demand (Brown 2001). For skills to have an impact on organisational or national performance, they need to be used in the workplace, and this depends on the way work is designed. By itself, human capital theory is an imperfect tool for encouraging and exploring skill. It explains some pay premiums extremely well and helps to differentiate between individual contributions. But the market for skills is not a perfect one and contributions are shaped by factors other than individual expertise.

Skill in the job

The idea that individual people can be skilled is a familiar one and it is this area of skill that attracts most attention from official interventions. Education, apprenticeship, training and qualification all focus on developing and maintaining individual skill. But, as both Cockburn (1983) and Littler (1982) have argued, skill is also an aspect of jobs and work can be designed to make use of, demand, develop and deploy skills, just as much as it can minimise the need for skill. McDonald's famously and relentlessly standardise every aspect of their product. The Operations and Training Manual (known to staff as 'the Bible') provides detailed prescriptions for every aspect of working life. Its 600 pages include full-colour photographs illustrating the proper placement of ketchup, mustard and pickle on every type of burger, set out the six steps of counter service and even prescribe the arm motions that should be used in salting a batch of fries. Kitchen and counter technology reinforce these instructions as lights and buzzers tell workers when to turn burgers or take fries out of the fat, ketchup dispensers provide measured amounts of product in the requisite 'flower' pattern and lights on the till remove the need for serving staff to write out orders as well as prompting them to offer additional items (Leidner 1993; Ritzer 1996; Royle 2000). Nor are such rigid regulations and narrowly defined tasks restricted to any one industry. Delbridge's (1998) account of women working in 'Nippon CTV', a factory in Wales, describes the way tasks were timed down to a tenth of a second. Workers on the conveyor belt were required to insert a set number of components into panels. Operators' tasks were set out in the 'manual', displayed above each worker's head and the average insertion time for each component was 2.7 seconds (see also Pollert 1981; Webster 1990).

Designing work in this way may have organisational advantages. It can ensure consistency of product, as McDonald's do, or make production more efficient. Adam Smith's ([1776] 1993) description of pin manufacturing estimates the capacity of individual craft workers at less than twenty pins a day. Ten workers, each endlessly repeating one part of the manufacturing process could produce between them some 48,000 pins a day. Work is completed more quickly and satisfactory outcomes are no longer dependent on workers making the right decisions. Frederick Taylor's (1949) desire to 'reduce every act of every workman to a science' (p. 64) was intended to increase work rates and replace skilled workers with unskilled. Workers are not expected to know about the product they are producing, or make decisions on how they might best work or judge the quality of their labour. Their role is simply to follow orders; in the words of one member of a typing pool, 'Janey gives us the work and I sit down and type all day' (Webster 1990:51).

Box 2.1

A McDonald's observation checklist used for the toasting and preparation of buns

PREPARATION AND TOASTING	Possible	Actual
1 Buns are selected using FIFO	3	
2 Empty as well as full bin trays are stacked where they are not a hazard and sorted according to colour code	2	
3 Trays of buns are stacked so that buns are not crushed	3	
4 Appropriate bun board used and toaster set at 420°F (±5°F)	3	
5 Bun trays are flat, clean and dry	3	
6 Macs/Regulars: Buns person directs grill person to achieve perfect timing and co-ordination. Buns are never pre-staged in toasters	3	
7a Regular bun crowns or Big Mac club and heel sections: placed in toaster immediately on call from production person 7b Quarter bun crowns: placed in toaster immediately; after 30 seconds duty timer sounds	3	
8a Regular and Quarters: when buzzer sounds, toaster handle is lifted immediately and heels are placed in toaster before crowns are removed	3	
8b Big Macs: when buzzer sounds, toaster handle is lifted immediately and crowns are placed in toaster before clubs are lifted out using a spatula, and placed on tray with heels. Tray is placed on dressing table	3	
9 Bun surface is caramelised to a uniform golden brown	3	
10 Bun is not crushed by excessive compression or damaged in any other way	3	
11 Bun person keeps up with production demand	3	
12 Good communication and teamwork exists (i.e. 3 Cs: Communication, Co-operation and Co-ordination)		

GENERAL		
1 Uniform is neat and clean (wearing apron). Name badge is worn	3	
2 Hands are washed before commencing work on this station	3	
3 Clean white/blue border cloths are used and kept in the appropriate pan	2	
4 Only countable waste is placed in the red bin	1	

OVERALL GRADE

(A) x 0.75 =	(C)	TOTAL (pass = 40) 44
(B) x 0.25 =	(D)	
OVERALL = C + D		SCORE (A) 100%
	Pass = 90%	

COMMENTS

Taken from Royle (2000:50).

However, while tight control systems and regimented work practices have advantages they may also create problems. Adam Smith ([1776] 1993) after describing the way that reorganising work in the pin factory could exponentially increase production, went on to point out that this would have a devastating and dehumanising effect on the workers. Interestingly, his solution was to increase education, not so that workers could contribute vocationally but to rehumanise them, as a form of civilised entertainment. Within work, rigid control mechanisms can have a range of results: turnover may be high. According to the *Economist*, American call centres have turnover rates in excess of 90 per cent (2004) and this example is not an isolated one (see also Royle 2000; Korczynski 2001). Absenteeism may rise and employees may misbehave or resist the regulations imposed (Edwards and Scullion 1982; Ackroyd and Thompson 1999). Moreover, tight controls are rarely put into practice as easily or as unproblematically as descriptions of the systems themselves may suggest (Doray 1988).

This 'workmanship of certainty' (Pye 1968) which eliminates skill can be contrasted with the 'workmanship of risk' in which the result depends on the judgement, dexterity and care of the worker. The consultants studied by Grugulis *et al.* (2000) enjoyed a great deal of discretion. Their work involved designing computer systems, writing and installing a range of applications, setting up websites and bidding for client contracts. They had the freedom to choose whether to work from home, a client's site or the office (and even where in the office to sit). They could take the initiative in acquiring new forms of expertise, ordering software or pulling together a team to bid for a client contract. But this autonomy in the job was secured by long working hours and a high degree of control over the consultants' social lives. As one of Kunda's (1992) interviewees remarked elsewhere: '[Y]ou can choose which twenty hours of the day you work' (see also Kidder 1981).

Box 2.2

Instructions from Nissan's operations manual

Extend the right hand	Take screw in the right hand	
Pick up a screw		Insert screw through the seal with the right hand
Insert through seal	Insert screw through the seal	

Taken from Garrahan and Stewart (1992:78).

Box 2.3

Workers may be given a great deal of autonomy in their jobs. 'Webboyz', a small software development company, encouraged their programmers to innovate by (according to the CEO) sitting 'them down in front of a computer and say[ing] "come up with a product" and then we'll sell it through our internet distribution channel.' Staff suggestions were rewarded with electronic toys such as Playstations or Gameboys and users who contributed were given T-shirts and a free copy of the programme. According to one of the project managers:

> If any of the guys has a good idea basically we let them do it if they haven't got anything else to do. A good example is one of the guys wanted to do some sort of graphics oriented programme and he's got these mathematical algorithms that generate random organic tileable backgrounds. That has been turned into a product that we've said we'll run with and we've wrapped another product around it . . . All the e-mail addresses we collect from the distribution of the product we use for direct marketing to sell our other products. So it helps us in the end because we can commericalise those ideas that come out of our development team . . . all with no money spent at all, apart from the developer's time.

Taken from Barrett (2004:784).

Levels of control, freedom, prescription, skill and expertise are not preset and jobs with similar (and occasionally the same) job title can be designed to demand higher or lower levels of skill. So the regulations laid down for cooks by McDonald's might be contrasted with those of privately owned restaurants where chefs' skills are at a premium (Ritzer and Stillman 2001). Even software development, popularly associated with high levels of autonomy, can be subdivided and controlled. Barrett's (2005a, 2005b) work in three different companies contrasts the work of programmers adapting secondary products who simply cut and paste prewritten code with developers writing their own code who were given far greater freedom (see also Swart and Kinnie 2003; Andrews *et al.* 2005). Moreover, levels of control and routinisation may change over time as credit scoring in banks replaces managers' lending decisions and knowledge of local companies (Hasluck 1999) and preset measures remove the onus on engineers to shape metal (Ainley 1993).

There is skill in the job, just as there is skill in the individual, but the distinction between them is often clearer in theory than it is in practice. Some forms of work, such as call centres, are very tightly regulated with computer prompts and company scripts guiding workers through appropriate responses and actions (see Taylor and Bain 1999; Korczynski 2001; Wray-Bliss 2001; Callaghan and Thompson 2002; ; Taylor *et al.* 2002). But such rigidity is rare and most work is subject to regular revision as tasks are allocated and responsibilities given or withheld. This means that skill levels can grow as individuals gain knowledge of the organisations they work in, see the way that systems operate, experience problems being solved successfully and learn which of their colleagues to approach with particular requests. Felstead *et al.*'s (2000) analysis of survey data reveals an increasing demand for skills even when respondents have held the same job for five years, suggesting that workers gain in skills and experience over time. Elsewhere, work on organisational innovation by Martin *et al.* (2001) argues that formal courses are far less valuable than advice from knowledgeable and supportive co-workers, chance queries and informal meetings (see also Zhou and George 2001). Again, these internal friendship networks might be expected to grow (in both breadth and depth) and strengthen over time.

Then too, the responsibilities, interest and status of a particular job do not depend entirely on skill. Webster's (1990) research on office workers shows how personal secretaries and departmental assistants might be responsible, as the workers in the typing pool were, for typing documents, corrections and presentations; but they were also expected to answer telephones, keep diaries, do filing and act as a store of organisational expertise for visitors. Assuming responsibility for such a range of tasks added little in the way of skill but it did provide elements of control and variety, a factor Webster calls 'porosity' in the job. Decisions had to be taken about which work to prioritise and workers gained a certain degree of physical mobility, both of which made a great deal of difference to the way work was experienced. As Burchell *et al.* (1994) argue, it may be helpful for the notion of skill to be broadened to include responsibilities (for resources, for records and information, for people, for output/standards).

Given this interplay between the skills possessed by workers and the way work is designed it is instructive to review the way jobs are changing. As Felstead *et al.*'s (2002) extensive survey *Work Skills in Britain* has shown, most jobs in Britain do not require skilled people to carry them out. Even when we add the number of jobs that demand higher level qualifications to those that require intermediate ones they are still outnumbered by posts for people with few or no qualifications (11 million and 13.3 million respectively, p. 104). Most work still demands few skills, with 61 per cent of jobs requiring less than three months' training and 20 per cent less than one month's experience to do well (compared with 26 per cent which require more than two years; p. 28). 'iMac' jobs have not yet entirely replaced 'McJobs' (Warhurst and Thompson 1998).

More optimistically, while the base is low the trajectory of skills is encouraging (Felstead *et al.* 2004). The qualifications required for jobs, the training needed and the length of time an individual requires to be able to do a job well all generally rose between 1986 and 2001 (Felstead *et al.* 2002:44).

Research with employers estimated that skill requirements had risen 'a lot' in 30 per cent of the jobs in their establishments over the preceding five years, with 55 per cent of jobs seeing a significant increase in the importance of computing skills, 49 per cent a rise in the need for planning skills and 31 per cent an increased need for writing skills (Green *et al.* 2003:23). Positive as these results are, they do need to be set against the findings that 37 per cent of employees are *overqualified* for the work that they do, a figure that has risen consistently since 1986 (Felstead *et al.* 2002:48).

But not all newly created jobs require skills of the people recruited to fill them. Despite a significant increase in demand for professional workers in the USA less than 40 per cent of American employees work in professional, managerial or technical occupations, a figure equally true for Germany, Japan, and Singapore (Brown *et al.* 2001). There has been a revival of sweatshops in New York and Los Angeles (Brown 2001) and in Britain the rise of the service sector has created much unskilled work (Rose *et al.* 1994), with job growth dominated by jobs in security, care work and hairdressing (Nolan 2001; Head 2003; Thompson 2004).

There is also one extremely worrying development. While every other measure of skill is rising, the levels of discretion employees can exercise is falling dramatically. This trend is most marked in professional workers. In 1986, 72 per cent of professionals exercised 'a great deal' of discretion over their work; by 2001 this figure had fallen to 38 per cent (Felstead *et al.* 2002:71). Overall the proportion of workers feeling that they had a great deal of choice over the way they did their job fell from 52 per cent to 39 per cent (p. 68); though the number claiming that they had no discretion at all also declined from 10 per cent to 6 per cent (p. 150). There was no one simple cause for this, with respondents citing increases in control over their work from clients, supervisors, fellow-workers, payment and appraisal systems (p. 73).

Discretion is a key element of skill. It allows workers space to develop their expertise and to exercise judgement and features heavily in academic attempts to theorise skill. Friedman (1977) draws out the differences between 'low-autonomy' and 'high-discretion' work (see also Braverman 1974; Fox 1974; Streeck 1987). Many of the jobs described here as 'low-skilled' or 'unskilled' deserve the label because they are routinised. The skills needed for successful execution are taken away from the job and built into the control system. Buns for McDonald's burgers arrive pre-sliced and the rule book tells workers how long they should spend toasting them. One of the defining features of professionalism is discretion, to the extent that professional expertise is generally described as resistant to both rigid specification and close supervision (Abbott 1988; Freidson 1988, 1994; Evetts 2002).

This is not to argue that there is a linear relationship between discretion and skill. As Noon and Blyton (2002) point out, a gardener will exercise a great deal more autonomy and work unsupervised for longer time periods than an anaesthetist, yet few would argue that the anaesthetist is less skilled. Moreover, it is just as difficult to design a job that is so wholly routinised that all discretion is removed, as it is to create work that has no constraints. Managers may not be required to clock in and out but they are likely to be ruthlessly policed on meeting client deadlines (Kunda 1992; Watson 1994; Anderson-Gough *et al.* 2000). Workers in McDonald's whose official tasks are prescribed in detail may prove surprisingly skilled at maintenance and problem-solving when machinery breaks down (Sennett 1998), and call centre representatives juggle tasks in ways unanticipated by formal control systems (Wray-Bliss 2001). Yet even given these reservations, the links between discretion and skill are strong ones and it is often the element of discretion in work which provides the space to exercise and develop skill. When levels of discretion are falling across all occupations there are grounds for concern.

Skill in the setting

The third element of Cockburn's (1983) definition is skill in the social setting. Here the status of an individual or group may bestow or protect skill, just as skill itself confers status. To a certain extent, skill, status and control are necessarily linked; expertise may require control over work and this brings with it higher status. But they are not equivalents, nor are the links necessarily simple or one-way. Aspects of social life that are unrelated to skill but which confer status (such as class or gender) impact on the way that skills are perceived. The Registrar General's classification was initially devised to measure the social standing of occupations and only later changed to a ranking of skills. Yet this transition was achieved with 'curiously little reorganisation of its constituent categories' (Gallie 1994:47).

This means that workers acknowledged as skilled may be able to defend their status even after changes to technology or work processes remove the original skills. Steiger's (1993) work on the construction industry reveals that, while most crafts gained status through a 'toolbox ideology' (possession, deployment of and expertise in the tools of their trade), plumbers, after the advent of plastic pipes, required little more than a hacksaw and a ruler to carry out their tasks. Despite this, and despite the fact that the plastic pipes were genuinely easier to install, plumbers lost none of their status, position or autonomy and, turning the tables on their colleagues, cited their ability to improvise and do a quality job without the proper tools to legitimise their standing. According to one (p. 539): 'anybody can do it with the proper tools. A good mechanic can get by without the proper tools'. Elsewhere, Bacon and Blyton's (2003) longitudinal study of a Corus steel plant shows how the introduction of team-working and single-status employment worked to the advantage of the skilled craftworkers (who became team leaders) rather than the less-skilled process workers.

Just as positive legacies can confer advantage so negative ones may be difficult to overcome. Nineteenth-century cotton production was based on subcontracting with 'spinners' or 'minders' dividing their tasks out between assistants: the 'big' and 'little' piecers. These workers, particularly the 'big piecer', were often as technically skilled and experienced as spinners but were formally classified as semiskilled and paid very different rates (Penn 1984). In marked contrast to plumbers, labourers working in construction were unable to negotiate craft rates, even when capable of doing craft work, because they were not required to bring tools to the site and tools were taken as signs of skill (Steiger 1993:538).

Unsurprisingly, occupational groups may seek to influence these processes by regulating and developing the skills of their members, restricting entry or work to approved individuals, and controlling work processes and defending their members' status. One consequence of this is that professional bodies and trade unions have been among the most active defenders of vocational training in Britain (Rainbird 1990; Keep 1994; Heyes and Stuart 1998). Turner's (1962) historical study of the cotton unions shows how 'strippers' and 'grinders' gained status by increasing the breadth of their occupational role and tightly restricting entry to the job; while both engineering and printing unions sought to restrict certain tasks to 'time-served men' who had undertaken a full apprenticeship (Cockburn 1983; Penn 1984). Such restrictions continue today and medics, accountants and engineers go through long periods of initial training and are then required to maintain their skills through regular continuing professional development. Not all occupations are so tightly regulated, and in many the training and examinations provided by professional associations are substantive and symbolic aids to progression rather than necessary prerequisites. In banking, insurance and personnel management (among others) professional bodies and examinations exist but while ambitious entrants may be encouraged to sit these examinations (Crompton and Jones 1984) rank is not dependent on them (see Abbott 1988; Freidson 1988; 1994 for accounts of 'professionalisation' and 'quasi-professions).

Skill and gender

These links between skill and status mean that people with power in the labour market have the capacity to defend their skills. But the corollary of this is that those of lower status find it far harder, both collectively and individually, to have their skills acknowledged and rewarded, something that can readily be seen in the way women's work is classified, controlled and compensated. In the nineteenth century, when secretarial work was undertaken by men, it was considered an excellent preparation for top management (Crompton and Jones 1984). As it became the preserve of women this link was severed (depriving organisations of an effective means of career development) and the work declined rapidly in status. Secretarial progression, even in bureaucracies, is feudal rather than structured, with secretaries gaining preferment as a result of 'their' manager being raised in the hierarchy (Moss-Kanter 1977). There is probably as much variety in the work of secretaries (from typing pool to assisting a board director) as there is in that of engineers, but few of these skills are acknowledged (Phillips and Taylor 1986).

More recent examples are not difficult to find. Rubery and Wilkinson (1979) compare the work done by women making paper boxes with that performed by men producing cartons. Since carton production was more highly automated the men needed less concentration and fewer skills than their female counterparts. Yet despite this, their work was classed as semi-skilled while the women were labelled (and paid) as unskilled. School caretakers, who are generally men, perform a wide range of discrete tasks but these jobs are gathered together to make up a full-time contract. Work done by women as cleaners, cooks and playground attendants is divided into part-time jobs with lower wages and lesser terms and conditions.

The Equal Pay Act 1975 made it illegal for an employer to pay men and women different wages for undertaking the same work and eliminated the old engineering pay scale of skilled, semi-skilled, unskilled and women. But it allows different pay for different work and, as Phillips and Taylor argue (1986:63), 'skill is defined against women – skilled work is work that women don't do'. 'Feminine' skills such as dexterity are downgraded against typically 'masculine' skills such as strength (p. 60). Part-time work, which is disproportionately done by women, is almost by definition low-skilled (Felstead *et al.* 2002) and the gulf is widening as full-time workers gain new skills or improve existing ones and part-timers do not (Felstead *et al.* 2000), a split which has worrying implications for the future of women's skills (Horrell *et al.* 1994).

The workplace is also still broadly segregated, with women still confined to or choosing 'women's work' (Bradley *et al.* 2000). Because these jobs are being done by women, they are classified as low- or unskilled. The European courts recently ruled against the different pay scales used by a hospital trust in Carlisle which resulted in male workers being paid up to 50 per cent more, working fewer hours and getting higher overtime rates than their female colleagues. Women domestics washing floors were paid £7505 for a 39-hour week. Wall-washers, all of whom were men, earned £9995 for a 37-hour week. A D-grade nurse earned £13,900 after qualifying at degree level and spending five years in the job. She could supervise up to 15 staff in life-or-death clinical situations. After three years a craftsman supervisor with a joinery apprenticeship can pull down £19,100 for overseeing a maximum of two. A cook, who needed the same level of qualifications and served the same length of apprenticeship as a plumber, earned £172.62 for a 39-hour week. The plumber earned £272.11 for 37 hours (see an article by A. Browne in *The Observer*, 15 July 2001).

This is not to argue that skill is entirely socially constructed, a marketing device deployed by craft associations and professional bodies. Skill is not simply the product of a perception of skill. Rather, judgements on skill are not constructed in a social vacuum and do not always emerge as objective and hierarchical rankings predicated on expertise. Jobs may be judged differently depending on the way they are valued socially or economically and vice versa. As with other issues involving social status, this means that judgements about skill may conflate skill levels with gender, class or race, further rewarding those already advantaged in the labour market.

The reason skills are a definitional minefield is because the exercise of skill is embedded in the employment relationship. Skills, expertise and know-how are not additional factors grafted onto workplaces but an integral part of working life. The way work is designed, controlled and regulated will impact on the skills employees can deploy – just as the skills used affect the way work is designed, controlled and regulated. This has implications for some of the regularly feted remedies to low skills employment. Supply side solutions, which focus on increasing vocational or academic participation, are welcome interventions but in isolation have limited potential to change skills in the workplace. HRM and technology, which target the way people work directly, may have a greater capacity to change the way people work, but even here the trajectory is not always upwards, nor are the results inevitably positive.

Skill and HRM

In theory, the 'development of resourceful humans' (Storey 1992:27) is at the heart of HRM, and the shift from personnel management marked a rise in structured development, 'learning companies' and commitment-oriented practice (see, for example Guest 1987; Legge 1995). Such links are certainly logical. When the key differential in organisational competitiveness is human capability and people are resources rather than costs then skills and training are the pivotal element of practice (Keep 1989:109). Workers who are skilled can work flexibly and autonomously; they have more to contribute to decision-making or employee involvement schemes; and when workers contribute more, this individual input can be acknowledged and rewarded with performance-related pay (Adler 1992; Spenner 1990). When employees are not skilled, when jobs are designed to minimise workers' contributions or when labour is treated as a cost then human resource practices are wasteful and expensive luxuries (Keep and Mayhew 1996).

There is empirical evidence of a link between skill and HRM. Arthur's (1999) research into US steel mini-mills shows that firms which specialised in small batch production required greater skills of their workers (and designed jobs more broadly). Switching between different types of steel or different shapes required close monitoring by melt-shop employees. The exact nature of changeover activities was difficult to predict and downtime expensive, so both quality and quantity of production relied heavily on the skills of opera-tors and maintenance workers. These small batch producers tended to have human resource systems which focused on generating commitment: wages were high, workers skilled and participation was emphasised (whether through trade union representation, social activities or formal consultative structures). By contrast, in firms where production runs were large and few changeover activities were needed most work was routine. Here human resource practices aimed to control employees: jobs were designed to incorporate the minimum amount of skill and discretion, wages tended to be low and investment in training, consultation and involvement was generally seen as counter-productive.

Such links between production, strategy, skill and HRM are intuitively attractive, but they are not inevitable. Skill is not the only driver of human resource practice: employers can follow fads and fashions, may wish to be seen as 'good employers' or can use HRM to 'reward' employees. Batt and Keefe's (1999) work on the fragmenting US telecommunications industry found that HRM was linked far more closely to how profitable a company's customer base was than to its employees' skill levels. Rubery et al.'s (2004) work in a multi-client call centre shows that pay rates and the deployment of 'soft' human resource practices were dependent on the attitude of employer and client, rather than the difficulty of the task. Aldi, a discount supermarket chain which competes by 'piling it high and selling it cheap', also consistently pays its employees above the sector average and provides high-quality training. And Kinnie *et al*.'s (2000) work shows the way that sophisticated HRM was used to entertain workers and distract them from alienating and tightly regulated jobs. It seems that HRM, like training, is a beneficiary of profits (Keep and Mayhew 1988).

Then too, employment practices are not simply 'read off' from organisational strategies and, even given the same market, employers may choose to compete in very different ways. Boxall and Purcell (2003) cite the example of British Oxygen and Air Products, two rival firms in the same industry which made very different decisions about the skills they required in their employees. Air Products opted for deskilling and outsourced its haulage and distribution to save delivery costs, with external drivers who knew little of the bottled gas industry beyond basic health and safety rules. British Oxygen decided to make delivery drivers key staff in ensuring customer satisfaction and securing repeat orders. Drivers were trained in customer relations, cab-based information systems and product knowledge, ensuring that customers were satisfied and encouraging them to trade up wherever possible.

It is not clear, despite the repeated emphasis on commitment, learning and employees' contribution, that HRM *inevitably* involves upskilling. This is partly, of course, because there is little consensus on which good, 'best' or strategic practices constitute HRM or even whether there is such a thing as HRM for them to constitute (see among others Noon 1992; Legge 1995; Pfeffer 1998; Storey 2001). But it is also because the way a practice is introduced and controlled can vary dramatically from workplace to workplace. Even multi-skilling is not always as skilful as the name suggests. It may involve a general increase in skills (Bacon and Blyton 2003) or allow

---

Box 2.5

The status and content of work may also be politically determined as Kessler *et al.* (2005) and Hyde *et al.* (2004) have shown in their work on teaching assistants, social workers and NHS staff. While, according to Kessler and his colleagues, there was a considerable degree of similarity between work undertaken by professionally qualified teachers and social workers and that done by the assistants the (overwhelmingly female) assistants, were generally less well qualified and much less well paid.

Taken from Kessler *et al.* (2005) and Hyde *et al.* (2004).

---

employees to control their own jobs, making informed decisions about which tasks to prioritise as Webster's (1990) personal secretaries did. But multi-skilling may also require workers to take on additional tasks with inadequate preparation under managers who have unrealistic expectations about the number of jobs that can be mastered (Clark 1993; Hendry 1993; Wilkinson and Willmott 1995). A chemicals company studied by Heyes (2001) altered its training systems so that trainees, who might have previously taken five or six years to learn one craft, were expected to develop a working knowledge of all relevant trades and processing skills in just two years. As a result, craft workers felt their skills were being devalued and training was becoming increasingly superficial and once on the job, workers would take longer to work out what was wrong with a particular piece of equipment. Elsewhere multi-skilling has succeeded far better in providing employees with a glimpse at more interesting work that is rarely part of daily responsibilities, but this has not always been welcomed by management. The managing director of GKN Hardy Spicer protested that multi-skilling production workers to fix the line when it broke down resulted in far more downtime because the workers wanted to use their newly acquired skills (Hendry 1993).

There are links between skill and HRM, to the extent that many human resource practices make little sense without knowledgeable workers who are able and willing to contribute. Moreover, workplaces dominated by skilled and professional workers are more likely to use sophisticated soft human resource practices (Cully *et al.* 1999). However, this does not mean that HRM increases skill or that skilled employees always enjoy favourable terms and conditions of employment.

Technology

Technology has long been seen to have the power to change the way people work. Automation and increasing numbers of computers have the potential to eliminate routine low-skilled work at the same time as actively creating jobs for knowledge workers, such as developing the computer systems themselves or analysing the data they provide. Bell (1973; 1974) even predicted that these developments would fundamentally alter society. Power derived from property and position would be replaced by power derived from knowledge and scientists and engineers would displace entrepreneurs to the extent that, according to Trist (1974:112), 'the learning force was already greater than the workforce' (see also Grugulis *et al.* 2004).

That particular social revolution has failed to materialise but technology has indeed created high-skilled jobs. Software development, systems analysis and designing multimedia applications all require expertise unheard of a century ago. Software that carries out complex statistical analyses is readily available and can be run on most home and office computers, facilitating statistical work and supporting the financial markets in their production of ever more complex derivatives; manufacturing is increasingly automated and the availability of laptop computers and mobile phones makes it even easier for workers to stay in contact with employers and colleagues.

But the impact of automation and new technologies varies (see, for example Corbett 1996; Rubery and Grimshaw 2001) and the introduction of technology is not uncontested (Ogbonna and Harris 2005). New jobs have been created but others have been destroyed and the traffic has not been one-way. Some knowledge work is indeed supported by computers but this is matched by skills that have been destroyed and by the increased opportunities for surveillance (and corresponding limits to discretion) offered by technology. Cockburn's (1983) study of workers proficient in Linotype and hot-metal printing shows how redundant their skills were once computers, QWERTY keyboards and photo-composition were introduced. Call centres are technologically extremely sophisticated workplaces but, despite the optimistic hopes of Frenkel et al. (1999), few could be considered sites of 'knowledge work'. Rather, the sophisticated technology is used to control employees and limit the skills they can deploy and the discretion they may exercise. As one call centre operative commented, 'we are basically the monkeys, the computer is the organ grinder' (Taylor et al. 2002:143; Callaghan and Thompson 2002).

Computers are associated with rising skill levels and there is an identifiable wage premium available for individuals working with them (Krueger 1993; Haskel 1999; Haskel and Heden 1999), perhaps because introducing technology changes the way people work. As a baker, in a piece of research by Smith and Hayton (1999:265), commented, 'We don't just lob a $160,000 piece of equipment on the floor and walk away.' However, technology does not automatically upskill. Wage premia similar to those available for people working with computers can be found for using a calculator, a telephone, a pen and even for sitting down (DiNardo and Pische 1997; Rubery and Grimshaw 2001). It may be, as Machin (2001) suggests, that computers are now so widespread in the workplace that simply counting them is not a meaningful measure of skill, particularly since not all computer use is complex (Tijdens and Steijn 2005). Felstead et al. (2002) reinforce this, pointing out that 77 per cent of people who work with computers use them for only simple or moderate tasks (printing out an invoice, or using word processing, spreadsheets or email). Only 6 per cent of workers are involved in 'advanced' computer work (p. 60).

Discussion and conclusions

Skill is embedded in the employment relationship and increases or decreases in skill levels do not rest simply on individuals' expertise or the introduction of new technology but on the way those skills are used and the technology is designed. These are not value-free and the links between various forms of skill, status, discretion, and the extent to which workers are trusted, are often circular. Professionals enjoy high status because they possess expertise and this expertise both justifies and is developed through, discretion. Workers in low-discretion jobs are tightly supervised and their jobs rigidly defined through rules and procedures with coordination done by others. Little trust is allotted to them and the official response to failure is punishment. By contrast, high-discretion work implies a moral commitment by employees to the organisation. It may require lengthy training in specialist skills, with workers 'professionalised' and 'socialised' into roles. Workers in these jobs can exercise initiative and may be motivated to do so for reasons of advancement. Disagreements here are treated very differently from those with workers in low-discretion jobs; professionals and top managers are both acting in the organisation's 'best interests'; they simply disagree over the form that 'best interest' should take. As a result, high-discretion workers are generally assumed to be doing their honest best at tasks (Fox 1974:25–37; see also Streeck 1987). According to Fox (1974:76):

> This explains why the characteristic top management exhortation to rank and file employees to 'trust the company' is often received with cynicism. In the very way it structures work, authority and rewards it excludes them from its own high-discretion, high-trust fellowship, yet asks them to submit to its discretion in handling their interests and destinies. In other words: 'we do not trust you, but we ask you nevertheless to trust us.' Mere verbal exhortations or formulae cannot – in Western-type society, indefinitely disguise this imbalance of reciprocity though . . . power may enforce it.

Essentially, questions of skill are inextricably intertwined with issues of workplace governance, product markets and organisational strategies.

This has implications for existing official interventions which seek to target only the supply side by increasing the numbers of people participating in education or raising levels of vocational education and training. Such developments are welcome, for reasons that extend beyond hoped-for gains in productivity and profitability. Education is a moral good and participation may improve an individual's life chances as well as preparing them for citizenship. However, while there has been no shortage of supply side interventions covering the education system, local labour markets and particular occupational groups, in all this activity, too little attention has been paid to the demand side.

Such neglect is understandable. Policy-makers can launch a training programme for the young unemployed far more readily than they can control or dictate employers' demand for skills. Moreover, previous activity in this area has often met with a startling lack of success (Sisson and Timperley 1994).

Individual firms may well adopt exemplary practices but these are likely to be both ad hoc and short-lived. It may be, of course, that external developments will provide enough momentum for positive change. Given the dramatic increase in educational participation, employees of the future will be far more highly qualified than their predecessors. Assuming that their credentials certify genuine improvements in knowledge, skills and competence then these workers should be more capable of contributing in the workplace. Since most jobs are not rigidly defined (it is a truism of industrial relations that the employment contract is 'incomplete') this could result in a 'grass roots' revolution: employees 'growing' their jobs, taking on more responsibilities and reshaping not only the way they work but also the basis on which the firms that employ them compete. There is already some evidence of this in the graduate labour market. Here, massive increases in the number of graduates entering the labour market seems to have met with some success. Immediately after graduation many graduates are working in non-graduate jobs but this, for the majority, is a transient phase (although opinions vary on whether it is growing over time). Over 90 per cent of respondents employed in 'traditional' graduate jobs, such as the established professions or further and higher education, reported using their qualifications, subject knowledge and skills in their work. But even in Elias and Purcell's (2003) new categories of modern graduate jobs, new graduate jobs and niche graduate jobs more than two-thirds of graduates used their subject knowledge and over 80 per cent used their skills (see also Purcell *et al.* 2004). Set against this, data from the *Skills Survey* suggest that less than 15 per cent of graduates employed were using their degree (Green *et al.* 2003:21).

So much for optimism. There is also a pessimistic scenario. We know from the evidence presented here that external developments are not deterministic and that each may result in a number of different outcomes. Our utopian vision of the future relies on individuals reshaping the work they do. Yet, as Felstead *et al.* (2002) observe, discretion is rapidly declining. When individuals have no choice about what they do or the way they do it it is difficult to see how the skills developed in the education system can be exercised in the workplace. Trapped in jobs that underutilise their skills and that they have little power to change, people are likely to become only stressed and frustrated (Green and Gallie 2002; Rose 2000). In practice, each of these predictions is likely to be realised in the labour market of the future: it would be nice to believe that it is the positive developments which will outnumber the negative ones.

3

International comparisons: skills and employment systems

> A deregulation approach and an enskilling one tend to embody opposite logics. In the former case all emphasis is on ease of disposal; for the latter it is important that employers regard employees as a long term investment resource, since a high rate of inter-firm mobility usually makes employers reluctant to carry out much training. (Crouch 1997:369).

Skills extend beyond individual expertise. The job that someone does, the way that job or the social group the workers belong to is perceived, the way work is designed and controlled and the markets firms compete in can and do all affect what skills workers possess, how much they are valued and whether (and in what direction) they are developed. So too can the national system in which those skills are developed. While almost every government applauds the idea of skills- and knowledge-based competition there are a wide range of very different approaches to the form that encouraging such competition should take (see, for example Crouch *et al.* 1999). These national systems still have a considerable influence since, despite the hope and hype over globalisation there does not yet exist one homogeneous international system of employment and skills (Bradley *et al.* 2000; Lauder 2001; Haworth and Hughes 2003; Rubery and Grimshaw 2003; Crouch 2005). Indeed, as Ferner (1997:19) comments, '[t]he notion of the global corporation transcending national boundaries is, very largely, myth'. Even in multinational companies where work is (at least partially) standardised and employment practices may be set at the centre, national variation creeps in and practices and policies are adapted to fit local custom, expectations and experience (Edwards 1998; Ferner and Quintanilla 1998; Ferner and Varul 2000a; Ferner and Varul 2000b; Edwards and Ferner 2002).

But the factors that influence skills development are not confined to national systems of VET. These are certainly important and may play a significant role in both developing and certifying skills, but the way skills are exercised in the workplace also depends on a country's approach to regulation, management and industrial relations. The point of reference, as Ashton (2004) argues, is not just the system of VET but the relationship between capital, labour and the state. Labour market structures may support progression in occupations or allow movement unfettered by checks on qualifications or competence; pay may be individually or collectively negotiated, and may make reference to seniority, skill or the market; and the form and content of training courses and qualifications may rely on whatever expertise there is in each individual firm or be set centrally following a collaboration between employer bodies and educationalists. The various approaches to each of these aspects of employment have very different implications for skills.

Voluntarist and regulated approaches

In this relationship between capital, labour and the state one of the key differences between nations is the extent to which the state intervenes in business and the form that intervention takes. While there is a general international consensus on the importance and value of training and development, this is not matched by agreement about how best to encourage good practice. At a national level the two principal approaches are voluntarist (also known as liberal or market-based) and regulated (educational). Both the USA and Britain are broadly voluntarist. The principal assumption behind such systems is that organisations operate more effectively when unfettered by regulation. Market pressures (to remain competitive, produce quality goods and run efficiently) will ensure that, where training is appropriate, firms will invest in it and, in the absence of expensive and cumbersome official bureaucracy, investment can be accurately targeted to respond to market needs. As Ashton (2004) points out, in such countries economic development tends to be led by a business elite. Trade unions are generally subordinate and the state's role is limited to providing legal and other frameworks which guarantee the free play of market forces. This is not, of course, the same as creating a level playing field since the free play of market forces means that the business elite continues to dominate.

By contrast, in a regulated system, as in much of continental Europe, vocational education and training is supported by the state. Regulation may take a variety of forms. In France, employers are required to support training or pay a levy of 1.5 per cent of turnover plus an apprenticeship tax of 0.5 per cent of turnover to the state. In Austria, Denmark, Germany, the Netherlands and Switzerland, there are systems of extensive and rigorous apprenticeships which attract high proportions of young people entering the labour market

(Steedman 2001), coupled with 'licences to practise' for particular occupations. The assumption is that vocational education and training is a public good and it is in the long-term interests of all to have a highly skilled workforce – but that, left to themselves, individual firms will prioritise profitability and may not invest in skills development or may fund only short-term and low-level training; according to Streeck (1992:17): '[F]irms that create only those skills that they need may well end up with less than they need. Cost- and profit-consciousness are more part of the problem than of the solution.'

Training and development is, after all, only one way of securing skilled workers and firms may choose to recruit workers trained elsewhere or deskill production instead. By providing an appropriate infrastructure (or a system of levies, or by regulating practice) the state ensures robust skills development. In these corporatist economies the state plays a greater role and economic growth is secured through cooperative relationships between capital and labour. This focus on consensus and the existence of a nationally recognised apprenticeship system means that the systems of employment are much more 'institutionally dense' (Ashton 2004). Industrial relations are more regulated and workplace learning is part of a general consensus between employers, unions and the state.

Both voluntarist and regulated approaches can be successful. Silicon Valley, California provides an excellent example of the way skills can be developed in a market-based system. Silicon Valley is famously the site of a cluster of extremely high-tech computing firms. These are supported by the proximity of universities (the University of California campuses in Berkeley, San Francisco, San Diego and Los Angeles and private institutions such as Stanford University; the University of Southern California and the California Institute of Technology), that supply expert labour, share research and stimulate startup companies. Stanford (whose graduates include William Hewlett and David Packard) even set up the first university science park to provide fledgling firms with support services. The infrastructure is conducive to growth with good local transport, an international airport and a state-of-the-art telecommunications system while the availability of venture capital, low levels of regulation and limited penalties on bankruptcy encourage startups. These small and often highly focused firms prosper through interdependency, forming partnerships with other organisations and participating in employer groups to pursue initiatives such as improving technical training in city colleges that are to their mutual benefit. Individuals also collaborate through professional associations, continuing education courses and alumni associations. In firms there is little formal training but skills and expertise are developed through project work on cutting-edge technical challenges. Even labour mobility, a point of concern elsewhere, assists knowledge diffusion here and increases personal and professional networks (Finegold 1999).

Such an unstructured 'ecosystem' is most effective at developing and supporting the most expert who work at the cutting edge of their profession. However, the USA as a whole is far less successful in training and development for the majority and it is here that a more regulated system triumphs. The highly regarded German apprenticeship is one of the best-known routes to achieving vocational qualifications. Full apprenticeships last three years and participants spend one or two days a week in the classroom and three or four in the workplace. Trainees are taught technical skills which are subsequently developed through participation in a series of problem-solving activities, graded in terms of difficulty. Care is taken to ensure that apprentices are exposed to a full range of different work situations, with central training centres supplementing workplace experience and providing additional workplace settings for trainees to learn in – an arrangement which gives smaller employers the capacity to offer high level training. Technical training is supplemented with knowledge of work control and design (manufacturing qualifications involve familiarity with costs, design and planning, and administration and production) and, in addition to this, all apprentices are required to continue to participate in further education for the duration of their vocational studies (Streeck *et al.* 1987; Lane 1989; Marsden and Ryan 1995; Crouch *et al.* 1999; Steedman 2001).

This system has also demonstrated its responsiveness to new occupations (in contrast to criticisms by Scott and Cockrill 1997). In the past Germany certainly struggled to provide qualifications for developing industries such as ICT since the tripartite arrangements for agreeing standards were so time-consuming that qualifications in fast-developing fields were out of date before they were launched. However, this development process has been shortened considerably and the dominance and longevity of systems like Microsoft mean that computing skills that do not date rapidly can be supported (Bosch 2003). Four new technical apprenticeships were launched in 1997 and proved so popular that, even in work with no tradition of apprenticeships, 60,000 young people were in training by the end of 2001, and this figure was in addition to the 10,000 apprentices enrolled on the 'old' ICT apprenticeship (Steedman *et al.* 2003:13).

Singapore, Taiwan and South Korea represent a different form of the regulated approach, the 'developmental state' (Ashton and Sung 1994; Ashton and Green 1996; Green *et al.* 1999b; Ashton 2004). These South-East Asian late industrialisers were largely 'state-shaped' (Lauder 2001) since national governments were involved in both the delivery and certification of skills. Sometimes they then withdrew (as in Japan and Korea where concentrations of capital were created) but in Singapore and Taiwan they have remained involved (although see also Debrah and Ofori 2001). The Taiwanese economy is dominated by small and medium enterprises (SMEs), that successfully resisted the introduction of a levy for vocational education and training in the 1970s. Yet, despite this, it has managed to introduce extensive vocational skills development, increasing the amount of technical vocational education and the numbers of scientists and engineers through the education system. Demand for education was for academic education (and this would have been cheaper to provide), but access to academic courses was officially restricted, more than half the schoolchildren were channelled into technical training and, at university level, more courses were made available for scientists and engineers and new institutes of technology launched. Student numbers, textbooks and curricula were state-controlled and this meant that Taiwan both succeeded in producing low-cost industrial products for export and also managed the transition from this to higher value-added production across many if not all sectors without significant reported skills shortages (Green *et al.* 1999a).

Interrelated systems

Perhaps the most notable feature of these examples is that they are systemic and that provision goes beyond the simple supply of high-quality training (indeed, in the US example, formal training is one of the least significant elements of skills development). The high skills ecosystem of Silicon Valley is made possible by the fact that recruits are already extremely highly educated on entry (and many of them are IT experts). Good intermediate skills training is facilitated in Germany by the existence of employers' associations, trade unions and vocational colleges that are prepared to collaborate, and in Taiwan by the government's readiness both to pay for skills development and to take decisions that may be unpopular with individual students and their families.

This is an important point and a key element of the success of each of these approaches. It also has implications for attempts to identify and transplant 'best practice', which generally focus only on one narrow element of a successful system. Korea's attempt to replicate the German apprenticeship system is a case in point (Jeong 1995). This had government support and experienced German advisers were engaged. But little financial support was available; the firms employing the apprentices provided little training, and used them as low-paid and low-skilled workers; few college tutors were sufficiently skilled to make up this deficit; and seniority, rather than skill, remained the key element in promotion. As a result, the initiative failed.

In Germany the apprenticeship system supports and is itself underpinned by the wider framework of societal relations. Qualifications are designed by consensus with input from employers' associations, trade unions and educationalists. Once launched they are rigorously policed by the chambers of commerce which have extensive powers to check on apprentices to ensure that companies are not exploiting trainees and that provision is of high quality. Such intervention is tolerated since the chambers are controlled by the employers themselves and they also provide a basis for sharing information on good practice. Sanctions against firms that fail to train range from formally removing apprentice training powers or depriving them of access to technology transfer networks as well as (widely used) more informal deterrents. This collective regulation and power to sanction serves a dual purpose. It ensures that standards are preserved, but it also means that there is less risk that some firms will refrain from training and poach staff – 'that other employers are not defecting from the game of skill provision' (Culpepper 1999:45).

The influential and active German employers' associations are complemented by powerful trade unions. Pay is negotiated sectorally so there is less incentive for newly qualified apprentices to gain a premium on their salary by moving employers (during their apprenticeship, young workers are paid about a third of the adult wage). Works council involvement in recruitment reinforces this. Such collective agreements also mean that firms do not compete by slashing wages and prices. The funding institutions provide further support for long-term investments (which include investment in skills) since German firms tend to be financed by long-term bank loans. This means that they are not as vulnerable as equity-financed organisations to investor panic at short-term underperformance and can demonstrate long-term results rather than quarterly profits. Cross-shareholdings between the banks make hostile takeovers a rarity (Crouch *et al.* 1999; Culpepper 1999; Rubery and Grimshaw 2003).

The final element in this equation is that way that German firms use labour, with many firms competing on the basis of incremental customisation rather than Fordist production or radical innovation (Culpepper 1999), so workforce skills are used to provide value-added elements in production. The fact that these structures and social supports are in place means that, even when work is reorganised, one of management's aims will be to use labour effectively. Lane's (1987) study of the banking and insurance industries shows how automation was used to eliminate almost all the low-skilled jobs. Other tasks were combined in a way that retained (and occasionally raised) skill levels, including a greater focus on customer service. In Britain, by contrast, the introduction of technology in banks resulted in work being standardised, with 91 per cent of clerks and 50 per cent of supervisors doing deskilled work (Crompton and Jones 1984:61).

Lloyd's (1999) comparison of the French and British aerospace industries reinforces the argument that institutional frameworks affect both employment security and skill. The French employment system is a regulated one. Redundancies of more than ten workers require consultation with works committee or employee representatives and firms must offer retraining. In

Box 3.1

In Denmark state intervention takes a very different form. Denmark tradition- ally has high trade union membership and a long history of collaboration between capital and labour which the state facilitates. The content and deliv- ery of all workplace learning programmes (including apprenticeship) is influ- enced heavily by both trade unions and employers and provision is subsidised by the state. As a result, standards can be set centrally while operations are highly decentralised. At the workplace workers are given a great deal of auton- omy and many workplaces contain 'mini-enterprises' where operations are under the direction of a skilled worker who has a great deal of autonomy over operations, maintenance and innovation so support for skills. There is strong and ongoing support for formal training and development, but the system is not so good at recognising non-formal learning, which is often seen as threat by powerful skilled unions.

Taken from Ashton (2004).

addition, French firms with more than ten employees must provide a training plan and consult the works committee on this when one exists. Unsurprisingly then, while the French organisations studied kept up training in the recession, often as a way of using staff who had little else to do, their British counterparts cut back on both staff and training programmes, stopping all apprenticeship and graduate training. While the French firms were well placed to cope with increased orders when the economy improved, the British ones were faced with skills shortages and went on a major recruitment drive, with one travelling as far as Australia to hire qualified staff. It seems that an organisation's effective use of skills both hinges on and influences its employ- ment contracts (though see also Guerrero and Sire 2001). As Bosch (2004:627–8) comments in a discussion of the shape of possible future employment practices in Europe:

> If a high-road strategy based on skills, flexible work organisation and internal flex- ibility is chosen, job tenure will remain stable. If a low-road strategy based on low skill, easily replaceable workers and a Taylorist work organisation, external flexi- bility might gain in importance and job tenure will be shorter than in the past.

These successful systems are not simply a result of well-designed initial VET programmes (though these are important), nor of individual firms' approaches to employment, nor the product and labour markets; rather they are a prod- uct of the institutional framework and wider societal relations within which the employment relationship is enacted (Buechtemann 1993). The successful

Box 3.2

This different organisation of work extends beyond manufacturing. In a study of hotel workers Finegold *et al.* (2000) found that all German front and back office staff spoke two languages and nearly two-thirds spoke a second foreign language. Their British and American respondents were far less linguistically capable, with 48 per cent of Americans and 39 per cent of British hotel staff speaking one other language. Once in work the training provided reinforced this skill difference between the nations. While the USA and Britain provided management training for a small group and vocationally relevant but narrow training for many (on work such as making a bed), 18 per cent of Germans went through a formal apprenticeship and ongoing training was broader (although in Germany work as room attendants was often outsourced to female immigrants who were kept outside the skills development loop).

Taken from Finegold, Wagner and Mason (2000).

implementation of flexible specialisation is the cornerstone of German prosperity and the application and utilisation of firm-specific skills is a central precondition of this. This needs cooperation between employees and employers to safeguard the investments of both sides, and works councils guarantee the necessary cooperation (Backes-Gellner *et al.* 1997; French 2001; FitzRoy and Kraft 2005).

It seems that when firms cannot dismiss workers, they are more likely to treat them as a fixed factor of production which encourages investment in skills (Streeck 1997), so work is organised very differently. Mason *et al.'s* (1996) study of biscuit manufacturing contrasts German production, where 90 per cent of workers were craft-trained bakers, with British, where almost no process workers and few supervisors had relevant qualifications. In Germany skilled workers would be responsible for several lines. In Britain one member of staff was devoted to each line. Even in industries such as ceramics, where neither country employs technically qualified workers, British jobs are more tightly controlled and discretion is limited with German workers taking responsibility for two to three machines while British workers stay on one (Jarvis *et al.* 2002). Ironically, in Jarvis and her colleagues' study, the striking difference between the way British and German firms organised production was that British firms had many more workers not attached to a specific line but responsible for quality control, inspectors, selectors and checkers, further deskilling the production tasks. In Germany, where apprenticeship instilled knowledge about and pride in work (the idea of the profession or *Beruf*), apprentice-trained workers were responsible for quality (see also Prais and

Wagner 1985; Prais and Wagner 1988; Mason and Finegold 1995; Clarke and Wall 1996, 1998, 2000; Finegold and Wagner 1998; Crouch *et al.* 1999).

Such devolution of responsibility did little to harm the products, indeed the quality of goods produced was far higher in the German firms than in the British ones. Additional workers were concentrated in areas that added value to the product (adding additional fillings and layers in the biscuits, planning and targeting ranges for ceramics). More highly qualified German supervisors would suggest changes to work organisation or machine configuration. In-house technicians and engineers not only ensured that routine maintenance was carried out but also gave investment advice to firms purchasing new equipment and forged relationships with equipment suppliers. British firms bought individual items ad hoc from firms that simply installed the machinery and left; these unmaintained machines broke down regularly, keeping their technicians more than fully occupied with troubleshooting activities and leaving lines inactive and workers idle. German equipment not only broke down far less often but was also configured to the needs of the firm since German suppliers provided packages of technology, assimilation advice and know-how.

As Lane (1987) argues, these high and clearly labelled skills in Germany benefit employers as well as employees. Recruitment costs are lower, labour is more flexible, work attitudes are more disciplined and motivation is higher. Firms offer a greater security of employment and employees stay in jobs longer (because sectoral pay bargaining means that there are fewer financial incentives to switch employers); even among young workers in the hotel sector, an area with traditionally high turnover, German workers enjoy higher wages and have much lower labour turnover than those elsewhere (Finegold *et al.* 2000).

Box 3.3

High workforce skills have implications for productivity and management. Clarke and Wall's (2000) study of construction in Britain, Germany and the Netherlands shows how both Dutch and German construction workers were more highly skilled and more specialist than their British counterparts. Yet despite the fact that managing continental building sites involved many more specialist workers and more complicated technologies than their British counterparts, it was Britain that had both the highest ratio of managers, 1 for every 24 workers compared with 1:33 in Germany and 1:49 in the Netherlands; the slowest work rate, 73 m^2 a day as opposed to 104 m^2 or 252 m^2; and the greatest number of faults.

Taken from Clarke and Wall (2000).

This systemic approach is apparent in Japan too, though here it takes a different form. There is considerable state investment in applied research and development as well as a highly regarded education system, which means that company expenditure can focus on the skills needed by the firm. Lifetime employment, minimal turnover and frequent retraining through a mixture of on- and off-the-job activities over an extended period ensure that there is a broad range of vocational skills and materially help problem-solving activities. A promotions system heavily dependent on seniority provides further incentives for workers to stay with the same employer (Dore and Sako 1989; Cole 1992; McMillan 1996; Sako 1999; Thelen 2004; Keizer 2005) . Such a system was only ever fully followed by a small minority of the largest firms (see Kondo 1990 for an account of work in a small, family-owned firm) but was extremely influential and allowed a great deal of functional flexibility within firms.

Such official involvement contrasts markedly with the USA. There there is little state involvement in learning and Rubery and Grimshaw (2003) describe the economy as an archetypal decentralised, market-led system. Almost all decisions on skills development are taken by individual firms or individual workers. There are some areas where training is sectorally regulated, but these are being abandoned rather than extended, as in the construction industry. There, once the regulations ceased to apply, training levels slumped, as did investment in physical capital and productivity (Bosch 2003). One brief attempt to devise national skill standards never got off the ground (Ashton 2004). In the absence of nationally recognised qualifications most learning is by doing, quality is uneven and provision polarised. Workers not already qualified at degree level are unlikely to receive firm-sponsored training and, when they do, the opportunities they are presented with are often narrowly based, while firms complain that much of their training spend is remedial. Many organisations rely on outside training providers or immigration to supply them with skills (Rubery and Grimshaw 2003). These are severe problems, and skills distribution is poor. Nonetheless, the USA enjoys both high capital productivity and reasonably high labour productivity in most sectors and is particularly effective at producing highly skilled elites in financial services, aero engineering, entertainment, biotechnology and software.

Systemic problems

There are problems with every type of system. In market economies the most severe problem is often the lack of skills development. Collectively employers have a clear interest in ensuring that a stock of appropriately skilled workers exists; individually it may be more attractive to poach trained workers from

Box 3.4

The danger of market systems is that skills training may not happen (because the cost is too great, for fear of poaching or simply because firms believe they can recruit appropriately skilled individuals when necessary). Clarke and Metalina's (2000) work in Russia's new market economy shows how little training the new private sector companies do, relying on what was provided by previous state employers or choosing to send only managers on skills development activities. One knitwear firm in Kemerovo got a new computerised knitting machine but sent the designer rather than the operator on courses so were never able to use it to full capacity (p. 26):

> In most new private enterprises, personnel selection and the use of probation is a substitute for training. If high-skilled employees are needed then the firm will advertise through newspapers or employment agencies and will select from the candidates on a competitive basis, paying wages at a sufficiently high level to recruit and retain people of the required standard. If the skills can be learnt on the job, then the new private-sector employers try to hire young people with relatively high levels of education and employ them on probationary terms, retaining those who have mastered the job within the probationary period. If the job does not require any particular skills, then the employer will seek out those with no skills and qualifications and pay them low wages, most often with a system of penalties and bonuses to encourage diligence and hard work, and put up with high labour turnover.

From Clarke and Metalina (2000).

elsewhere, spending some of the savings made by not providing training on salary premia. So in Finegold *et al.*'s (2000) comparative study of work and skill development in hotels, Britain experienced chronic skills shortages (particularly for chefs and front-of-house staff), which were partially solved by recruiting apprentice-trained staff from abroad. Since the German apprenticeship gave workers experience of every department this was also popular for managerial recruits. Similarly, in Lloyd's (1999) study of the aerospace industry, while France developed skills in-house, Britain poached.

Unsurprisingly such behaviour makes it less attractive for organisations to train staff (Keep 1989; Booth and Snower 1996). According to Becker (1964), such an omission should not matter, since as skills become scarce and employers pay more for them employees will step into the breach, funding their own development in anticipation of higher earnings. Few economies work this rationally and few workers are so perfectly well informed. Even when skills premia are publicised, some form of institutional support is needed to ensure that training is robust (whether through professional associations, trade unions, the state or universities and colleges). Moreover the people most likely to take advantage of such provision are those who are already highly educated and probably already in secure and skilled work where they are more likely to receive employer funded training. As Rubery and Grimshaw (2003) point out, this 'solution' simply divides insiders from outsiders, further polarising provision. It also does little to address the need for intermediate-level skills. The existence of labour market groups who are 'skills–poor' also raises issues above and beyond the economic needs of firms since these workers are likely to be poorly paid or unemployed, socially marginalised and (in the USA) deprived of welfare benefits. Some government-funded programmes are targeted at people who are disadvantaged in the labour market, but these tend to be narrowly based and contribute little to skills development (see, for example Butterwick 2003; Lafer 2004).

Compared with this, it would seem that the corporatist model for developing skills has considerable advantages. Employer bodies have the capacity for strategy at the collective level that individual firms lack, coupled with a proximity to business that the state does not have (Crouch *et al.* 1999). Yet corporatist systems are not without problems. They may avoid the conflicts and contradictions over the provision of skill that market economies experience, but their challenges tend to occur at the level of the sector or national economy (Rubery and Grimshaw 2003). In Germany questions have been raised about both the viability of apprenticeships and the wider system of employment regulation that supports it. There is a tension between generating a small number of good jobs or a large number of bad jobs (Ebbinghaus and Kittel 2005; Maurin and Postel-Vinay 2005). The market economies of Britain and the USA have clearly chosen the latter option. There unemployment is low and record numbers of new jobs are being created but, as the *Economist* noted in the style of the traditional good-news–bad-news Jewish joke, when 10,000 new jobs were created in the USA the bad news was that you needed three of them to live. In Germany where wages are high, jobs tend to be skilled and individual workers are still productive unemployment stands at 3.86 million (Federal Statistical Office 2005). In the service sector in particular there are some signs that employers are responding to this by taking on more low-paid and unskilled workers. In hotels room attendance is outsourced to female immigrants (Finegold *et al.* 2000) while in retail the highly skilled apprenticeship-trained workers are now 'anchor' staff surrounded by unqualified 'pairs of hands' (Kirsch *et al.* 2000). If more of the growing service sector in Germany adopts this type of Anglo-American numerical flexibility the systems of employment protection that underpin apprenticeship could be threatened.

Then there are problems with the apprenticeship itself. Qualifications are drawn up by consensus and so take a long time to develop, which may result in the skills taught being dated. The system has also been criticised for being too rigid and inflexible; as workers acquire and take pride in particular occupational identities and skills their flexibility to take on other skills decreases (Finegold and Wagner 1997; Scott and Cockrill 1997). Set against this are the recent successes in providing support for new, technological occupations and the regular links between general and practical skills that are built in to the apprenticeship. Since a trainer (*Meister*) spends most of their time doing normal work they are more likely to be up-to-date with the employer's needs and changing practices than their specialist counterpart in Britain or the USA (Crouch *et al.* 1999). However the unification of East and West Germany has placed the apprenticeship system itself under strain. Aside from the costs of unification to Germany as a whole (and these are considerable), tensions between works councils (which wish to see individual enterprises survive, possibly at the expense of pay settlements) and trade unions (which wish to preserve sectoral pay levels) may threaten the consensus that currently exists. In old East Germany 80 per cent of apprenticeships are offered by the state, which means that apprentices lack productive experience and which contradicts the principle of the dual market (Sloane and Ertl 2003). That said, large firms based there are taking steps towards introducing the full apprenticeship system including employment supports, rather than using the old East Germany as a trial for more-flexible, less-regulated policies (Culpepper 1999). This skills transfer also occurs in some partnerships between German firms and those based in Central Europe. Indeed, according to Bluhm (2001) it is the larger German firms (which are supposedly under most pressure to adopt the 'Anglo-Saxon' model), that are most likely to preserve the distinctive 'German' model of production.

The number of apprenticeship places have declined and some firms do seem unwilling to take on trainees, but this decline is from a record base and, with the increasing participation of young women in apprenticeships, nearly 70 per cent of school-leavers enrol on programmes with supply as popular among young people as ever (Crouch *et al.* 1999; Culpepper 1999). The German high skill equilibrium looks set to continue (Finegold and Soskice 1988). Indeed the most severe criticism of the German skills system is not the way it operates but that it does not go far enough. While apprentice training is systematised and highly regulated, continuing professional development is as fragmented and variable as it is in Britain and the USA. Extending the German model beyond apprenticeship would be widely welcomed (Crouch *et al.* 1999).

Innovations – working towards high skills

It seems that governments of all nations are prepared to intervene to support skills, if only to a limited extent. Even such market economies as the USA,

Britain and Canada have state-funded provision for groups disadvantaged in the labour market, although the quality and cost of such schemes may vary (see, for example Rainbird 1990; Payne 1991; Peck 1993; Cohen 2003; Lafer 2004). The issue is not whether an economy should be mixed but the form that mix should take. This is important, since, as the examples above have demonstrated, much of the success of various attempts to increase skills, in both market and regulated economies, is systemic. The advantages of Silicon Valley and the strengths of the German high skills equilibrium (Finegold and Soskice 1988) are not simply the result of improved vocational education and training.

Yet still, in many market economies intervention is often restricted to the supply side. Such interventions may be very successful. A small number of software companies in Ireland have turned to cooperative and collective action to address skill formation issues (McCartney and Teague 2001). And Buchanan and Evesson describe the way group training programmes in Australia combine the role of temporary employment agencies and skills developers, ensuring that young people have structured training, pastoral support and developmental work placements (2004a, 2004b). However it cannot be assumed that ensuring a supply of skilled workers will create its own demand (Brown 2001; Lauder 2001). Indeed, in Britain, one of the main problems with attempts to raise skills is that the country either does not or cannot compete effectively in high-quality production (Finegold and Soskice 1988;

Box 3.5

Group training organisations
One of the Australian responses to the problem of providing high-quality vocational training in a voluntarist state are group training organisations. These state-funded, often charitable companies offer accredited vocational training and pastoral support to trainees, who are classified as employees. They also hire their trainees out, at a price, to local firms, effectively acting as temporary employment agencies and providing the trainees with (supported) work experience plus an opportunity to impress a potential employer. About 200 group training organisations exist and between them they cater for 35,000 apprentices (13 per cent of the national total). There have been some problems with this system – in particular some of the organisations attempt to place workers by undercutting their peers, effectively forcing down the quality of provision; but in general it has been extremely successful at supporting training delivery while maintaining employment standards and offering trainees protection.

Taken from Buchanan and Evesson (2004b).

Nolan and Slater 2003). Accordingly, it may be useful to explore some skills based interventions which aim to change the demand for skills as well as the supply.

Hannon's (2005) research in the Irish dairy industry, historically a low-skills and low-quality sector, shows the way government-sponsored research institutes, targeted technology transfer and grants to firms helped several organisations switch to 'value-added' production from 'commodity' milk, butter and cheese markets. The new products included probiotic yoghurt drinks, 'functional' foods, continental cheeses and supplies to the ice cream industry. Such changes advantaged the firms, where margins and viability had been under considerable pressure from powerful retailers, by enabling them to produce 'value-added' products and giving them access to less-competitive (and higher margin) markets, but the impact on employees' skill levels was rather more mixed. One firm did indeed set up a research institute to support the development of 'functional' foods employing fifty science and technology graduates but in several of the others while what was being produced changed, the mode of production did not and workers were engaged only in low-skilled work.

Norwegian attempts to increase lifelong learning and improve skills in work made use of trade union involvement. After signing pacts on wage restraint in 1992 the unions started to bargain on skills development issues. At the end of the 1990s over 600 skills development projects were launched covering more than 50,000 employees. However, the least-advantaged workers were also least likely to take part in these. Programmes were popular with participants and successes in skill development were reported, but these were limited. It is not clear how much these initiatives improved matters for the 'learning-poor'. Most were small projects and few formal plans existed to ensure that good practice could be spread. The unions, one potential conduit, did succeed in winning various rights but only a few, such as electricians, who operated in a sector where the pace of change was rapid, let competence bargaining have priority over distributional issues. There were many positive developments from these schemes, in a country where people were already highly educated and already valued continuing workplace development, but more needs to be done to embed lessons learned and ensure that the positive results are extended beyond the life of this official intervention (Payne 2005).

In Finland a similar scheme aimed to make further and full use of staff know-how as well as (unusually) seeking to provide a balanced development between quality of working life and productivity. They too had a range of workplace-initiated projects funded by government. Numerous successes were reported, including a municipal meals service where kitchen workers became involved in planning menus, purchasing and budgeting. This not only increased productivity; it also helped to boost staff motivation. The initiative was limited to two sectors, engineering and local government, and the quality of consultants involved was uneven, but results were generally positive (Keep and Payne 2002; Alasoimi 2003; Payne 2004).

Each of these examples is limited in scope. The dairy industry in Ireland represents only one (small) sector and the Norwegian and Finnish programmes, while numerous, were all comparatively small-scale. However, in marked contrast to the British interventions, they do show governments attempting to stimulate the way skills are used as well as the way they are developed. This is important. 'High-skills eco-systems' can and do occur through a combination of market factors, as Silicon Valley and the Hollywood film industry in the USA demonstrate (Finegold 1999). However such occurrences are rare and countries or regions that wish to compete in skills and knowledge-intensive markets are well advised to take action to support this. Hannon's (2005) research compares the Irish dairy industry with its English counterpart where state intervention was limited. The Milk Marketing Board, which had provided a strong collective voice for the industry, was dismantled in 1994 and a dedicated R&D group at Reading University shut down. The little protective regulation that still existed (the Office of Fair Trading code of practice, designed to protect companies from excessive cost pressure by retailers) was not being enforced. Unsurprisingly efforts to upskill production or compete on a different basis were not successful. Several firms went bankrupt and the only evidence of high skills activity and advanced dairy products were found in foreign firms, which set up some extremely successful operations.

Discussion and conclusions

The high-skills society is a common aspiration but, as Green and Sakamoto (2001) point out, there is often little precision in debates about what is meant by this term. They observe four different models: an economy in which highly skilled creative elites, such as symbolic analysts, sell high-priced labour in international markets which generates most of the value added; an economy with a wide distribution of skills and relative equality of income distribution; an economy with high levels of technical skills and knowledge specialisation; or an economy with a wide spread of generic competences which provides the basis for future learning and civic participation. Each has very different implications not only for skills but also for society as a whole, since every form of skills development has implications that extend beyond the boundaries of individual firms (Lane 1987). Reich's (1993) *The Work of Nations* refers optimistically to 'symbolic analysts', the knowledge elite who make money by manipulating ideas, but also expresses concern that, since they are linked to global professional networks, such workers will have few ties to their localities, may live in gated communities and secure separate schools for their children and hospitals for their sick, leaving their compatriots condemned to generations of poverty. The 'hourglass economy' observed by Nolan (2001) in Britain where incomes polarise is also apparent in the USA. In continental Europe, where many more people are skilled, wage distribution is much more even (Diprete 2005; Gangl 2005).

Such fears are particularly acute now as the entries of China and India into the global labour markets effectively double the number of workers but have only a marginal effect on the supply of global capital. This 'great doubling' fundamentally changes the capital:labour ratio and potentially weakens labour-power. It could potentially lead to falling or stagnating wages in the developed world, a decline in the power of trade unions and huge increases in in-country inequality. Alternatively, instead of this 'bad transition', countries might plan for a 'good transition' using technological advances to increase productivity and lower prices so that purchasing power is maintained; and providing a social service infrastructure and a social wage to preserve living standards (Freeman 2005).

This is a genuine option. In Sweden many service sector jobs are located in the welfare state with the result that they are relatively well paid and secure. In the USA low-end service workers are typically employed in the private sector. They are poorly paid, with no job security and generally excluded from benefits (Esping-Andersen 1999). Spreading the Swedish, rather than the American, model of service sector jobs would raise living standards and reduce social polarisation. This would mean, in Green and Sakamoto's (2001) terms, switching from one type of high-skills society to another, and one with greater benefits for the majority of citizens.

Such a shift would require other changes too since, as this chapter has argued, the successes observed here are systemic ones. Germany's excellent supply of robust, intermediate-level vocational skills provides shopfloor-level expertise that can be harnessed through consultative processes while job security and seniority- and skill-based payment systems provide both firms and individuals with structural incentives to acquire and develop skills. Transplanting the apprenticeship system without the corresponding employer and union associations, wage agreements, bank financing and job security is unlikely to produce the same results (as Korea discovered). The institutional infrastructure that supports apprenticeship also makes it viable by ensuring that individual firms train young workers for the sector, rather than simply poaching skilled employees from elsewhere. Following this model, productivity and skill can be secured through cooperation, regulation and high wages (Turner 1962). Indeed, a recent ten-country study by Vernon and Rogers (2005) clearly links productivity growth with regulation and trade union density.

Regulation, it seems, not only supports skill development; it also (relatedly) underpins more cooperative industrial relations, higher wages and better terms and conditions for employees. The most clear disadvantage is the claimed link with unemployment. German jobless figures are high and the 'lost decade' of Japanese stagnation has lasted since 1989 (Keizer 2005) while the British and US economies have boomed. It may be that there is a choice between high skill, high wage and high unemployment or low skill, low wage and high employment. Yet this seems to be too pessimistic a conclusion. Intensive R&D and high worker skills mean that German labour productivity is still extremely high, despite the levels of unemployment and fewer working hours. Given its many advantages, it is still far too early to write off corporatist industrial relations (Visser 1998; Culpepper 1999; Crouch et al. 1999; Green and Sakamoto 2001). Market systems and competition based on numerical flexibility may raise greater problems. Britain in particular has always struggled to compete on the basis of high skill and high-quality goods and services (Finegold and Soskice 1988; Del Bono and Mayhew 2001; Keep and Mayhew 2001; Caulkin 2005). The existing voluntarist approach to skills development does little to enhance either skills or innovation, while repeated rounds of redundancies effectively intensify work and 'de-knowledge' firms, all of which makes the country less able to compete on quality (Ackroyd and Procter 1998; Littler and Innes 2003; Walker 2004).

But interventions that target the supply of skills in isolation are not sufficient. Britain has had a plethora of them, with the result that more than a third of workers report that their skills are underutilised at work (Felstead et al. 2002). Just as successful skills development is systemic, so too must successful intervention be. This is particularly necessary since skills-based competition at firm level does not necessarily translate into high skills for workers (Hannon 2005). While Streeck's research shows the links between individual workers' skills and skills based competition by firms (Streeck et al. 1987; Streeck 1992), such a link cannot be assumed.

Brown (2001) provides an excellent route forward as well as a detailed analysis of the existing situation. He argues that high skill formation also depends on building societal capacity; that the social foundations on which skills are built will also affect whether those skills can be effectively utilised. He proposes a framework of seven 'C's for high skills, as follows:

- *Consensus* – with all major stakeholders (government, employers and trade unions) committed to upgrade skills.
- *Competitive capacity* – best achieved by 'value-added' rivalry between firms rather than zero-sum competition and downsizing; cost-cutting may meet the short-term demands of the shareholder but not the long-term needs of society and the economy.

- *Capability* – a view of human capacity which assumes that the majority (rather than simply the elite) are capable of high-skilled work.
- *Coordination* – of supply and demand for labour, including stimulating demand for highly skilled workers and encouraging partnerships between municipal authorities, businesses and communities.
- *Circulation* – with skills diffused beyond a few companies.
- *Cooperation* – and high trust relations,
- *Closure* – avoiding the fallacy of blaming the individuals who do not find professional or managerial jobs for this and consider how work is defined and rewarded.

This is a valuable framework. It emphasises the importance of intervention and of high-trust relations through which skills can be developed and exercised, skills diffusion and positive partnerships. And it could provide a basis for consensual skills development even in the absence of full corporatism (see also Baccaro 2003). It would be nice to believe that governments, faced with the perennial task of building skills, would take this model to heart.

4

Vocational education and training in Britain

> The skills of our people are a vital national asset. Skills help businesses achieve the productivity, innovation and profitability needed to compete. They help our public services provide the quality and choice that people want. They help individuals raise their employability, and achieve their ambitions for themselves, their families and their communities. Sustaining a competitive, productive economy which delivers prosperity for all requires an ever growing proportion of skilled, qualified people. We will not achieve a fairer, more inclusive society if we fail to narrow the gap between the skills-rich and the skills-poor. (Department for Education and Skills/DTI/HM Treasury/Department for Work and Pensions 2003:7)

As Chapter 3 demonstrated, the difference between voluntarist and regulated approaches to VET is clearer in theory than it is in practice. Singapore's 'developmental state' also supports locally designed, employer-led training (Ashton and Sung 1994; Debrah and Ofori 2001; Ashton 2004:15); and the well-developed German training programmes lapse into fragmented market-driven activities once workers have passed their apprenticeships (Crouch *et al.* 1999). Equally in Britain, where the system is broadly voluntarist and successive governments have argued that decisions on training and development should be left to employers, officials are not passive and there is (often extensive) state intervention.

This chapter provides more detail on the British experience of VET considering both its advantages and its disadvantages. Unlike corporatist or developmental states, market-led VET is by its nature not systemic, at least in the sense that practices are seldom specifically set up to complement each other. Yet despite repeated commitments to voluntarism (Department for Education and Skills/DTI/HM Treasury/Department for Work and Pensions

2003; DfES 2004a), governments of different political orientations have made VET a key aspect of their activities, acting, if not arguing, as though VET is much too important to be left to the market.

State support and infrastructure

British VET has been voluntarist since 1814, except in the brief period following the 1964 Industrial Training Act during which, first, sectoral Industry Training Boards, ensured that training was provided and set levies on firms that did not participate (Sheldrake and Vickerstaff 1987) and then the boards' replacement, the Manpower Services Commission, attempted to develop a national system of training to agreed standards, focusing particularly on the young and the unemployed (Ainley and Corney 1990). As the last chapter argued, in theory this should mean that training is more flexible and more responsive to employers' needs (since they, presumably, will design or approve it) but it may also result in activities that are fragmented, a level of provision that is variable and extensive poaching.

Yet in Britain, over the last twenty years, voluntarism has taken an unusual form as successive governments of different political persuasions have observed the ample evidence of market failure in VET and intervened. The extent, and the confused nature, of this intervention can be seen from the list of government departments with responsibility, accountability or interest in VET. Training issues are dealt with by the Department for Education and Skills, the Department for Work and Pensions, the Department for Trade and Industry, the Treasury, the Office of the Deputy Prime Minister, the Cabinet Office, the Home Office and the prime minister and his advisers. These, together with local authorities and regional development associations, intervene in education (to make it more vocationally oriented) and colleges, provide business support, and offer training for both the unemployed and those in work. In order to do so, they have established a range of quangos and state agencies including one national Learning and Skills Council, 47 Local Learning and Skills Councils, the Learning and Skills Development Agency, the Qualifications and Curriculum Authority, the Adult Learning Inspectorate, the Office for Standards in Education, the Sector Skills Development Agency and a network of sector skills councils (Keep and Ashton 2004).

The cost and scale of such operations is significant. The Learning and Skills Council is the largest quango in Europe, controlling a budget of £8.5 million, and because people are appointed to quangos rather than elected, they are accountable only to the relevant secretary of state (Keep and Ashton 2004). Unsurprisingly, such a plethora of bodies makes coordination difficult and

Box 4.1

Competing on cost

Outsourcing (an increasingly popular activity) may magnify pressures on organisations to deskill and compete on cost. In 1997 British Airways outsourced provision of in-flight meals to Gate Gourmet, then started to press for price reductions. In August 2005 at the peak of the holiday season Gate Gourmet brought in 130 temporary workers, mainly Eastern Europeans and Somalis, as cheap labour (Toynbee 2005a). Concerned, existing staff refused to carry on working and, within hours, 639 had been dismissed by megaphone. These workers were already poorly paid. The workforce consisted mainly of middle-aged women from the local Sikh communities and their take-home salary of £10,000 to £12,000 was less than half the London average (Townsend 2005). Within a day, ground staff at British Airways (many of whom were the fathers, husbands and brothers of these women) had come out in sympathy, more than 700 aeroplanes were grounded and passengers were stranded (Tran 2005). After nearly three weeks of dispute Gate Gourmet rene-gotiated its contract with British Airways, gaining an extra £10 million, and offered voluntary redundancy for which 700 workers applied (Hencke 2005). Ironically, the additional funds provided by British Airways exactly equalled the amount spent by David Bonderman, the founder and chief executive of Gate Gourmet's parent company, on his own birthday party (Toynbee 2005b). Throughout these activities the company's website boasted its faith in its 'most valuable resources – our employees' and claimed that it was 'keeping our employees passionate about what they do' and attempting to 'infuse our employees with enthusiasm and eagerness' (Walsh 2005).

working in the area of skills and training extremely complex (Pring 2004). As a result, a great deal of effort is dedicated not to increasing skills but rather to guiding others round the system or putting various groups in touch with one another (the sector skills councils, for example, provide no training themselves and exist simply to pass on information, bring interested parties together, gather labour market intelligence and develop qualifications).

More worryingly, the system is an extremely changeable one. Since state intervention and centralisation became a major feature of British VET at the start of the 1980s there have been a vast number of VET programmes. Some, such as the Training Opportunities Programme described by Joan Payne (1991), have been successful. Providing several weeks of intensive skill devel-opment, coupled with a small stipend, this scheme enabled many people to find or change jobs. Indeed, it is one of the few that attracted participants who were already in work and who gave up employment to participate. Others, like the Youth Training Scheme, were widely criticised (Keep 1986, 1987; Cockburn 1987; Ainley and Corney 1990). It existed largely to provide the young unemployed with training in work (hopefully leading to jobs) but, like many schemes for the unemployed, it was targeted at people who wanted work rather than training and the standard of provision varied greatly. While some employers offered high-quality skills development with the prospect of future secure employment, often linked to old apprenticeship programmes, others used the scheme to supply them with subsidised, unskilled labour, firing the trainee once the subsidy expired. But good or bad, such schemes had an extremely limited life expectancy. The TOPs programme was halted at the start of the 1990s while YTS was extended from one year to two, then changed to Youth Training, National Traineeships, Other Training, Foundation and Advanced Modern Apprenticeships and has now been revised and repackaged as junior, foundation and advanced apprenticeships (Keep and Ashton 2004).

The system is in a continuous state of flux. According to the Cabinet Office's Performance and Innovation Unit, in 2001 there were 54 separate workforce development initiatives (Performance and Innovation Unit 2001). Small wonder that most of the participants have difficulty negotiating it (Matlay 2002; Coffield 2002); as Keep and Ashton (2004:2) note:

> The authors cannot think of a single other European country in which the training system has been subjected to such a profound and sustained series of institutional changes. The process has meant a limited half-life for major institutions, qualifications, inspection regimes and programmes, with associated problems of stability and recognition (not least among small employers, parents, students and others who need to use the VET system). Even those who are paid to observe and analyse the system find it problematic to keep track of, assimilate and make sense of the many changes that are constantly taking place at the behest of government.

Extensive efforts are made to involve employers, through qualification design, participation in the ever changing quangos, monitoring and assessment (Keep and Stasz 2004), though trade unions may be excluded from consultation and involvement (Peck 1993). But this is not, nor is it intended to be, the type of social partnership observed elsewhere. Rather, discussions are limited to VET (rather than employment conditions or ways of working) and the agenda is set by the state (Keep and Ashton 2004).

Education

Official activity generally stops short of actual legislation, with regulation limited to areas such as health and safety, food standards and care work. But there is extensive regulation in one area that has a significant impact on VET, namely the education system. The state's increasing involvement in and centralisation of VET has been undertaken in tandem with a centralisation of compulsory education. The government has become increasingly involved in schools and further education at all levels – setting a national curriculum; introducing a new national qualifications framework and new qualifications (as well as abolishing many existing ones); setting centrally designed, national tests for pupils at prescribed stages; rationalising the exam boards and markedly reducing their autonomy; and effectively changing the British system from the one with least state involvement to that with most (Keep and Ashton 2004).

At the same time, as noted in Chapter 2, more British students are staying on in full-time education, gaining qualifications in school and going on to further or higher study (though it seems unlikely that the central government involvement has either contributed to or caused this rise). One issue that has attracted a considerable amount of discussion is the extent to which school pupils should receive a vocational education (Hayward and Sudnes 2000; Brockington 2002; Grubb 2003). Realistically, the lines between schooling and VET have always been blurred. The success of Silicon Valley rests on the influx of bright, well-educated graduates; the expert workers in Arthur's (1999) steel mini-mills depend on US universities' engineering courses, since employer-provided VET tends to be weak; and Taiwan's skills base is largely supported by government investment in technical schools and colleges. Schooling certainly influences VET provision, not least because an influx of well-educated recruits into the labour market makes VET far more effective. However, the effectiveness, relevance and rigour of VET in schools is open to question (Stasz and Wright 2004; Stasz et al. 2004). At best, VET in schools can provide pupils alienated by traditional academic routes with a robust skills base and nationally recognised qualifications to ease their progress in the job market. At worst it offers out-of-date, low-level activities which take up time that might otherwise be used gaining academic certificates that would add significantly to lifetime earnings and provides access only to unskilled jobs. Such provision also raises the danger of moral hazard, that employers may reduce their own training activities and see schools as the only provider of skills. The regular complaints that school-leavers cannot 'hit the ground running' and are not sufficiently ready for the world of work (see for example Stewart 2005) may reflect a corporate reluctance to train, rather than declining standards in education. It is far from clear that the main role of the education system is (or should be) to equip students with vocational skills, and several commentators have been highly critical of the transfer of responsibilities from employers to taxpayers that this implies (Keep 2001).

Investors in People

In the workplace, official VET programmes and initiatives change regularly (and often dramatically). Two of the most widespread, and long-lived, programmes are Investors in People and National Vocational Qualifications (NVQs). Both are voluntary and, while some official funds are provided, to market these schemes and (occasionally) subsidise accreditation, each relies on advertising rather than compulsion.

Investors in People is a quality kitemark awarded to firms that meet certain standards in human resource provision. Specifically these include linking training to business strategy, ensuring that practices such as appraisal, involvement and communication are in place for the whole workforce and checking that these are appropriate by evaluating the processes implemented. By August 2004 just over 37,000 organisations covering 38 per cent of people in employment had gained Investors in People accreditation (http://www.iipuk.co.uk). Successes have been reported in terms of employee motivation and morale (Hillage and Moralee 1996) and reduced levels of absenteeism and turnover (Alberga et al. 1997). Comparisons between firms with and without Investors in People accreditation seem to indicate that those with the award enjoy higher levels of profit.

According to its proponents, gaining the award sends an important, symbolic message to staff. The assistant chief executive (personnel) of a hospital trust seeking reaccreditation argued that (Grugulis and Bevitt 2002:48):

> I think it is important to demonstrate to both the world outside and the staff within that we do have the HR/personnel policies and procedures – training and development policies and procedures – that are designed to support them in the work that they are doing and to help them achieve.

In this trust, staff motivation, job satisfaction and commitment were all extremely high. Staff spoke very positively of 'their' hospital. Extensive training was available, much of it leading to qualifications, and staff could and did progress from unskilled ancillary posts to skilled nursing positions. However, it was not clear how much of this could be attributed to the Investors in People award. The National Health Service in Britain, in common with much of the public sector, has long enjoyed a good reputation for training and development. When employees were asked about the reasons underlying their high commitment to work they spoke of the hospital as a service for the local community and the importance of doing meaningful work. Only 13 per cent claimed to be motivated by the Investors in People award and most completely failed to recognise the staff development policy, the staff charter and the training charter (all of which were lynchpins of the trust's accreditation). According to one radiology sister (p. 55):

I think they're a waste of time personally. I mean the object of a hospital is to treat people and get them better, you don't really need it written down do you . . . we don't need to be *told* we need to treat them to the best of our ability because it doesn't *make* you treat them to the best of your ability by telling you that you need to do it.

It may be that such recognition of policies is unnecessary to success. Staff, after all, may feel the effects of these documents without being aware of their existence. Alternatively it may be that Investors in People accredits well-managed firms, but does little to encourage or enhance their success. Firms with Investors in People accreditation are more profitable, more successful and have more highly motivated staff than those without. However, these differences may be attributable to the nature of the firms that seek accreditation rather than to the Investors in People award itself. It may be that successful firms were already actively engaged in training and development and that the kitemark simply rubber-stamped existing practice (Grugulis and Bevitt 2002). According to Hoque (2003), factors such as industrial sector, the expertise of the personnel department, ownership and size (all of which Investors in People does little to change) have the greatest impact on a firm's decision to seek accreditation. Once this has been gained it does not necessarily act as a stimulus to further progress since training activity does not necessarily increase after the award has been achieved. Large firms (which may already possess sophisticated human resource systems) gain awards faster than small ones. Moreover, recent evidence suggests that either organisations are becoming more adept at assessment, more realistic about the prospect of succeeding, or the award is becoming easier to gain since far more organisations are successfully accredited now than when Investors in People was launched (Fernandez *et al.* 2005).

The impact Investors in People has on practice is not necessarily positive. Ram (2000a), in a study of three SMEs that had either gained or were working towards Investors in People, argues that the award was valued because it could help them to win business from government bodies, rather than for the impact it might have on skills. Indeed, changes tended to be sham exercises. One company director, who had pinned mission statements onto the office walls before an assessor's visit, commented (Ram 2000a:280):

We had a mission statement devised very quickly for Investors in People and basically we had to have all these statements stuck around the room, so that when the assessor came in he was able to see these, which really I think qualifies my argument that we are doing it for a paperwork exercise. I am sure if he walks round this building and says to people 'what is our mission statement?' I can almost guarantee that 90 per cent, maybe 95 per cent, of our employees would not know what it was.

It was not that these organisations did not value training and development – they did, and all engaged actively in it – but rather that the accreditation process was bureaucratic and did not fit their current practice particularly readily. As a result, gaining the Investors in People award became a 'mock' exercise with the activities necessary for accreditation divorced from reality. It seems that, while the Investors in People award can be valuable it does not necessarily extend training and development activities beyond organisations that already train actively and that the bureaucracy involved in accreditation may cause problems (Hoque *et al.* 2005).

National Vocational Qualifications

While Investors in People is targeted at the level of the firm, NVQs provide a system of qualifications that cover almost all occupations and all levels of achievement from level 1 (the most basic) to level 5 (the most complex). By March 2004 nearly 4.5 million NVQs had been awarded, over 75 per cent of which were at levels 1 and 2 (http://www.qca.org.uk). NVQs were intended originally to provide an umbrella framework against which all vocational awards could be measured (Raggatt and Williams 1999). Such clarity was (and is) badly needed since vocational qualifications in Britain are a cottage industry, designed, delivered and accredited by a range of bodies including professional associations, colleges, trade unions and employers. As a result, provision is often fragmented. In 1990 there were 279 different certificates available for secretaries at five different levels (Employment Department 1992; Keep 1994). However, in practice, NVQs became a radical new form of qualification themselves. Their distinctive feature was lists of the behaviours workers should demonstrate, so that people who had become competent through years of experience on the job could be assessed as easily as those who had undertaken formal training.

This was a radical departure from existing practice. The demands of the workplace and demonstrations of competence in work are key features in most forms of vocational education and training but rarely had they been the sole means of assessment, though their attraction is easy to see. Qualifications rarely measure workplace performance directly. Most aim to improve it by increasing candidates' knowledge or technical competence, so the prospect of somehow certifying workplace performance itself is enticing. Nor is this a new debate. Indeed, over the last century there have been various attempts by utilitarian vocationalists to capture and certify *only* those skills that are immediately useful for work (see Hyland 1994).

The NVQ system rated achievements at five different levels and this framework was intended to cover work-based qualifications for everyone from apprentice to board director. Large numbers of NVQs were developed with impressive speed. By 1992 NVQs had been designed for occupations that covered 80 per cent of the workforce (Raggatt and Williams 1999). While this achievement was laudable, the National Council for Vocational Qualifications had not, as originally intended, provided the means to accredit existing qualifications. Rather, they anticipated that all qualifications could and should be recast into NVQ format. It was hoped that the NVQ framework would become well understood and easily recognisable by dominating provision rather than because it rated existing qualifications in relation to one another (Fennell 1993).

This structure created problems. Each qualification set out, in detailed lists of 'competences', exactly what behaviours a competent person should display in the workplace (Burke 1989), couched in a specialist (and highly regulated) language. This 'NVQ-speak' is described, even in official reviews, as complex, confusing, difficult to understand or relate to work, and inappropriate, criticisms that are extended to the guidance provided with it (Beaumont 1995). Such a use of language, coupled with NVQs' emphasis on the workplace, means that candidates are required to demonstrate competence in particular ways. These ways need to be conveyed and studies suggest that teaching candidates the administrative demands of the NVQ system (how evidence should be presented and 'portfolios' assembled) is time-consuming. As a result, teaching time is taken up with administrative necessities rather than substantive, occupationally relevant knowledge (Hyland and Weller 1994; Grugulis 1997; Fuller and Unwin 2001). Nor does an NVQ increase the individual's autonomy and discretion. The specification of NVQ 'standards' effectively achieves a Taylorist separation of conception and execution, with the NVQ's designers deciding which actions constitute competent performance and candidates simply demonstrating that they can perform actions.

More fundamentally, their impact on skills is questionable. Senker (1996) observed that NVQ level 3 in engineering covered only two-thirds of the requirements of the traditional apprenticeship. Since an NVQ could be achieved after two years, while the 'full apprenticeship' typically took three and a half to four years this estimate probably errs on the side of generosity. Other studies note the lowering of standards in construction (Callendar 1992), hairdressing (Dispatches 1993; Raggatt 1994), management (Grugulis 1997) and electrical engineering (Smithers 1993).

Work done by Smithers (1993), which contrasts the old City and Guilds plumbing certificate with the plumbing NVQ, provides a dramatic illustration of the differences between the two qualifications. The City and Guilds qualification not only required a higher level of practical, technical expertise; it also tested knowledge of physics, electronics, maths, technical drawing and

Box 4.2

Designing qualifications as a series of 'competences' or statements of observable behaviours is also cumbersome. While traditional certificates rely on the expertise of assessors, guidance from the syllabus and informed holistic judgements of workplace competence, it is a requirement of NVQs that everything necessary to success must be explicitly specified in the qualifications' criteria and judged in assessment. As a result, all NVQs, at every level, are long and prescriptive lists of actions. The management NVQ at level 4 had 1 key purpose, 4 key roles, 9 units of competence, 26 elements of competence, 163 performance criteria and 338 range statements. Successful candidates were required to prove their competence against all of these. Yet extensive as these lists were, they provided little practical guidance on the depth of knowledge which candidates should possess. As Popham, an advocate turned critic of competence-based qualifications, argued (1984:39):

> Once upon a time, when I was younger and foolisher, I thought we could create test specifications so constraining that the test items produced as a consequence of their use would be *functionally homogeneous*, that is, essentially interchangeable. But if we use the difficulty of an item as at least one index of the item's nature, then it becomes quite obvious that even in such teensy behaviour domains as measuring the students ability to multiply pairs of double-digit numbers, the task of $11 \times 11 = ?$ is lots easier than $99 \times 99 = ?$. About the only way we can ever attain functional homogeneity is to keep pruning the nature of the measured behaviour so that we're assessing ever more trifling sorts of behaviour. That would be inane. [Emphasis in original.]

technology. The background to technology included physical qualities, electricity and magnetism, forces, pressure, heat, thermal movement, energy, principles of tool construction and materials technology, concepts in chemistry, applied chemistry and materials for industry. The NVQ which replaced it specified none of these and the lists of behaviours (or 'competences') NVQs prescribed proved cumbersome. According to Eraut *et al.* (1996) even at the lowest level, NVQs involved around 1000 separate assessment decisions.

More fundamentally, despite their claim to be 'employer-led', one of the most common criticisms of NVQs is that the process is cumbersome and bureaucratic, bearing little relationship to the 'real' world of work. There is some evidence to support these criticisms. NVQs make their claim to relevance on the basis that they describe the actions to be performed in any given occupation. Yet, as Senker (1996) argues, neither in theory nor in practice is work organised on a sectoral basis. Jobs may be and are designed in a different way from company to company and even from person to person. The employment contract is incomplete, since attempting to specify exactly what employees should do is likely to be dysfunctional. While it is clearly a valuable and useful exercise to consider the function of work, explore the aims of an occupation and review the rationale for particular tasks (not least because these processes may help to inform decision-making), such broad conclusions are probably beyond behaviourally specific 'competences'. These simply list actions and assume that anything which 'underlies' these actions (including motivation, knowledge and choice) can be 'inferred' through observation alone. Paradoxically, it seems that the concern to make these qualifications 'relevant' has resulted in their exclusive preoccupation with behaviours and actions (which are not centrally dictated) in place of more broadly constituted skills and knowledge (which might be of interest to a whole occupational sector or industry).

In NVQs, emphasis is taken from the overall meaning and function of work to the minutiae of its application. So the managers in Grugulis's (2000) study gained units towards their qualification for arranging their offices in an ergonomic way (with the computer, filing cabinet and telephone all within easy reach) or ordering name badges for staff rather than the more substantive managerial tasks (developing IT systems and negotiating pay rates) that each was involved in, because the first set of actions, though trivial, met the wording of the standards while the second set, though important and substantive, did not.

Nor were appropriate standards of performance immediately apparent to assessors working from NVQ performance criteria. Wolf (1995:25) provides a (dramatic) illustration of this by reproducing element 9.1, 'Obtain and evaluate information to aid decision making', from the MCI's NVQ level 5 for senior managers which is intended to describe high-level, complex work (see Box 4.3). These behaviours, ostensibly drawn from the activities of managers, could as easily be used to describe the responsibilities of the porter at an office reception desk. It is far easier to assess work when the assessors are also supplied with exemplars, set texts and guidance (Wolf and Silver 1986; Eraut and Cole 1993).

To what extent have NVQs succeeded? Qualifications have been awarded to many previously excluded from the system, which is praiseworthy. However, they have been widely criticised (see, among others Hyland 1994; Wolf 1995; Grugulis 2003) and, outside the public sector, the armed services and retailing, proved unpopular with employers. Moreover, compared with other qualifications, NVQs produce few financial benefits, with levels 1 and 2 giving no salary premium at all. In part this is because they are targeted at those at the lowest end of the achievement scale. Many advantages of higher-level qualifications stem from the fact that they mark individuals as belonging to the brightest group in society or the highest social class (Crouch *et al.*

Management, level 5 element 3.2
Element 9.1 Obtain and evaluate information to aid decision making

(a) Information requirements are identified accurately and re-evaluated at suitable intervals
(b) Information is sought on all relevant factors affecting current or potential operations
(c) Information is relevant and is collected in time to be of use
(d) A variety of sources of information are regularly reviewed for usefulness, reliability and cost
(e) Opportunities are taken to establish and maintain contacts with those who may provide useful information
(f) Methods of obtaining information are periodically evaluated and improved where necessary
(g) When normal information routes are blocked, alternative methods are tried
(h) Information is organised into a suitable form to aid decision making
(i) Conclusions drawn from relevant information are based on reasoned argument and appropriate evidence

1999). However, HNDs and HNCs also serve previous low achievers and yet they consistently produce financial gains. The explanation for this is probably that HNDs and HNCs have syllabi and attempt to teach candidates new skills while NVQs simply accredit what workers already do. Indeed, in Munro and Rainbird's (2001) research into low-skilled workers, none said they had learned anything from the NVQs they had taken. Qualifications need to be achievable, but they should also develop skills and it is here that NVQs fail. As Young (2001) argues, making the qualifications of those at the lowest level of the workforce so different from those at the highest simply reinforces disadvantage.

Apprenticeships

In Britain apprenticeships, which work so well elsewhere, have never played more than a marginal role in skills provision (Keep 1994). Their role was most significant, at least in terms of numbers, in the period after the Second World War (though see also Greenwood 1933/1993) but by the 1960s apprenticeship programmes were highly criticised. Since most were in male-dominated industries they tended to reflect (and occasionally exaggerate) the gender distribution of jobs, so few places were available for young women, time-serving was seen as an increasingly inefficient way to pass on skills and some programmes were seen simply as mechanisms for reproducing demarcation and restrictive practices (Fuller and Unwin 2004a, 2004b). The decline of manufacturing in the 1970s resulted in a dramatic fall in the number of apprenticeship places from 445,800 in 1968 (Keep and Ashton 2004:15) to 53,000 in 1990 (Fuller and Unwin 2004a:103), with engineering, which had previously accounted for a significant proportion of traineeships, particularly badly affected.

Following this decline, problems with youth training (Keep 1986) and a nostalgic view of the robust skills development of the good old days, apprenticeships were officially relaunched in 1994 as Modern Apprenticeships and Foundation Modern Apprenticeships. These new programmes have had some success in providing training for young people and extending provision to women (Gospel 1998; Department for Education and Skills 2001). Candidates work towards qualifications up to NVQ level 3 while holding jobs, and their wages are paid by their employer while the apprenticeship training is funded by the state. This scheme has been taken up by sectors with little tradition of apprenticeship including business administration, health and social care, and hairdressing. However, in contrast to experience elsewhere, few young people complete their programmes with only two sectors (engineering and travel services) getting more than half the candidates to the qualification stage. In retailing only 12 per cent complete the course (Fuller and Unwin 2004a:105). While there are, as might be expected, a range of reasons for this, a large proportion of leavers stay working for the same employer after withdrawing from apprenticeships, suggesting that one or both have decided that there is no reason to complete the programme.

Despite the attempt to regulate quality by funding only recognised qualifications, provision is extremely mixed. Some industries have very successful apprenticeship programmes but the spread is patchy and the best providers, such as manufacturing and engineering are often those with long traditions of apprenticeship provision (Fuller and Unwin 2001). Such schemes are much in demand; British Gas received more than 25,000 applications for 500 places on its apprenticeship scheme in 2004 (Kenyon 2005). But it is not clear how widespread such good practice is, and the difference between this and the worst provision is dramatic. In their study of apprenticeship programmes Fuller and Unwin (2004a) illustrate the different levels of skill development and access to career ladders. One case-study, a medium-sized manufacturer of bathroom showers with about 700 employees, provided four-year apprenticeships (with the first three years supported by the Advanced Modern

Box 4.4

Becoming a chef

NVQs were intended to provide consistent, national standards which would eliminate the need for time-serving for workers to be recognised as competent. Yet as James and Hayward show in their research into trainee chefs, spending time in the kitchen (traditionally chefs had a four- or five-year apprenticeship), working on tasks until successful completion becomes a matter of habit, displaying the right personal characteristics and a capacity for work and working with known chefs are the most significant elements in joining the profession. This is a learning process, but it also involves socialisation, with apprentices starting as peripheral members of the community, performing tasks that are real and useful but not yet central to its operation, then, gradually, as their competence increases and they become known, gaining full membership status (Lave and Wenger 1991). Tasks are structured and grow more complex as the apprenticeship progresses:

Apprentice (restaurant)	Two months	Six months	16 months
Jack (chives)	Breakfast Vegetable preparation	Breakfast Vegetable preparation Main kitchen	Breakfast Vegetable preparation Main kitchen
Daniel (chives)	Breakfast Vegetable preparation	Breakfast Salad preparation Some main kitchen	
Lawrence (gastron.)	Vegetable preparation Garde manager	Vegetable preparation Garde manager	Vegetable preparation Garde manager Dessert section About to begin on entremetier
Clint (sebs)	Salad preparation Vegetable preparation Parts of dishes from the main kitchen Pastry selection		

Taken from James and Hayward (2004).

Apprenticeship scheme). On completion, apprentices gained an NVQ level 3 in technical services, an HNC in mechanical and manufacturing engineering and several key skills units. Team-working enabled them to learn from colleagues on the job and monthly performance reviews helped to monitor progress and raise issues. Those who successfully completed their apprenticeships were given permanent jobs in the firm. The company also funded HND fees and allowed trainees one day a week to study, though they were expected to make up their hours by working longer on other days. In retailing the picture was very different and apprentices were expected to be productive workers almost from the start. Some attended their company's in-house training programme but for most their only link to apprenticeship was an NVQ assessor who visited every six to eight weeks to observe them on the job. Somewhere between excellent developmental provision and minimal on-the-job activity that should not disrupt work came banking. Traditionally banks have offered strong internal career ladders to (generally male) staff but providing discrete customer service apprenticeships effectively separated trainees from progression routes. Apprentices attended the bank's general induction for all staff but most of their training was carried out on the job with assessment for their NVQs undertaken by a private training provider. Those who successfully completed the programme were given the opportunity to stay on as cashiers. However, the opportunities for further development were limited and there was a clear division between the customer service workers and staff with specialist banking skills and knowledge. To progress to other jobs, apprentices would have to take banking qualifications and it was not clear how closely the customer services qualifications were linked to banking work.

Clearly young people's experience in each of these organisations varies considerably. The first employer, the shower manufacturer, comes closest to both traditional apprentice provision and practice overseas. Those who successfully complete their traineeships are offered work, additional skills development and the prospect of a career. In retailing and banking the position is rather different. The bank observed by Fuller and Unwin used apprenticeship as a means of recruiting young people rather than the first stage of a career in the industry, while the retail apprenticeship seemed little different from entry-level work. Then too, for the customer service qualifications, training provision was divorced from work; government-funded providers assessed and monitored progress towards the qualifications with little input from the employers.

The type of employer organisation which underpins training in Germany is largely absent in Britain (Steedman *et al.* 1998). The mechanisms in place to ensure quality, such as making sure that schemes offer NVQ qualifications, are not particularly effective and often demand more intervention by government or government agencies (James and Hayward 2004). As a result, quality varies considerably. While some schemes can and do offer robust skills development and access to career ladders this is not true of all, or even most. Worryingly too, much training is separated from work, raising questions both about its relevance to the industry and the skilled nature of the work itself.

Discussion and conclusions

It seems that government intervention UK-style has a mixed record. The education system is certainly producing higher numbers of more highly qualified people (though possibly at the expense of standards) but official involvement in workplace activity is less successful (Stevens 1999). Investors in People tends to be well received by organisations that have gained accreditation, but it may simply certify existing good provision rather than extend it. NVQs have helped many workers to gain certification, but do little to actively build skills and the support that exists for better and more rigorous qualifications is tenuous. Even the Confederation of British Industry (the closest body Britain has to an employers' association) rejected the idea that minimum periods of training or compulsory off-the-job training should form part of an apprenticeship (Steedman 2001). At national level, the extensive (if voluntarist) state architecture may be the least effective combination of systems. It assumes that there exists an unmet demand for skills and that, given suitable (weak) intermediary associations, this can readily be articulated and implemented by employers (Wright and Hayward 2003). But this assumption, and the initiatives that target the supply of skills, miss the point (Keep and Mayhew 1996), since many British firms can and do compete very successfully on the basis of low skills.

There are skills shortages, but skills are also underused and existing product market strategies may not necessarily require more or better skills of employees (Hogarth and Wilson 2002). Indeed there is considerable evidence that employers may not want and cannot use more highly skilled employees. Research conducted before and after the introduction of the National Minimum Wage, which was intended, at least in part, to encourage employers to use labour more effectively (and more skilfully) by making it more expensive, suggests that even employers who wished to increase employees' skill levels and compete on quality did not do so because they did not know how to change production (Edwards *et al.* 2002). Indeed, production changes following this legislation may have involved deskilling rather than upskilling as employers switched to younger workers (who were not covered by the regulations) and additional training was limited to induction (Heyes and Gray 2003). There were some schemes that assisted organisations in developing new ways of competing. The 'Clothing Partnership' set up by Coventry City

Council has managed to raise standards, improve work design and payment systems, increase skills and change the way firms compete, and all in an industry characterised by cost-based competition, through a voluntary association of firms (Edwards *et al.* 2002). But few programmes gave any assistance at all on the way businesses worked, focusing only on individual skills in isolation. It is possible to sympathise with the government's dilemma here. It is far easier to launch a new training programme than it is to fundamentally change the way jobs are organised within firms, switch the markets companies compete in or modify the goods and services they provide (and even when governments do intervene to manage demand, their record is rarely successful). Yet it is this demand for and use of skills that needs to be shaped, at least if interventions on the supply side are to have any prospect of success.

Worryingly, official intervention in Britain is both too extensive and too limited. The programmes that exist, Investors in People, NVQs and apprenticeships, have had some successes but fail to provide the consistent and high-level skills development seen elsewhere. Indeed, these programmes offer little guidance on developing skills, with the extensive intervention ceding to market-driven activities at the most crucial point in the process. As a result, rigorous provision tends to be observable in firms and sectors with strong traditions of VET. Flexibility, for organisations already expert in the style and types of training required, is welcome; but support is badly needed for those employers not familiar with VET, and this support should take the form of content as well as process. NVQs focus on accreditation, separate from any learning that may occur, Investors in People audit human resource systems, and official involvement with apprenticeships is often at the level of assessment and guidance in preparing materials rather than teaching new skills. Guidance in content and challenging syllabi would provide a more robust basis for skills development.

There are problems too with the infrastructure of quangos and agencies set up by central government. These set the agenda for VET, design the qualifications, carry out the assessments, monitor provision and suggest changes. It is an expensive process and one that is government- rather than employer- (or even employment-) led. In other nations when the state has intervened it is to create tertiary bodies that can then take responsibility for action, allowing the state to step back. In Britain the state seems locked into a cycle of intervention. It sets targets, which employers fail to deliver, so the state steps in again creating a situation of moral hazard in which employers realise that allowing the market to fail results in more extensive subsidy (Keep and Ashton 2004).

5

New skills for old?
The changing nature of skill

The . . . 'transferable skills' are so basic as to lend themselves to parody: learning to push, learning to pull. Learning to stand up without falling over? Life and social skills, intended . . . to be a core element of all . . . schemes, are widely regarded as a patronising slur on young people's personal qualities. Under this theme they are invited to improve their appearance, their interview technique and their approach to authority. The implicit message is that their unemployment is their own fault and the implicit promise is that they will thereby get a job (they will only compete better with the next younger person for the same dwindling stock of jobs). (Cockburn 1987:23–4)

The discussion of skill in the last three chapters has focused on the expertise possessed by individuals, the skills demanded by the job and the different national systems through which such skills and ways of working can be developed. It would be simplistic to describe these aspects of skill as 'technical'; skill in the social setting in particular is socially constructed and sustained. But they might reasonably be described as traditional. This typology of skill has helped to describe and understand the development of occupational and craft unions, the way workers have defended and developed expertise and how and why skilled workers take pains to exclude certain groups from membership or training (Turner 1962; Cockburn 1983). This way of understanding skills is still important. Rowena Barrett's (2005b) research into professionals working in the IT industry before and after the dot.com boom clearly shows the interplay between these three elements. However, as a description of skill for the twenty-first century it needs to be supplemented. Job adverts, job descriptions, shortlisting, interviews, appraisals, promotions, skills gaps and governmental solutions to the skills crisis all now focus on new criteria: 'soft' and social skills (Crenin 2003).

There are a range of terms for these in the literature: soft skills, competencies, personal attributes, generic skills, individual qualities, transferable skills, virtues and social skills. Few are defined (and when they are, these definitions are generally contradicted in the next study), the boundary between each term and the next is rather blurred and the rigour with which individual models and skill lists are developed varies greatly. Nonetheless, the terms and practices in this unwieldy agglomeration do have certain features in common, the most notable of which is a concern with personal qualities, particularly the way an individual feels about their work and *how* they work rather than *what* they do. This focus on character and attitude dominates practice at work. According to Hillage *et al.* (2002) two of the three skills most in demand by employers are soft skills: communication and customer handling (pp. 33–6). Cappelli (1995a), drawing on research that shows that the most common reasons for firing new hires were absenteeism and a failure to adapt to the work environment, argues that these figures show there is an *attitude gap* rather than a *skills gap*.

It seems that what is happening – in workplaces, at recruitment and promotion, and in policy-makers' documents – is a shift not only in which skills are important but in the use of the word skill itself. Many of the qualities and attributes that now feature highly on lists of the skills most needed by employers would not have figured at all in earlier accounts (Keep and Mayhew 1999). In part this move is a semantic one, with qualities employers have always demanded simply incorporated into the word 'skill', but it also marks genuine changes in the way people work and the way work is controlled and regulated. This escalation of skills has practical implications too. Soft skills are less easy to identify objectively and more readily observed through stereotypes than technical skills, and an emphasis on one can and does marginalise the other.

What are soft skills?

The consensus on the demand for soft skills (Cappelli 1995a; Cappelli 1995b; Hillage *et al.* 2002) is not matched by any agreement on exactly what such skills are nor how they should be demonstrated. Keep (2001), drawing on a range of studies, found many suggestions including positive attitudes towards change, self-confidence, self-promotion, exploring and creating opportunities and political focus. Research into the 'style labour markets' of the hospitality industry reveals a demand for a persona that is 'passionate, stylish, confident, tasty, clever, successful and well-travelled' (Nickson *et al.* 2001; Warhurst and Nickson 2001:14). Government documents recommend the development of positive attitudes to life and work, getting on with workmates, working as a

Box 5.1

What skills are really valued?
Most people claim to value their colleagues for their competence and the technical skills they bring to the workplace. However, according to Casciaro and Lobo (2005) in practice likability is far more important than competence. They rated workers on both competence and likability and found (unsurprisingly) that colleagues who were most highly valued were the lovable stars who were both nice and capable. However, in their absence most people would far rather direct their queries and pleas to 'lovable fools' than 'competent jerks'.

Likability

	Low	High

	Low	**High**
High Competence	**Competent jerk** Mostly avoided	**Lovable Star** Desperately wanted
Low	**Incompetent jerk** Desperately avoided	**Lovable fool** Mildly wanted

Taken from Casciaro and Lobo (2005).

team and getting information and advice (Payne 1999). In the USA employers seek work attitude, punctuality, loyalty (Lafer 2004); friendliness, teamwork, ability to fit in (Moss and Tilly 1996); and also dedication to work and discipline in work habits (Cappelli 1995a). The lists are lengthy and bring together a confused morass of personal traits, attitudes, qualities and predispositions (Brown and Hesketh 2004).

Conceptually this is messy. At one level, as Payne (1999) argues, an emphasis on the technical know-how, manual dexterity and spatial awareness of the skilled craft worker has given way to generic, transferable, soft skills, personal attributes, competencies and individual qualities. But the new skills demanded are themselves a curious mixture of robust, psychologically verifiable traits, attitudes to work and naïve wish lists. The different terms used – competencies, skills, traits and qualities – reflect this.

The origins of these new skills vary as much as the skills themselves. Boyatzis (1982) combines a psychological model of the individual with performance ratings over two decades of research. Salaman (2004) describes competencies drawn up from organisational strategies with priorities such as 'customer focus' or a 'concern for quality' to be achieved through staff measured on new criteria and behaving in different ways (see also du Gay *et al.* 1996). But not all preparatory studies are so lengthy. Rees and Garnsey (2003) observed one firm which spent eighteen months conducting detailed investigations into staff competencies, a rigour that seemed wasted when the consultant they employed prioritised qualities and clustered attributes without explaining any of her decisions. Another firm in the same study held only eight interviews before drawing up their required behaviours. And the number of desirable qualities can be extensive. Hirsch and Bevan's (1988) survey of 41 organisations produced nearly 1700 different traits as well as one organisation which claimed to measure its managers against no fewer than 71 different criteria. The authors commented that (p. 31): 'It is difficult to know whether the length of skill lists is determined by personal taste, theoretical considerations, the tolerance of managers or the size of a sheet of A4 paper.'

At stages this process seems almost random. Mangham and Silver (1986) discovered that, while there was a consensus over many of the qualities required of managers (a group that has been subject to efforts to manage desirable traits for longer than many others), such agreement was readily shattered by the introduction of new traits into the list since respondents agreed with these too. What employers say they want is not necessarily the same as what they actually want (Raffe 2004). It may be, as Lewis and Stewart (1958:100) argued that: 'Listing the qualities of a good manager makes an excellent parlour game in business circles. Soon all the main virtues will be mentioned and who is to say that any of them, except chastity, is not desirable?'

The attributes listed are often vague and highly subjective. It is difficult to avoid the conclusion that these models are 'highly vulnerable to the prejudices, values, personal experiences and ideas of particular individuals' (Boyatzis 1982:7). Or, as Lafer (2004) argues, that in practice soft skills mean little more than (p. 118) 'whatever employers want'.

This change in emphasis is a comparatively recent one. Payne's (1999, 2000) extensive review of policy documents notes that until the 1970s skill needs

---

Box 5.2

> You get a cv and the person has a great cv and they've worked for a high powered research agency, and that's brilliant, you've got to see them. But you know that there is a pretty strong chance that the moment you meet them you're going to know that they're not one of us.

Taken from Robertson *et al.* (2003:841).

---

were couched in technical terms. What was desired was technicians and craftsmen, mathematicians, chemists, physicists, accountants, economists and systems analysts. By the mid 1970s this was still true, but calls for rigorous technical skills were supplemented by demands for school- and college-leavers with the right attitude and disposition, a call that strengthened over the next few decades. Cappelli (1995a), in a study of US documents, observes that 'character' is the characteristic most often given primary importance in hiring decisions (by 48 per cent of employers) and that 80 per cent of employers were more concerned with worker attitudes and personalities than with basic academic skills.

This is a dilemma. At one level it is clear that what people do at work is important and all jobs involve a (fluid) mixture of both technical and soft skills. The midwives studied by Lave and Wenger (1991) knew about pregnancy and childbirth but were also very emotionally involved in the lives, hopes and anxieties of the expectant mothers in their community. Steiger's (1993) building-site craftsmen were willing to learn and able to work unsupervised. Kidder's (1981) account of innovation in the early days of computing shows how the designers became obsessed with their product, working through the night to hit deadlines. In all of these accounts, the way that individuals went about their jobs, the engagement they had with colleagues and clients and their approach to learning, problem-solving and innovation were inextricably intertwined with their knowledge of their specialism. But all of these are collective acts, so the soft skills described are an aspect of joint working rather than an individual quality. Soft skills are important at work but it is not clear whether they are generic, whether they are possessed by individuals, or whether they are amenable to measurement and assessment. Nor does it necessarily follow that shaping and assessing workers around one (or all) of the generic models of competency and soft skill would stimulate better performance or produce more able workers. Yet at the grass roots level, these skills and attitudes really are the factors employers say they want and claim to actively seek at all stages of the employment relationship.

Box 5.4

Brown and Hesketh's (2004) study of graduate recruitment shows that, beneath the jargon of assessment centres, the process is 'the science of gut feeling' (p. 10) where the subjectivity of judgements and discrepancies between assessors are glossed over and where raters have confidence in their ability to spot good candidates as soon as they walk through the door. What is required are 'oven ready graduates', who look good, exude enthusiasm and can 'hit the ground running' (p. 150). The graduate applicants themselves prove adept at working out the rules of this game and Brown and Hesketh divide them between 'Players' and 'Purists'. Players would tell any story, write any cv and act any part to get the job. They gear their activities to those that will look good in career terms, rewrite their family histories and even mimic the interviewers' accents. Purists by contrast see the whole assessment process as a technical one, designed to produce the best candidate for the job. According to one (p. 137): 'The only strategy I've got is to be me and if they don't want me then I don't want to work for them.' This is the recruitment of style over substance.

Taken from Brown and Hesketh (2004).

Soft skills in the workplace

Soft skills are clearly important. The ability to communicate with colleagues and customers, prioritise tasks and reshape work are necessary features of almost every workplace. In Shibata's (2001) study of a Japanese manufacturing firm and its American transplant, soft and technical skills were inextricably interlinked. All workers were trained in mathematics, quality circles and *kaizen* (continuous-improvement) circles, and production workers were expected to carry out routine maintenance in addition to their production duties. Here problem–solving and communication skills were harnessed to technical ones to predict breakdowns, analyse problems and solve them. Tellingly, the problems observed were not ones caused by a lack of soft skills; rather they were the result of technical deficiencies. In the Japanese plant where workers were more experienced and continuing technical training was mandatory line stoppages were rare. Workers could and did anticipate problems and resolve them fairly rapidly. In America, where workers were less experienced, participation in technical training was voluntary and job rotation meant that experienced production line workers voluntarily transferred to other sections, problems were more frequent. Production lines were often stopped, simple problems took longer to fix (an average of 6 minutes 52 seconds compared with 2 minutes 43 seconds in Japan) and Japanese assistance was required to resolve more difficult problems. In both countries workers were trained in ways of communicating with one another and problem-solving techniques; it was the greater technical expertise of the Japanese that secured them continuing productivity advantages.

Much of the interest in soft skills in manufacturing came with the rise of team-working and cellular manufacturing. In principle this replaced Fordist conveyor-belts and tightly defined jobs with empowered teams who would monitor the quality of production and remedy problems (see, for example Mueller 1994; Wickens 1987; Walton 1985).

These autonomous teams were intended to be self-managing, which meant that different skills were required from the workers (Thompson and Wallace 1996; Belanger *et al.* 2003). Thompson *et al.'s* (1995) account of truck and bus manufacture shows the importance of individual input to the production process. One of their interviewees, a production manager from frame assembly, was clear about the qualities he required (p. 735):

> The skill I am looking for is the ability of a person to completely motivate himself, use his initiative, have an understanding of what he needs to do and be able to complete it and overcome any of the minor problems which may crop up and have the nous to alert somebody if he still has a problem.

Box 5.5

The five minute meeting

It is 8 am and the start of another shift in the press shop at the Nissan car plant in Sunderland, Tyne and Wear. The supervisor and the twenty men (comprising two teams, each with a team leader) leave the meeting room where they have been chatting and reading newspapers prior to the shift commencing, and go out onto the shopfloor. They congregate in a circle by the presses while the supervisor discusses a problem they had encountered the previous day with some faulty pressings, which had got through as far as the paint shop. The upshot of this discussion is that one of the group is detailed to go down to the paint shop and go through the stack of parts waiting to be painted, in order to find the faulty ones (Wickens 1987:85–6).

Nothing very remarkable about all this one might suppose, except in one or two respects. First it is a scene that is being replicated simultaneously throughout the plant and one that is repeated at the beginning of each shift. Employees are required to be at their work area no later than the shift start time in order that the first few minutes of the shift can be used to discuss issues such as work schedule changes, work redistribution, process changes, training, social events or the introduction of a new member. The principal subjects of the discussion, however, tend to be quality-related.

Taken from Blyton and Turnbull (1994:18–21).

The human resource manager in the same plant expressed the same sentiment, but in rather more negative terms:

> They have a very high level of education but have, and this sounds awful, a blue-collar attitude. It is frustrating for me because they have got the intelligence to put forward their own argument but have an attitude which says, 'we are the workers, you are the governors'. Every craftsman, when he comes out of his apprenticeship, is sloppy, greedy and not particularly respectful of their fellow workers.

The very different attitudes described in these two quotations and the experience of team-working in practice, rather than in theory, also serve to shed some light on the way soft skills are used in the workplace. Team-working actually describes a whole range of different practices (Mueller 1994; Cully *et al.* 1999; Batt and Doellgast 2005). Some workplaces do indeed report successful team-working with workers welcoming the process (Findlay *et al.* 2000; McCabe 2000; Bacon and Blyton 2003) and gaining in autonomy, skill and interesting work (Wright and Edwards 1998; Jackson *et al.* 2000; Edwards and Collinson 2002). But the picture is not a universally positive one and team-working may also be a means of deskilling (Danford 1997; Wright and Edwards 1998), facilitate the deterioration of terms and conditions (Bacon and Blyton 2000), allow workers little control over their own work (Delbridge *et al.* 2000) and require work intensification (Martinez Lucio *et al.* 2000). Working together may provide support networks and sources of advice (Batt 2000; Lloyd and Newell 2000); but it can also replace management with peer surveillance (Garrahan and Stewart 1992; Geary 1995; Murakami 1997; Bacon 1999) and 'management by stress' (Parker and Slaughter 1988). Team-working can indeed provide the basis for making work more skilled, more human and more productive; but it can also be used to describe work that is tightly regulated, unpleasant and low-skilled.

Nor is team-working the only area where soft skills are seen as a potential substitute for technical ones, rather than a support for them. Whalen and Vinhkhuyzen's (2000) research provides an account of the way an expert computer system, designed to diagnose and suggest solutions for customer IT problems, was implemented. Since the computer system was intended to do all the skilled work, the IT call centre help desk was staffed by untrained, non-expert customer representatives whose task was limited to inputting callers' descriptions of their problems and relaying the solutions. Unfortunately, the diagnostic programme had been designed by computer experts who all used the same highly technical vocabulary, and who described faults with reference to a hierarchy of actions. Real users neither employed this vocabulary nor understood the system hierarchy. As a result their explanations were rambling and incoherent and the agents' attempts to guess the problems were rarely successful. Most calls resulted in agents arranging for a technician to visit the

Box 5.6

The different types of team member sought by Nissan

Doer

- Doers are action-centred people
- They constantly urge people to get on with the task in hand
- They tend to be totally concerned with the task ('the what') often at the expense of the process ('the how')
- They are often impatient with 'waffle' and tend to swing into action without thinking things through

Thinker

- Thinkers are good at producing carefully considered ideas
- Weighing up alternative courses of action based upon other people's ideas
- Rarely have much to say – they are often among the quietest members of the team
- When they do speak they are the sort of people who come up with winning ideas
- If they are listened to

Carer

- Carers are people oriented
- They tend to be alert to relationship issues within the team
- Good at easing tension and maintaining harmony
- Carers help the leader to counterbalance the doers and the thinkers who both tend to be task-oriented – not people-oriented

Taken from Garrahan and Stewart (1992:98–9).

---

customers on-site – the very thing the call centre had been set up to prevent. It is unlikely that the callers to this call centre would have been satisfied with the soft skills the customer service representatives demonstrated.

Skills and character

In some respects, little of this is novel. Employers have always required that workers get on with colleagues, obey orders or assume responsibilities. Paules (1991) after a magnificently detailed account of the working lives of waitresses in a down-market American diner draws out the similarities between what was expected of (though not necessarily forthcoming from) these workers and the demands made of servants in the nineteenth century. A 1906 government investigation into higher elementary schools, quoted by Reeder (1979), noted that employers sought 'a good character, qualities of subservience and general handiness'. Employers interviewed by Oliver and Turton (1982) lamented the shortage of 'stable', 'reliable' and 'responsible' workers (p. 199) and Steiger's (1993) account of work on a building-site reveals the importance of getting on with colleagues.

Then too, the dominance of the service sector (National Statistics 2005) means that many of the jobs being created now genuinely demand very different skills from those required in manufacturing. When the process of being served is as much a part of the sale as any physical products that may be involved, the way workers feel and the feelings they produce in others are important. Flight attendants are required to make passengers feel good and debt collectors 'create alarm' to persuade debtors to pay, while call centre workers must establish rapport then, just as quickly, emotionally disengage. People working in the most prosaic jobs, from bank clerks and waitresses to language tutors and bar staff, must demonstrate the 'right' emotional orientation, look and sound (see, among others Hochschild 1983; Trethewey 1999; Korczynski 2001; Grugulis 2002; Nickson et al. 2001; Bolton 2005a). In all of these instances, the product being sold includes some part of the employees. So now, gaining employment is about appearing and feeling as much as it is about doing and the effort bargain is extended to aesthetics and emotions (Noon and Blyton 2002).

The key element here is not that employers' requirements are changing but rather that demands vary from employer to employer and desirable personal attributes – the (elusive and changing) combination of qualities Oliver and Turton (1982) call the 'Good Bloke Syndrome' – are being relabelled as skills. This name change is more than a simple question of semantics. It obscures very real differences within and between these new skills, individualises responsibility for them and dilutes the technical aspects of work.

General definitions of valued attributes serve to convey the impression that the qualities described are generic: that communicating the location of baked beans in a supermarket is the same as communicating the rules of cricket or abstract theories in mathematics (for criticisms of this see Peters 1973; Keep 2001). Yet effective and sensible communication on any or all of these topics may also involve subject knowledge, an awareness of local processes and personal judgement, factors discounted in generic lists. Differences in degree also pass unnoted. The ability to sell may require very few skills when the product is a bar of chocolate or a biro. When what is being sold is a new and still evolving technology, winning sales is an involved process. Darr's (2002; 2004) studies of technical sales show how salespeople were technical experts and had wide social networks in which assistance with technical problems was a key commodity which could be bartered for information about companies, sales leads and actual sales. Selling an application in emergent technology often involved weeks and months of joint development work with the customers' engineers, configuring the system to their use. Yet in the generic skill lists both this and the bar of chocolate would count as salesmanship.

Conflating personal attributes and skills also individualises responsibility for them and neglects their reciprocal and relational elements. In his study of the skills required by US employers Lafer (2004) draws on research by Moss and Tilly (1996) in two warehouses in the same district of Los Angeles, both of which employed present and past gang members. While managers in one complained of high turnover, laziness and dishonesty, in the second, which paid several dollars per hour more, managers had few complaints and turnover was a modest 2 per cent. As Lafer (2004:117–18) argues: '[T]raits such as discipline, loyalty and punctuality are not "skills" that one either possesses or lacks; they are measures of commitment that one chooses to give or withhold based on the conditions of work offered.'

Tellingly, in Thompson *et al.*'s (1995) international study of truck and bus manufacturing the complaints about workers' lack of involvement and reliance on managers came from Britain and Belgium where no incentives were available for those taking on extra work. Indeed, the Belgian human resource manager, when asked whether his workers were happy with a contract which allowed the company to demand an extra five hours of work a week at normal rates and additional competences for no extra payment commented that: 'if they wanted to be happy they should go to the Bahamas' (p. 732).

The implication of this is that training and educational efforts should shift, as Ackers and Preston (1997) note, from training to character formation. Yet as Cappelli (1995a) observes, in his broadly sympathetic account of training for attitude, the history of previous attempts to do this does not inspire confidence. Bowles and Gintis's (1976) critical account of the US education system argued that schools were teaching compliance with authority as employers required but that this conflicted with individual personal growth and development and that the logical corollary to this was designing jobs which demanded only unquestioning obedience. Cappelli also notes the failure of programmes to socialise the long-term unemployed and some of the conflicts within 'character development' programmes in education.

Soft skills are not neutral requirements, necessary for the job in hand. They are often explicitly skewed towards a particular image of an organisation, a way of working or a desired culture. They may be sectorally specific, with private sector values generally triumphing over public sector ones or culturally specific, focusing on behavioural norms that are not readily transplanted

(Sturdy 2001, 1998). Rees and Garnsey (2003) argue that competency development is a political process. Their study included a university and a hospital but, despite the centrality of academic and medical skills in these environments, the skill clusters emphasised managerial attributes (see also Manley 2001; Bolton 2005b). Qualities are selected not simply because they are valued organisationally but for political reasons. This is reflected more widely in the public sector with the increasing emphasis on customer service. Customer service, though central to much private sector work, is, in the public sector, only one aspect of a complex and often politicised relationship. While contact with the 'consumer', courtesy and efficient service are important, they form only part of the 'service' process. The public sector, in structure, values and objectives, is inherently political and is responsible to a range of stakeholders beyond its 'customers', including parliament (Corby and White 1999; Martinez Lucio and MacKenzie 1999). Carlzon's (1987) 'moment of delight' at the point of contact between 'consumer' and 'service worker', through which the customer conflates the manner of service delivery with the product delivered (Korczynski 2002), is often only one aspect of an ongoing relationship. Public sector service may have objectives such as social justice, equity and democracy that are not readily achieved and for which the 'customer' cannot choose to go to another provider if they are dissatisfied. Understandably, demand for such services tends to exceed supply (Fountain 2001) and, while excellent service in the private sector may stimulate both demand and resources, in the public sector, good service may mean securing reasonable delivery when faced with declining or limited real resources (Rainbird et al. 2004). It is not clear that judgements about performance or lists detailing required skills can be reduced to customer satisfaction (Boyne 2003).

Discriminating skills

All forms of skill can discriminate and Chapter 2 demonstrated that women's skills, even when objectively more complex than men's, could be deemed lesser. This issue is even more acute when it comes to soft skills. Many technical skills are observable and measurable. It is possible to check with reasonable accuracy whether an individual can build a wall, weld two pipes together or fix a car engine. It is much harder to arrive at an objective and reliable conclusion on that same individual's commitment or loyalty, particularly since many workers realise quite rapidly which traits their employer values and are sufficiently 'maze bright' (Jackall 1988) to demonstrate them. Since personal attributes, attitudes to work and individual qualities are extremely difficult to evaluate directly, proxies are used. Even when examples of how to gauge soft skills are specified, it is extremely easy for judgements on their presence or absence to focus on the most visible aspects of an individual: their gender, race, class, appearance or accent. The stereotypes associated with each of these are familiar and often far more readily understood than the soft skills themselves.

Judgements based on gender have the added complication that the jobs people do and the way they are required to do them are themselves stereotyped with certain kinds of work or positions in the hierarchy considered typically 'women's' or 'men's' work (Kanter 1977; Skuratowicz and Hunter 2004; Hebson and Grugulis 2005). This means that women may have difficulty obtaining traditionally male work and also that men may have difficulty gaining traditionally female work. Collinson *et al.*'s (1990) study of recruitment revealed both how hard it was for women to gain access to highly paid positions in insurance sales (one candidate was described as 'ideal – if she had been male'; p. 150) as well as the resistance a male applicant faced when applying for work in a female-dominated catalogue company. Unlike his female counterpart, the male applicant was able to persuade the interviewers to give him a job. However, once hired, he was swiftly moved from the packing line, where he was the only man among 61 women, to the better-paid and male-dominated loading bay by the female supervisor. In her words (p. 116), 'I know I shouldn't treat anyone differently, but he just didn't look right on the packing line. I think this is a woman's job really.'

These gendered expectations of work are not confined to traditional jobs and persist through restructuring and job redesign. Skuratowicz and Hunter's (2004) account of work in an American bank shows clearly how jobs were redesigned around notions of masculinity and femininity when the new posts of customer relationship manager and personal banker were introduced. The customer relationship managers, described by one bank employee as a 'glorified Wal-Mart greeter' (p. 91), welcomed customers to the branch, dealt with basic queries and showed them how to use the various automated services. Personal bankers were the sales staff; they were set demanding targets and expected to work long hours for bonuses and commission. In the pilot branches the personal banker positions were illustrated by a small graphic representation of a man wearing a tie while customer relationship managers were depicted by a photograph of a woman with a telephone headset. Salaries were adjusted accordingly. Before the restructuring branch managers had been female-dominated and earned an average salary of $52,300. This was the population from whom customer relationship managers were recruited, average salary $28,300; platform jobs, from whom personal bankers were selected, had been paid $30,000; personal bankers could earn $44,000. Not only were the pictures in pilot branches gendered; so was recruitment and training for these new jobs. When women were appointed to the sales posts they were expected to work in tandem with a male partner and the skills each was assumed to possess were stereotypical (p. 93): '[H]e's a leader in investment sales, top lender . . . he's already dialling for dollars. She has customer trust, she soft sells and does more referrals.'

Men who became customer relationship managers were very much in the minority and were seen as either cynical careerists or homosexual. According to one woman personal banker (pp. 97–8):

> I met one customer relationship manager when I started training, to me he was a regular guy. He couldn't get hired as a personal banker because of his background, he was doing customer relationship management like a stepping stone to a personal banker. I talked to [another] customer relationship manager the other day . . . just from hearing him over the phone, he sounded gay to me. Which doesn't surprise me.

Nor are newly restructured organisations in Britain any different. Hebson and Grugulis's (2005) study of an outsourced housing benefit department in London showed how, despite protests, women caseworkers were sent to work on the newly created reception desk because they were less likely than their male colleagues to react with aggression to aggressive claimants. This move damaged the women's careers. Reception work largely involved acting as a postbox for other departments and caseworkers based here were out of touch with the (frequent) changes to casework. Refresher training was promised but never materialised.

Jobs are often designed around ideas of masculinity and femininity and people chosen for them because of their gender, rather than any individual skills they possess. Moreover, once in jobs, men and women are expected to behave in ways appropriate to their gender, with actions and qualities which run counter to expectations condemned, even when these are appropriate for the occupation (Collinson et al. 1990; Pierce 1995). So female (but not male) paralegals are expected to nurture (Pierce 1995, 1996); while women call centre representatives must be empathetic and men need only reach sales targets (Taylor and Tyler 2000). Competence in work is rated more highly when employees are the 'right' gender for that job (Fischer et al. 1997). And the tendency to recruit based on stereotypical assumptions may be exaggerated in the service sector where customers and clients also gauge competence through stereotypes. Erickson et al.'s (2000) study of women in the American security industry shows that the low-level work of monitoring cameras was a pink-collar ghetto and the competence of women security staff was frequently questioned by clients. But it also shows that the more women clients a firm had, the more women security staff and managers it was prepared to employ.

These gendered norms may also be seen in skill and competency lists. Rees and Garnsey (2003) describe one semi-privatised industry that rated managers against the following criteria: *stress tolerance; thrives on pressure and significance of work; in debate maintains logic and persuasiveness of argument despite heavy opposition.* These traits are stereotypically 'male' and specifying them as desirable competencies may advantage male managers. But also, since assertiveness and aggression tend to be judged positively in men and negatively in women (and since lower-level behaviours will be seen as aggression in women), men are likely to be assessed more sympathetically against this template than their female colleagues. Women who seek to develop and adopt the corporate persona may be marked down because such behaviour is 'inappropriate' for women. By contrast a cosmetics manufacturer and retailer, chosen for the study because of its high proportion of women managers, had as its competencies *employee motivation; open door policy; takes an interest in employees' lives outside; has concern for the well-being of individuals.*

Assessments of the soft skills individuals possess can also be made on the basis of race. Asian women may not be considered career-minded (People Management 2003) and black men are rated as less loyal and ambitious than their white colleagues (Maume 1999). In work groups, when there are small numbers of a minority group, evaluations of performance will be harsher than those for the majority group. However, as numbers grow and the proportion of minority workers in an occupation increases, individual evaluations harmonise but the status and pay of that occupation declines (Reskin *et al.* 1999).

Structural factors also mitigate against women and minority ethnic workers. Soft skills tend to be assessed during informal interactions and women and minority employees have less access to high-status networks (Miech *et al.* 2003) and are less likely to be employed in jobs which allow them to exercise discretion. According to McGuire (2000:518):

'Few white women or people of colour occupy the types of managerial positions . . . in which they can perform extraordinary tasks, for which they are likely to acquire the label of *high potential.*' [Emphasis in original.]

This exclusion and harsh evaluation can lead to a dialectic of defiance as less equal treatment means that the normative obligations that bind individuals to their work groups or their employers may be relatively weak (Vallas 2003). Even attempts to improve the position of disadvantaged groups can result in further marginalisation. Black and minority ethnic workers may be hired for 'racialised' positions to provide links to the community, run affirmative action programmes or link to clients. One of Jones's (1986) interviewees (cited in Maume 1999:489) described this process unfavourably:

Too often Black managers are channelled into The Relations as I call them – the community relations, the public relations, the personnel relations. These may be important functions, but they are not the gut functions that make the business grow or bring in revenues. And they are not the jobs that prepare an executive to be a CEO.

It seems that not only are women and ethnic minority workers likely to be judged more harshly than their male counterparts; they are also likely to be confined to jobs which either give them little opportunity to demonstrate their talents or restrict them to gendered and racialised silos from which it is difficult to break free. Even where recruitment is self-consciously aiming for diversity, setting out the qualities required as soft skills advantages white, male, middle-class candidates from traditional academic backgrounds (Brown and Hesketh 2004). Should women or ethnic minority workers become unhappy at this treatment their complaints are likely to be interpreted as confirmation that they did not possess the required soft skills in the first place.

Soft skills and disadvantage

If the success stories of soft skills can be found among skilled and expert workers, some of the problems are most vividly illustrated in accounts of those who have fewest technical skills. Skill has always been a key issue among the unemployed and the vulnerable in the labour market, with government schemes to enable people return to work focusing on retraining and raising skills. In this low-level skills training for the unemployed, soft skills, life skills, generic skills and attitudes to work have all started to feature heavily. Training the unemployed for work is an area that has always attracted a great deal of criticism. Budgets tend to be limited, and programmes short and often narrowly defined, while well-paid entry-level jobs are in short supply (see, among others, Keep 1987; Cohen 2003; Lafer 2004). Successful interventions, where they exist, tend to be longer and focus on building substantive and often technical skills (Payne 1991). However, as soft skills attract more attention from policy-makers these have started to dominate courses for the unemployed, often to the exclusion of all else.

There are some positive results here. Butterwick (2003) describes classes for immigrant women in Canada which taught them how to present their previous experience in the language of skill to make themselves more attractive to potential employers and to dress like businesswomen; classes for Aboriginal women which encouraged them to aim higher than they had done before and others which gave people who otherwise could not afford therapy access to a form of counselling. But despite these positive experiences the critics outnumbered those who praised the schemes. Counselling-based classes demanded a high degree of disclosure from participants, much of which was alien to the Aboriginal custom of 'maintaining', tutors were generally ill

Box 5.7

During the first week of [a US state funded training programme] about a dozen women and two men sit around a conference table at the Dane county job centre. The instructor, who introduces herself as Kelly, shows flashcards. One flashcard says, *You'll never amount to anything.*

'Has anybody ever heard this in your life?' she asks

No response.

'Good! Because it's not true!'

She holds up another flashcard: *You can do anything you set your mind to.*

'How about this one, how often do we hear this?'

No one says anything.

This is day three of the two-week . . . session. The topic: communication. From Kelly's point of view, things aren't going so well. 'People aren't talking a lot' she says.

Several participants are clearly trying though. Kelly holds up a flashcard that says *I'm so proud of you.* 'How do we feel when someone says this to us?' she asks.

'Good?' one participant offers.

'Yeah!' says Kelly. She hands out pieces of paper and asks everyone to write down the names of two people who have had a positive influence on their lives.

'It's the person who believes in you,' she says.

She writes 'belives' in magic marker on a flip chart, then crosses it out and writes 'beleives'.

'Don't tell her,' the woman in front of me whispers.

'What?' Kelly asks. 'Don't tell me what?'

'You still spelled "believes" wrong,' someone says.

Kelly stares at the flip chart.

'It's I before E except after C,' another participant explains.

'That's okay,' the woman in front of me says. 'That's a hard one.'

After a short break, Kelly lists some more rules for good communication. 'Here are two of the hardest things to say in the English language,' she says, and writes 'Thank you' and 'I'm sorry' on the flip chart . . .

I interview some participants after class. 'I don't want to knock the programme or anything – maybe someone is getting their self-esteem raised,' says one . . . 'But . . . they've given me an ultimatum: you either go to this class or it's your check.'

Conniff (1994:18–21) in Lafer (2004:121).

equipped to cope with any serious issues this process might reveal and many participants felt blamed for their own unemployment. As one said critically (p. 172): 'I'm not having problems with my life, I'm having problems with my career.'

Most worryingly, these interventions replaced any more substantive form of skills training. One tutor in Butterwick's (2003) study was so annoyed with this that in the life skills classes she was required to teach she taught students about the economy, labour market structures and practices, employment standards, work rights, racism, discrimination and how to tackle these issues. But this was the (somewhat illicit) exception. In the area of return to work training it seems that skill development has become a zero-sum game, with 'a combination of harsh discipline and hokey motivational seminars' (Lafer 2004:120) replacing more substantive content.

Discussion and conclusions

So, soft skills and competencies are important, they are both necessary and useful in the workplace and they are an integral part of employment. But they are also difficult to measure, with most devices from the self-report psychological test to the critical incident technique and simple interview relying on interviewer and respondent using a shared vocabulary with the same meanings, interpreting actions and answers in the same way and being truthful. Even when these occur, there may be little consensus over which skills are valued and valuable (Mangham and Silver 1986) and the 'official' skills language may not be the key element in the decision-making (Hirsch and Bevan 1988:68–9):

> [O]ne organisation (which had come to believe most of its managers were rather 'stodgy') actually looked for 'sparkle' in making appointments – an attribute which appeared on none of its . . . public lists of skill requirements! Another organisation which had staff posted all over the world had well developed formal . . . languages for both managerial and professional skills. However, its [informal] language spoke of 'gin and tonic' people (suited for jobs in developed countries or large cities) versus 'bush' people (who could function in much less well supported environments). These distinctions were well understood and clearly relevant to the organisation, but had only a vague linkage to listed attributes used in performance appraisal.

Employees may be judged on their looks (Barnard 1962), their gender (Kanter 1977), their relationship with their line managers (Jackall 1988), the impression of competence they convey (Heller 1972, 1996; Gowler and Legge 1983), their membership of certain groups (Dalton 1966) or the stories other employees tell about them (Lewis and Stewart 1958). It is difficult to argue that this is an objective gauge of an individual, though the majority of firms using such systems believe that it is, no matter how random their development process was (Rees and Garnsey 2003).

There is a circularity about this process. Skills are assessed and jobs are designed in ways that both draw on and contribute to stereotypical assumptions about workers such that it is difficult to disentangle the gender, race or class of the individual doing the job from the character they are assumed to have. This has social implications, since workers may find it challenging to construct their own identities in traditionally atypical work (Cockburn 1987; Williams 1992) and the disadvantages faced by workers who are not in the majority or most high-status social group are well known (see, for example Kanter 1977; Cockburn 1983; Reskin and Roos 1990; Glass 1999; Skuratowicz and Hunter 2004). However, when workers are expected to possess soft skills these disadvantages are mutiplied. When gauged against stereotypes, individuals may be judged unfit for particular jobs because they are a certain gender; when they live up to the competencies required by the job they may be condemned for acting in ways 'inappropriate' to their gender. Objections or discontent at less-equal treatment may mean both that workers feel less loyalty and that they are deemed to possess fewer soft skills, effectively reinforcing their disadvantage.

Moreover the very way that soft skills are defined and assessed means that the relationship is an asymmetric one. Technical and professional expertise may be the product of politics and consensus, but it is generally agreed by professional bodies, educationalists or experienced and expert workers (Abbott 1988; Freidson 1988, 1994). Soft skills, in marked contrast to this, are defined by the employer who also specifies how they should be demonstrated and the means by which they may be assessed. There is generally no wider occupational, craft or professional body to adjudicate on whether a particular action really does show flexibility or how enthusiasm should be demonstrated.

Nor are soft skills necessarily skilful. The firms studied by Thompson et al. (1995) and Shibata (2001) required expertise and knowledge of their workers. Other workplaces do not (see, for example Callaghan and Thompson 2002; Taylor et al. 2002). Indeed, an emphasis on soft skills may actively serve to marginalise technical skills in workplaces as in training for the unemployed. In Grugulis and Vincent's (2004) study of work at Post Office counters, person-nel's enthusiastic embrace of customer service skills meant that the technical side of the work, which covered more than 170 different transactions, was neglected. According to a regional network manager (p. 21): '[A]lmost anybody, realistically, could do the transactions over the counter . . . But to do the other things, the selling and the customer care, it takes a certain kind of personality to do that' (regional network manager, Post Office, female).

Despite the emphasis on the 'natural' aspects of customer service skills and the demand for a 'certain kind of personality', the customer service side of Post Office work was designed to minimise employee input rather than harness the talents sought in recruitment. In all outlets, the form these 'new', sales-oriented skills took was scripted and synthetic. According to the offi-cial check-list, employees were required to make eye contact with customers, give a polite greeting, serve the customer immediately, give them their full attention, offer other products and make a pleasing closing statement. Name badges were worn and mystery shoppers monitored staff on scripts, product knowledge and cross-selling. These formalised controls could and did cause problems. Several small sub-offices and franchises had received critical reports for not offering products specified by that day's mystery shopper checklist but which the Post Office would not let them sell, and the scripts were widely resented. Some prompts secured such trivial increases in sales that they seemed designed simply to ensure obedience to the idea of cross-selling. During this research, books of stamps were redesigned into groups of 6 and 12 rather than 4 and 10 and staff were instructed to offer a book of 12 stamps to a customers asking for 10. A regional network manager, arguing that increasing sales was easy and could readily be incorporated into every transaction, pointed out how little extra time it took for clerks to mention that stamps now came in books of 12. A sub-postmaster, on the front line himself, was less positive and saw this exercise, 'for which you earn 0.0000lp', as meaningless.

These skill-less skills are apparent in low-level vocational training where technical content and substantive input are replaced by confidence-building sessions and low-level, unlicensed therapy (Butterwick 2003; Lafer 2004). This is rather worrying. Traditionally skills have provided workers with bargaining power and have acted as a basis on which higher wages, control over the workplace or an input into decision-making can be negotiated (Turner 1962; Cockburn 1983). The power conferred by soft skills is a great deal more fragile and exists largely in the eye of the beholder, advantaging workers when it is acknowledged by employers and not otherwise. As Grugulis and Vincent (2004) point out, in their account of an environment where loyalty was valued, not everyone who demonstrated loyalty got rewarded. These skills convey only a courtier's ability to please, not an artisan's power to produce. Indeed, contrary to the normal laws of economics, there is little correlation between demand, supply and wages. Employers have long claimed that there are too few workers with customer service skills, but customer service jobs are generally low-paid (Dickerson and Green 2002; Bolton 2004a). It may be that this is because such skills are deemed 'natural' (particularly for women) or because they are demanded at high levels in work that is done by women, and women are rarely paid high rates. The key soft skill which does attract a salary premium is the ability to do PowerPoint presentations (Felstead *et al.* 2002), a premium far more likely to come from the correlation of this activity with status than anything to do with the complexity of the skill itself. Within firms, soft skills enjoy only a precarious position, since their value lies less in their exercise and more in their recognition and positive interpretation.

Finally it may be worth returning to the question of whether these qualities of commitment and loyalty, or communications and customer service or problem-solving and entrepreneurship, really are skills. Relabelling them is a confusing process that individualises responsibility, reinforces disadvantage and sidelines technical skills. Are they skills? Probably not, and there are many other words that describe these attributes better (Keep and Mayhew 1999; Payne 2000). However, in reality the idea of attributes, competencies and personal qualities as skills has gained so much currency that it seems unlikely that this particular exercise in rebranding will be reversed. It may be more sensible to live with the linguistic inaccuracy and to concentrate on ways of introducing soft skills to the workplace skilfully.

6

Emotions and aesthetics for work and labour: the pleasures and pains of the changing nature of work

[W]hen the product – the thing to be engineered, mass produced, and subjected to speed-up and slowdown – is a smile, a mood, a feeling, or a relationship, it comes to belong more to the organisation and less to the self. And so, in the country that most publicly celebrated the individual, more people privately wonder, without tracing the question to its deepest social root: What do I really feel? (Hochschild 1983:198)

I don't take any nonsense from no-one . . . I don't take no junk . . . because I demand to make sure that I treat you fair, you treat me fair . . . So . . . I told him [a customer] I said, 'Don't you dare talk to me this way, cause I take this pot of water and I throw it right in your damn face.' (Paules 1991:1)

Organisations exist, as their name implies, to provide structure and control. Traditionally these controls have been rational ones, exemplified by Weber's bureaucracy from which personal feelings have been purged (Gerth and Wright Mills 1948; Fineman 1993; Domagalski 1999); though see also du Gay (2000) for a spirited defence of the type of emotions and actions approved by Weber. In practice it is unlikely that the lived realities of work have ever been rational. Yet, if bureaucratic work design does not produce 'rational' workers (Mant 1977) it certainly affects the control systems employed, the skills shaped and the legitimate limits of the managerial prerogative.

Current accounts of work organisation, by contrast, set emotions in centre stage. The way workers feel and the feelings they produce in others have become, for many, the main aim of work. Recruitment campaigns, selection processes and control systems focus around the identification, moulding and

Box 6.1

At the Orange call centre in North Shields, the manager told me they never recruited someone for their technical skills. What they were looking for was a particular personality: cheerful, outgoing, flexible, good natured, adaptable – because these were the characteristics which they couldn't train. It is an approach shared by B&Q, the DIY retail chain which uses an automated telephone personality test to recruit employees with the right kind of emotional characteristics; applicants have to press their telephone keypad to answer questions such as, 'I prefer to have my closest relationships outside work rather than with a colleague.' . . . Identifying the right personalities has become a big industry, with a turnover of £20 million a year; over 70 per cent of companies in the FTSE 100 now use psychometric testing. In this labour market women and young people are favoured, while the shy, the reserved and those who find it hard to adapt to change are disadvantaged.

Bunting (2004:68–9).

managing of employees' emotions with capturing hearts and minds depicted as the solution to all organisational ills (Anthony 1994; Brown and Hesketh 2004).

Much of this is due to the growth in the service sector. When customers purchase the process of being served as well as (or instead of) a physical product, employees become an integral part of the sale. The implications of this are wide-ranging. As work changes, so too does the way that people are managed, the skills they are expected to demonstrate and the way they experience work. This switch in emphasis can provide a welcome corrective to rational and mechanistic accounts of employment (Fineman and Gabriel 1996; Fineman 1993). And incorporating emotions and aesthetics into work can be pleasurable. According to the gurus, work becomes a nice place to be and working a pleasurable activity. Even controlling this process is gratifying because managers' jobs become 'more fun. Instead of brain games in the sterile ivory tower, it's shaping values and reinforcing through coaching and evangelism in the field – with the worker in support of the cherished product' (Peters and Waterman 1982:xxv). More robust studies have also shown that employees take pride and pleasure in the emotional and aesthetic aspects of their work (Leidner 1993; 1996; Korczynski 2001; Nickson *et al.* 2001); and this emotional emphasis may allow organisations to relax bureaucratic or hierarchical controls (Grugulis *et al.* 2000).

However, the way emotions and aesthetics are incorporated into work is rather more complex than the enthusiasts assume. Acting out social roles is neither unnatural nor particularly unusual (Goffman 1959). Expressing warmth towards and establishing rapport with customers may provide a genuine source of pleasure for workers. Yet in practice emotions are incorporated into organisations within very strict limits. Emotion work does not necessarily legitimise the expression of human feelings in a way that supports the development of healthy individuals; instead it offers these feelings for sale. Work is not redesigned to accommodate employees' emotions: rather, employees are redesigned to fit what is deemed necessary at work (Putnam and Mumby 1993). This may involve experiencing and projecting enthusiasm, warmth, empathy, commitment, sincerity or anger, but such emotions are prescribed rather than 'natural'.

Moreover, as with domestic servitude, the emotional exchange is an asymmetric one, with frontline workers exempt from most considerations of courtesy or etiquette. Service workers are required to show respect, or care, or attentiveness without expecting to receive these courtesies in return. Their first names are announced by name badges and scripts, but they may not know their customers' names and the emotional outlets considered necessary for customers such as anger and abuse are denied to those that serve them. Turning emotions into commodities changes them and the conscious control of feelings in the workplace has negative, as well as positive, consequences for those who are controlled.

Working with emotions: labours of love?

Essentially, emotion work demands that employees feel particular emotions themselves in order to produce specific and desirable reactions in others. This means that areas in which individuals have traditionally exercised their own judgement, such as when to smile, what to feel, what to do and how to appear, may now be controlled by their managers. This is something that is most dramatically apparent in places like Disneyland where staff are hired on the basis of looks and work is presented as an 'act'. Ride operators and assistants are single white males and females in their early twenties who are above average height, below average weight, with straight teeth, conservative grooming and good posture (Van Maanen 1991). At work they are expected to immerse themselves in their 'roles' when 'onstage', smiling, following scripts and adhering to rigid and detailed rules about their appearance (covering hair, spectacles, earrings and other jewellery, make-up and fingernails).

In some respects, Disneyland is a special case, representing entertainment rather than industry; its recruits are aware of what will be demanded of them and its staff willingly complicit in the 'acts' they portray. In others, it simply illustrates controls that supermarkets, restaurants, call centres, banks and airlines exert. Here too employees are encouraged to feel emotions to order and to act them out in specified ways. In all of these sites, workers selling their feelings discover that this sale impacts on their home and private lives. The truly remarkable feature of emotion work is its sheer ordinariness, the extent to which it has permeated most forms of work, and to which it is deemed natural (Noon and Blyton 2002). The form that this emotional engagement takes differs and the 'scripts' used vary from job to job. There is the smiling 'have a nice day' warmth of McDonald's serving staff; the 'have a rotten day' discourtesies of debt collectors and the 'have a cool day' detachment and professionalism of accountants (Mann 1999).

There are pleasures involved in working with emotions and in being emotional about work. Tracy Kidder's (1981) account of the construction and programming of a 1970s computer is a story of hobbyists and enthusiasts inspired by their task and engaged with it for all hours of the day and night, while Kunda's (1992) ethnography of 'Tech' tells of skilled, well-paid workers caught up in their company's culture and deeply committed to their work. Nor is this pleasure restricted to professional employees. Many 'customer-facing' and 'front-line' staff enjoy their contact with people. Leidner's (1993) study of McDonald's describes how workers enjoy and take pleasure in the most routine of tasks. As 'Steve' and 'Theo' comment (p. 136):

> It's just fun, the people are fun! . . . They make my day, they really do. I mean, sometimes, I can come to work – like yesterday, I wasn't really happy. I was some-what in the middle. This guy came in, he was talking real low, and his friend said, 'Why don't you talk up?' . . . I told him to turn his volume up [I laugh], and he said something . . . and I just started smiling. Ever since then, I've been happy . . . The guests out here . . . they're friendly and fun. I just love to meet them, you know? I mean, it's nice working for them, it's nice serving them. Some, you know – well, I'd say one out of ten guests will probably try to give you a bad time. But the rest of them, they'll just make my day.
>
> Well, I enjoy working with the public, 'cause they're fun to be with. Some of them are a trip. So I enjoy it, find it very amusing.

Yet such conclusions should not be surprising. After all, the rapport and warmth that these workers are instructed to provoke in others may not leave them entirely untouched themselves. Smiling and making eye contact may evoke feelings of openness and warmth, the use of a name may suggest a rela-tionship of friendship or respect and an open posture may break down barri-ers between people. Companies go to a great deal of effort to train workers in the exhibition of 'naturally' warm and friendly qualities (Hochschild 1983; Nickson et al. 2001; Callaghan and Thompson 2002) in order to meet (or exceed) customers' expectations. But the reason these behaviours have such positive effects is, at least in part, because of the associations customers have of them in more innocent settings. These behaviours counterfeit friendship, warmth or respect, but the process of simulation may affect the employee who acts out the behaviours (however instrumentally) as much as the 'customer' who is targeted, with each experiencing pleasure.

Moreover, companies often go to great lengths to recruit suitably empathetic and emotional people with sophisticated role-playing and interviews for even the most basic of call centre jobs (Thompson *et al.* 2001; Callaghan and Thompson 2002) so that the people chosen for this work are those who gain most pleasure from, or are best at this aspect of work. In Korczynski's (2001) study, when asked what the best aspects of their work were, most customer service representatives claimed that it was the people factor (p. 93):

> When you satisfy a customer and get recognition from the customer
> I like talking to people all day.
> The best part is the customers, the things you can do for them, rapport with them.
> One of the plusses of the job is speaking with people.
> I love what I do – working with people.
> I love this job, because I like dealing with people, resolving issues. I feel very happy when I've resolved an issue.

These workers were expected to be friendly, to establish rapport and to be warm and helpful. The companies studied made special efforts to hire staff who naturally displayed these characteristics and the workers enjoyed this aspect of their work.

At this level, it seems that working with emotions is entirely positive; these actions are natural and may be intrinsically pleasurable, and people who work with their emotions report higher levels of job satisfaction (Wharton 1996). Then, too, companies that consciously control the emotional states of their employees may also manage their staff in more pleasant ways including dress-down days, games, prizes, informal working relations or emotional support from managers (Kinnie *et al.* 2000; Grugulis *et al.* 2000; Carroll *et al.* 2001). But acknowledging that emotion work can be pleasurable does not mean that it always is. Moments of genuine engagement and humour must be set against the permanent requirement to smile and the fact that those smiles are regulated.

Looking good for the money

Just as emotions are increasingly subject to managerial control so too are aesthetics, with the way that staff look consciously incorporated into organisations' brand identities (Nickson *et al.* 2001). While the Weberian bureaucracy emphasised technical skills and work roles, a focus on appearance is now more explicit. Indeed, so powerful is this association between employee image and corporate product that one American comedian joked that a downmarket restaurant chain deliberately hired the ugliest women it could find in order to make the food appear more appetising (Paules 1991:3). Some economists have even started to explore the way that beauty 'capital' increases both individual and corporate earnings (Hamermesh and Biddle 1994; Biddle and Hamermesh 1998; Pfann *et al.* 2000). Employers now appear to have assumed a legitimate interest in the way employees look. According to the *Observer* (2002) even officials for the 2002 Commonwealth Games were selected on the basis of appearance. Not only are more attractive employees hired, but also employers may seek to control and improve the appearance of those already employed. Retail outlets that specialise in women's clothes now keep stores of make-up and accessories in their back rooms for inadequately prepared (or groomed) staff to draw on. An employee with laddered tights, unshaven legs or an 'inappropriate' hairstyle may be required to change their appearance (see, for example, Hochschild 1983; Paules 1991; Nickson *et al.* 2001).

This management of aesthetics has been observed in a range of environments. Nickson *et al.* (2001), conducting research into many of the most fashionable and exclusive bars and restaurants in newly prosperous Glasgow, noted the existence of a 'style' labour market. Recruiters expected prospective employees to be 'stylish', 'tasty', 'of smart appearance', 'trendier people' or 'very well presented' (pp. 179–80). Once hired, training enhanced their natural attributes. Waiting staff in one 'boutique hotel' were given a ten-day induction in which they were aesthetically groomed. Men were taught to shave properly and women coached in how to apply make-up. All were taught about haircuts, personal style and controlling their moods: '[Y]ou have to understand

---

Box 6.2

'Different companies favour different variations of the ideal type of sociability. Veteran employees talk about differences in company personality as matter-of-factly as they talk about differences in uniform or shoe style. United Airlines, the consensus has it, is "the girl-next-door", the neighbourhood babysitter grown up. Pan Am is upper class, sophisticated, and slightly reserved in its graciousness. PSA is brassy, fun-loving and sexy. Some flight attendants see a connection between the personality they were supposed to project and the market segment the company wants to attract. One United worker explained: "United wants to appeal to Ma and Pa Kettle. So it wants Caucasian girls – not so beautiful that Ma feels fat and not so plain that Pa feels unsatisfied. It's the Ma and Pa Kettle market that's growing, so that's why they use the girl-next-door image to appeal to the market"'.

Hochschild (1983:97–8).

what "successful" looks like … what "confident" looks like' (p. 181). Subsequent haircuts or changes of image had to be approved by the managers and grooming was regular monitored.

Nor is this managing and moulding of images restricted to hotels or catering. Aesthetics are as much an issue for professional workers as for those employed in clubs, shops and bars. Most of the main accountancy firms (including KPMG, Coopers & Lybrand and Ernst & Young) hired image consultants to advise their professional staff (PriceWaterhouse extended this to advice on dining etiquette for prospective partners). The Law Society publishes guidelines on the way solicitors should dress and Barclays Bank provided grooming sessions for all employees when they introduced a new uniform (Anderson-Gough et al. 2000; Wellington and Bryson 2001). Even when professional image consultants are not employed, appearance can form a key aspect of work. In McDowell's (1997) research into investment banks in the City of London, where high-flying employees were expected to appear 'seriously sexy in a self-confident, moneyed way' (p. 185) her male interviewees talked of the pressure they faced to diet, exercise, dress well and exude self-confidence. This also became part of the way that senior (male) bankers managed their staff (p. 187): 'I tell people in my team to look after themselves, sort out their BO or weight. You have got to look good.'

While professional guidance (and guidance for professionals) may take the form of tips on, and expectations about, personal grooming, the appearance of lower-ranking workers is often far more stringently regulated. The 'cast' at Disneyland are provided with detailed aesthetic regulations that cover fingernails, teeth and jewellery (Van Maanen 1991). Andy's restaurant chain in the USA insists that waitresses' uniforms must be no higher than 1–1½ inches above the knee, they are not allowed to wear elaborate make-up, or dark tights, or dark red or brown nail polish, and neither their hair roots nor their tattoos should be visible (Paules 1991:103). Nor is this particularly unusual. McDonald's, the Red Lobster Restaurant chain and Delta Airlines provide similar prescriptions (Hochschild 1983; Paules 1991; Leidner 1996). Flight attendants were also expected to keep their weight below a managerially set maximum and exceeding this was a disciplinary offence. Women who worked for PSA also had their bust, waist, hips and thighs measured on a regular basis. Those whose bodies ceased to conform to corporate norms were sacked (Hochschild 1983).

The way this control of appearance is received varies. The young people working in Glasgow's fashionable bars and restaurants, who may have wanted to look 'stylish' and 'tasty' anyway, tended to welcome the hints and tips they received. Managerial 'uniform police' (who reprimanded the less well groomed) were seen as supporting those staff who did make an effort. Not only was an employee's appearance seen as a legitimate arena for managerial concern and control, but also intervention could actively advantage workers, particularly when one shop equipped its staff with designer clothes in place of a uniform (Warhurst and Nickson 2001). By contrast, the 'sexy' high heels demanded by Delta Airlines meant that flight attendants had to cope with both instability and fatigue on long flights. Discontent here was shown by 'shoe-ins' (in which staff came to work wearing more comfortable shoes), wearing an extra piece of jewellery, a slightly shaggier beard, lighter make-up or a new hairstyle (Hochschild 1983:126; see also Paules 1991). But here employees' hard-won freedoms were usually followed by corporate crackdowns.

At one level this interest in aesthetics seems trivial. The length of a skirt and the style of a beard may not merit a major protest. At another, these are deeply personal issues and managerial regulation here affects individual freedom both inside and outside work. It also raises questions about the nature of work itself. Instead of regulating tasks, technique or knowledge organisations now attempt to control presentation.

Customers in control?

Service work has yet another element distinguishing it from manufacturing: the role of the customer (Sturdy 2001). In it, not only is the process of serving part of the product being purchased, but also (and relatedly) customers are implicated in the very management of the service process itself in a range of different ways (Bolton and Houlihan 2005). An inclusion which affects both the practice and theory of service sector work. Traditionally, work has involved an employer's control of an employee affected and experienced through loyalties, commitment, misbehaviour and resistance. In service sector work the relationship is a triangular one incorporating customer, employee and employer (Leidner 1993) with shifting alliances and allegiances. This way of organising work has implications for both the traditional control pattern and the established model of resistance. So employees of McDonald's are accountable to every customer who enters the restaurant for their appearance and expressions (Leidner 1996), Disneyland staff are expected to stay in character (Van Maanen 1991), flight attendants may be taken to task by passengers for not smiling, or not smiling enough (Hochschild 1983), and call centre workers may be blamed for mistakes that they had little to do with (Carroll et al. 2001; Korczynski 2001).

This triangle of relations is dynamic, with alliances and allegiances neither straightforward nor fixed. Employers and employees may find common interests 'against' their customers to increase sales or because working together encourages solidarity against the strangers. Alternatively, managers may elicit customers' help in setting or monitoring service standards and customers may volunteer this assistance. And finally, employees may take pride in the service they offer, allying themselves with customers against management. To make this shifting pattern of alliances more confusing, the demands of each of these parties may not be clearly articulated, and customers can exist in both a notional and a real form. This means that all three parties can lay claim to the right to speak for customers and set out whatever it is customers really want. Since serving the customer is, rhetorically at least, the principal aim of service work, this appeal is a powerful legitimatory device.

The most common, and recurrent, of these alliances is that of employer and employee 'against' customer. Indeed, it might be argued that such is the nature of service sector work, which aims to please but exists to extract money from those who 'consume' it. Employers design work to achieve these ends and employees carry it out. So, the insurance sales staff studied by Leidner (1993) saw the scripts that they were required to learn by rote (jokes, pauses and all) not as alienating or deskilling but as a codified form of expertise that was tried and tested and would help them to make more sales. Alliances can take a human as well as a structural form. Waitresses in 'Route', a down-market American restaurant chain, were more likely to receive sympathy than blame from their managers when customers complained of poor service (Paules 1996).

But while this may be the 'natural' or expected state of work, it is not the only one. Work processes are designed to please customers (rather than employees). Since customers know this many will volunteer opinions and criticism (Van Maanen 1991; Lopez 1996). Managers can also actively involve customers in the control process. Such involvement may be reactive, with management simply responding to comments and complaints. One restaurant chain aggregated positive and negative feedback and published the ratio between each for every employee on its corporate website (Fuller and Smith 1996). Delta Airlines filed all letters received about flight attendants: complimentary ones were known as 'orchids', critical ones, which often attracted disciplinary action, 'onions' (Hochschild 1983). Satisfaction surveys and mystery shoppers, the logical extension of this, have pervaded almost every area of work (Noon and Blyton 2002). 'Customers' of various different institutions may be asked (Fuller and Smith 1996:80):

> Were your nurses *concerned*?
> Were you greeted *graciously*?
> How was your salesperson's *appearance*?
> Was our employee *cheerful*?

Or even (Hochschild 1983:120):

> How were the magazines handed out?
> With a smile?
> With a *sincere* smile?

Through these managers may gain an ever-present and unpaid extension to their numbers and employees' actions can be tailored more precisely to the likes and dislikes of survey respondents. Even professional appraisal in accountancy firms covers serving the client (Anderson-Gough *et al.* 2000).

Equally, employees may ally with customers against managers. After all, working on the 'front line' involves close contact with one another and employees can gain great emotional satisfaction from pleasing customers (as well as having to face irritation and anger when they do not). This can find expression through simply avoiding a sales pitch that will advantage the organisation but annoy the customer. McDonald's staff, despite being urged to offer larger portions, fries or dessert with orders, frequently did not when out of earshot of supervisors since such requests added nothing to their own pay packets and annoyed customers (Leidner 1996). It can also result in workers becoming customers' champions against management. 'Route' waitresses, who relied on tips for much of their income, would serve larger portions, provide extras free or 'forget' to charge for particular items in order to please the people they served (Paules 1991). Workers in British Telecom call centres even called a one-day strike over managerial insistence that calls should last no longer than 285 seconds, so affecting employees' abilities to deal with callers (Independent 1999).

This choice of sides, coupled with a rhetoric of customer focus that over-lies (and often legitimises) the desire to increase profits, productivity or sales

---

Box 6.3

While flight attendants are told to imagine that their passengers are emotionally vulnerable, a major aspect of nursing involves dealing with patients who are genuinely ill or dying, all of which presents the individual nurse with intense emotional demands. Most have a great deal of autonomy in the way they deal with this and may establish close relationships with patients, but nurses are not always free to set their own rate of emotional 'exchange'. Some hospitals and managers have started to prescribe how such interactions should take place and often the work is so fast-paced that little time is left for emotional engagement, making the reassurances offered labour rather than work. Yet nurses still value the way they make an emotional difference to patients and their families and continue to see this as one of the most important aspects of their work, even when promotions distance them from it for much of the working day.

Taken mainly from Bolton (2005a) though see also (James 1993; Brown and Kirpal 2004; Bolton 2005b).

can also result in the idea of the customer being used to evade responsibility for actions. Constraints on call times (set by management) limit the extent to which call centre workers can establish friendly relations with or solve complicated problems for, callers. Yet call centre managers present this as a weakness of staff (who should learn to establish rapport quickly and efficiently). Junior accountants repeatedly told Anderson-Gough *et al.* (2000) that they worked long hours for the clients who wanted them to deliver projects or audits on time; none mentioned the fact that their seniors (who negotiated these agreements) were also involved in setting these deadlines.

This shifting pattern of linkages and loyalties means that service work is very different from manufacturing. Commitment, compliance, resistance and misbehaviour are all less straightforward. Deadlines, emotional demands and performance indicators may be set, policed or varied by either customers or employers and pleasing one of these actors may alienate the other. Yet service workers negotiate this complexity in their daily lives through the most mundane of triumphs and disasters.

Emotion work and emotional labour

So, working with emotions may be welcomed by employees, and relationships with customers may give pleasure and satisfaction. To a certain extent too, such behaviours are natural. In many of these organisations, the fact that work is about being and feeling as much as it is about doing, that workers are expected to feel as part of the wage effort bargain and that they may embody their organisations seems both natural and welcome to employees and managers. It is certainly true that there are expressive and performative elements in almost any form of social life and, according to Goffman (1959), everyone is involved in the conscious and unconscious management of impressions. A husband and wife will postpone their quarrel when in the presence of casual acquaintances and a boss, accustomed to familiarity with his subordinates, will act with courtesy and formality when visitors are in the office, setting the cue for the way the visitors should behave. In Goffman's account, the world of work is simply an extension of this natural behaviour where subordinates will simulate 'busyness' when supervisors are near, where mental health nurses will avoid being caught striking patients, and where waiters will assume a dignified and stately calm before customers that is far removed from the passion displayed when reprimanding erring juniors 'backstage'.

Understood in this way, emotion management is a natural process (or its unnaturalness is extended to all aspects of social life). The moment a society becomes complex, its members will relate to roles rather than to the individuals who take on those roles and dramaturgical elements will enter the relationship. This is not to say that there are no times when people go 'off-stage' – indeed, acting becomes apparent largely when it stops and behaviours change – rather, it means that acting is an inevitable part of life.

Yet what Goffman fails to take account of are the power relations that exist in the workplace (see Hochschild 1979, 1983; Paules 1991, 1996). Expressive and performative elements may be a normal part of any life but when they are used in the workplace under the direction of management they become commodities. Emotion work is not about making workplaces more human or sensitising organisational analysts to non-rational activities; it is the valorisation of human feelings (Thompson and McHugh 2002). In the private sphere, roles may be subject to renegotiation and change. They may vary and, at least in theory, are controlled by the individual adopting them. Those in the workplace are fixed and regulated by the firm. As Höpfl (2002:261) argues: 'That social life is regulated in a similar way is not in question. The issue here is the locus of regulation; the individual or the organisation.'

So, Hochschild's flight attendants act out their roles because they wish to be good at their work, the 'professionals' that their trainers describe, but they also perform their acts because each detail of action and behaviour is prescribed by the twenty-four men who work in method analysis and it is this separation of conception and execution that transforms the process from work to labour. These flight attendants are not allowed to make their own decisions, to judge situations as they see fit and rely on their own abilities and experience: they are instructed to perform to a script. In Delta Airlines almost nothing was left to the discretion of the individual worker, with feelings and forms as tightly controlled as the shovelling done by Taylor's Schmitt (1949). So too in call centre work encounters may be prescribed and customer representatives required to establish emotional rapport to a set routine. Yet the rapport so established and the emotions acted on are intended to be only 'virtual relationships'. Call centre workers are required to establish a warm and friendly relationship with callers but must also terminate the call as soon as possible. Nor are they allowed to give their direct line or encourage callers to wait to speak to their 'friend' the next time they call. since this would interfere with the management of the work processes. Call centre computers direct calls to the next available worker, not the one the caller is friendly with, although some customer representatives managed to have 'regular' callers despite this (Korczynski 2001; Wray-Bliss 2001).

Such virtuality raises questions about the impact of these specially counterfeited emotions. After all, if staff enjoy emotions (Leidner 1993; Wharton 1996; Korczynski 2001) might they be alienated by 'virtuality'? Both Korczynski's call centres and Leidner's fast food restaurants experienced massive staff turnover. High satisfaction is normally correlated with employees staying, but here, workers 'were so satisfied with the job that they were

Box 6.4

Emotional labour is not always about faking pleasant emotions. Hochschild's (1983) study also incorporated debt-collectors whose task, according to a sign on display in the collection office, was to 'create alarm' and deflate the customer's status. A prompt card urged them to 'Catch your customer off guard. Control the conversation.' Collectors get the customer to identify themselves then adjust the degree of threat to fit the debtor's resistance. While flight collectors were required to believe that the customer was always right, so trust could not give way to suspicion, collectors could not allow suspicion to give way to trust. The boss, who worked in the back office, would scream abuse at collectors who were not sufficiently aggressive to clients, 'Can't you get madder than that? Create alarm!'

Taken from Hochschild (1983).

leaving in considerable numbers' (Korczynski 2001:92). While in Goffman's studies participants *chose* to act and might step away from their performance with few ill consequences (other than, perhaps a quarrel), emotion workers have few such rights. They are there to take care of the customers and it is the customer's emotional rights that dominate. So, flight attendants are told to imagine that passengers are guests, or children, or have received traumatic news, placing an onus on them to behave with a care and courtesy that they know may not be reciprocated (Hochschild 1983). Similarly, Harvard clerical staff, upset at students' rebukes, were advised to 'think of yourself as a trash can. Take everyone's little bits of anger all day, put it inside you, and at the end of the day, just pour it into the dumpster on your way out the door' (Eaton 1996:296). As one trade unionist pointed out, if the customer is always right, those who serve them are always wrong (p. 304). There is a great deal of difference between choosing to act and being told to act, just as there is a great deal of difference between enjoying emotions and selling them. Work that focuses on customers' desires and needs often does so at the price of the employee.

Emotions and gender: women's work and women as workers

Emotional labour commodifies feelings and positions employees' emotional rights below those of customers. Most of the workers subordinated in this way are women. 53 per cent of service sector jobs in Britain are held by women and 91 per cent of jobs held by women are in the service sector (National

Statistics 2005:21–2). Moreover, this extensive participation of women in employment itself fuels demand for more service sector employees as the work that women have traditionally done in the household for nothing must now be purchased in the labour market (generally from other women). So, people eat out more, supermarkets sell more pre-prepared and partly prepared meals and the demand for carers, cleaners, child-minders and cooks rises.

While the increasing numbers of women in paid employment is often welcomed and does provide an element of economic power, the way these jobs are designed and controlled both advantages and traps the women who do them. Women are considered to be 'naturally' better at subordinating their own emotional needs to those of others, at being nice, at nurturing and, fundamentally, at being feminine. As one manager, charged with recruiting call centre staff who were empathetic, admitted (Taylor and Tyler 2000:83–4):

> The vast, vast majority of the agents we select are women . . . it's not as if we don't get men applying for the job . . . they just seem to fit it better, they're better at it . . . we are looking for people who can chat to people, interact, build rapport. What we find is that women can do this more, they're definitely more natural when they do it anyway. It doesn't sound as forced, perhaps they're used to doing it all the time anyway . . . women are naturally good at that sort of thing. I think they have a higher tolerance level than men . . . I suppose we do, yes, if we're honest about it, select women because they are women, rather than anything they've particularly shown at the interview.

Not only are women considered more suitable for service work (Paules 1991; Pierce 1995; McGauran 2000, 2001) but also, because they are assumed to be better at the emotional aspects of work, women will have more emotional demands placed on them than male colleagues and they will be monitored more stringently on the way they carry these emotional demands out. While male workers can define (or redefine) their jobs as unemotional, less emotional or differently emotional, women workers have no such freedom. They may find themselves trapped in a vicious circle that first prescribes then demands a particular form of gender relations. So the women paralegals in Pierce's (1996) study were expected to nurse and nurture their (mainly male) lawyer bosses in a process that could be like 'babysitting' (p. 207). Women who did not become affectively engaged in this way were penalised when it came to appraisals, pay rises and promotions. Male paralegals, by contrast, were expected only to be courteous. Similarly the women customer service representatives observed by Taylor and Tyler (2000) were assessed against both emotional and sales targets, while male colleagues who reached the sales targets could get away with ignoring emotional demands.

Emotional labour may also be sexualised, with advertising and notions of service deliberately linked to erotic imagery (Hochschild 1983). As a result, women's work becomes officially intertwined with male sexuality, an eroticised subordination with women workers in all occupations required to respond positively to uninvited sexual encounters as part of their job (Adkins 1992; Thompson and McHugh 2002). These range from being asked out on dates (Korczynski 2001), to harassment (Filby 1992), with workers told to encourage and put up with sexual harassment from callers in the hope that they might make a sale (Taylor and Tyler 2000). Nor is this restricted to low-level workers, as one woman investment banker commented (McDowell 1997:141): 'It's so difficult to strike a balance – if you are seen as feminine or desirable they think you're available, and if you are not they call you a dyke' (woman, 28, trader, Northbank).

When this form of titillation is used as a marketing device it is hard to pretend that the sexualised images and actions imposed on women staff are enjoyable or consensual. Women can and do use their sexuality to their own advantage in organisations and draw clear lines between instrumental flirting and harassment (Paules 1991) but they may also be systemically denied the opportunity to resist or rebuff advances.

Just as women are expected to provide emotional support 'naturally', because they are women, so they are judged more strictly on their grooming and the way they embody their organisations. The male investment bankers interviewed by McDowell (1997) all mentioned appearance and weight, but male fashions are far more forgiving to the imperfect figure than female ones, and the way that women look is far more closely regulated. Hancock and Tyler (2000) report that applicants for jobs as flight attendants were rejected because they were too old, their skin was blemished, their hair was too short, messy or severe, their nails were too short or bitten, their posture was poor or their legs chubby, their weight was wrong, they lacked 'poise' or 'style' or they had a common accent (p. 118). Even in work that ostensibly has no aesthetic dimension, women applicants and employees are judged on appearance in ways it is difficult to imagine happening to men. One woman candidate to National Westminster Bank with an IQ of 172 was told by an interviewer that her weight of 16 stones made it unlikely that she would be offered a job (Cook 1997). Overweight women might also be denied promotion or kept away from public or prestigious work (Trethewey 1999) and images of what is acceptable are restrictive. Women professionals must be feminine and well groomed but not overtly sexual ('Leah' in Trethewey 1999:443):

> Don't let your skirts be too short, don't let the top be too low, um make sure that the material isn't see through. Don't let your hair be too wild, you need [a style] that when you go to work you can make it calm and more professional. Because you really want people to know what you're saying, not your clothes, because they'll be distracted by your clothes.

It seems that women must both live up to, and live down, sexualised images in order to be seen as workers (Trethewey 1999:443):

> Thus, women choose their professional attire very carefully. It must be stylish, but not trendy, says Suzanne. It must be pretty, but not too feminine, contends Success. It must be interesting, but not suggestive, claims Lara. Additionally, clothing must be tailored but not too tight. In short, women must reveal their bodies in very specific and specified ways.

This has particular implications for women. First, arranging this type of aesthetic display of the self is clearly very time-consuming. Effective grooming, making up (and making down) and finding clothes that meet the organisational demands (as well as, hopefully, fitting and flattering their own notions of themselves) is a demanding process leaving women less time to work on organisational, technical and social skills (Brodo 1989). Second, despite repeated references to the ideal body as 'fit' (Trethewey 1999; McDowell 1997), notions of female beauty revolve around increasingly slimmer forms. Airlines' weight limits for flight attendants can be as much as ten pounds below the medically recommended weight and all the women contacted by Brewis and Sinclair (2000) reported that they were, or had been, unhappy with their weight and the size of their body. Yet the boyish slenderness demanded by the fashion industry may physically weaken (and, through this, disempower) those women who achieve it (Orbach 1978). Conforming to these demanding aesthetic ideals makes women less, rather than more, capable of coping with organisational pressures.

Even once these displays have been achieved, women are still expected to perform tasks and inhabit their jobs in ways not required of their male colleagues. Successful performance may result in emotional and physical exhaustion, and is likely to impact on home life. It may also mean that the woman worker displays behaviours that are entirely inappropriate for promotion. This is a Catch-22 situation. To succeed in their jobs women must be nice, nurturing, submissive or feminine. Yet few senior vacancies favour this particular blend of attributes. Women who do not have these qualities, or who choose not to display them at work, may be seen as bad at their jobs or (worse) bad at being women and they too are unlikely to be promoted.

Acknowledging the gender implications of emotion work also raises questions about Goffman's (1959) assumptions of the 'naturalness' of performative and expressive activities. His work, based on observations made in the 1950s, consistently and repeatedly portrays women as subordinate and submissive. So high school pupils fake ignorance of mathematics to allow their (male) dates to feel superior, wives listen attentively to jokes that their husbands have told a thousand times before and courtship rituals are described as a man's 'attempts to manoeuvre someone for whom he must at first show respect into a position of subordinate intimacy' (p. 190). The one brief mention of women with more power and status than men is quickly switched to male myths of sexual conquest over such women. Yet while women adopt roles to make life more pleasant for men, there are few instances of men adopting roles to make life more pleasant for women. Goffman exposes the gendered nature of these interactions through his descriptions and draws on the work of Simone de Beauvoir, but his analysis neglects the extent to which performances are one-sided.

Labour pains: resistance and misbehaviour

So, acknowledging emotions at work may encourage a more human environment; people who work with their emotions not only report higher levels of job satisfaction (Wharton 1996) but claim that the emotional element is the most pleasurable aspect of their work (Leidner 1993; Korczynski 2001); and this type of simulated performance is a common feature of human interaction (Goffman 1959). However, as Thompson and McHugh (2002) argue, emotional labour is not some catch-all term for emotions in the workplace: it commodifies human feelings. Through it, emotions are managed, monitored and measured, often with little regard for the person who feels them. But workers are not passive recipients of management's prescriptions. They can and do protest against emotion work, resisting and misbehaving as well as cooperating and complying. Some of their triumphs are dramatic but most are ordinary, everyday achievements.

Fundamentally, emotional labour involves workers in simulating emotions they do not always feel and subordinating their needs to those of customers and clients. This may, as shown above, bring pleasure, but it also brings pain. Abusive customers can spoil workers' days (Hochschild 1983; Korczynski 2001). Acting as an emotional 'trash can' (Eaton 1996) may involve penalties. One call centre worker interviewed by Callaghan and Thompson (2002) pointed out how difficult it was not to take abusive customers personally (p. 245):

> If they raise their voice at me, I keep the same volume in my voice. It can be quite nerve-wracking. As I said, with the businessmen, they can be quite sharp and it can be quite demeaning to you, because you're there to do a job and they won't let you do it. But I try to keep the tone and volume of my voice about the same, so that they're not getting at me. Maybe they have a grievance with the bank, but it's not with me.

Small wonder then that one of the distinctive features of emotional labour is training workers to 'cope' with this abuse without ever reacting to it:

imagining the abuser as a guest, a child or someone who has been bereaved, getting co-workers to talk an employee out of their anger, rather than sympathising with them and even taking ten minutes off for vigorous exercise with skipping strongly recommended (Hochschild 1983; Eaton 1996; Pierce 1996). Only customers' feelings are legitimate. The effort required to simulate and conceal feelings can be exhausting and employees may react, burn out or find themselves unable to engage with the original and uncommodified emotion. Emotion workers may arrive home on a 'high' so manically and happily talking that they cannot engage properly with friends and family (Hochschild 1983), or over long shifts of forced cheerfulness, lose their ability to smile away from the workplace or respond to partners and spouses only in the language and ways appropriate to work colleagues (Casey 1995).

This is quite a serious issue. Emotions are an important element of personal life and it is difficult to simulate feelings for long hours at work without a corresponding impact in the home. Interestingly, freedom from emotional control, as Goffman (1959) points out, is often the freedom to be rude, surly or unhappy. In addition to this it is very difficult for those accustomed to dealing with emotions as commodities to accept them in their uncommodified form. Giving emotions a market value endangers their use value. When smiles are bought and sold it is harder to accept them as gifts.

But workers are neither passive victims nor 'emotional dupes'. They can and do react to corporate control by reasserting their own rights to control and define their work. They reshape what they do. Much of this takes the form of simple everyday actions to exert control over, for example, the pace of work. On the Fordist conveyor belt of service work there are tactics to help the fight back. So flight attendants, trying to cope with serving large numbers of passengers with food and drink avoid meeting people's eyes to cut down on additional requests (Hochschild 1983), call centre staff cut callers off 'in error' (Ackroyd and Thompson 1999) or do not hang up after finishing a call (Wray-Bliss 2001) and waitresses avoid clearing and re-laying tables during busy periods to delay new customers sitting down and demanding service (Paules 1996). Undramatic as these are, they do offer individual workers very real freedoms.

Workers also redefine the work that they do. Some women paralegals, faced with high demands on their technical expertise and emotional engagement, coped by portraying their relationships with their lawyer bosses as 'personal' and 'special', others by belittling the demands and competence that these lawyers demonstrated (Pierce 1996). Maids and au pairs sought to redefine their work through its technical components as 'professional' rather than emotional (Macdonald 1996). Flight attendants emphasised their extensive expertise at emergency procedures and first aid (Hochschild 1983).

Other reassertions of control over work show disapproval: 'smile strikes'

A single gate agent was re-booking a long line of inconvenienced travellers after the cancellation of a crowded flight. Suddenly an angry passenger pushed his way to the desk. He slapped his ticket down on the counter and said, 'I HAVE to be on this flight and it HAS to be FIRST CLASS.'

The agent replied, 'I'm sorry sir, I'll be happy to help you, but I've got to help these folks out first, and I'm sure we'll be able to work something out.'

The passenger was unimpressed. He asked loudly, so that passengers behind him could hear, 'Do you have any idea who I am?'

Without hesitating, the gate agent smiled and reached for her public address microphone.

'May I have your attention please?' she began, her voice bellowing throughout the terminal. 'We have a passenger here at the gate who does not know who he is. If anyone can help him find his identity, please come to Gate 17.'

With the passengers behind him in line laughing hysterically, the man glared at the gate agent, gritted his teeth and swore, '[Expletive] you.'

Without flinching she smiled and said, 'I'm sorry sir, but you'll have to stand in line for that too.'

The man retreated as the people in the terminal applauded loudly. Although the flight was cancelled and the passengers were late, they were no longer angry with the airline.

Macdonald and Sirianni (1996:ix–x)

(Fuller and Smith 1996), 'going into robot' by performing the actions required but in ways that are totally emotionally disengaged (Hochschild 1983) or reasserting control over appearance by breaking the dress code (Hochschild 1983; Paules 1991). Humour too becomes a weapon to restore pride and there are several examples of unofficial house journals with articles that reveal inconsistencies and ironies in organisational practice or jokes that show the triumph of the exploited over the exploiters. *Chaos* in British Airways and the *PanAm Quipper* in one of their rivals are both passed round, samizdat-style. One (probably apocryphal) story, that captures the emotional labourer's discontent perfectly is reported by Hochschild (1983:127):

A young businessman said to a flight attendant, 'why aren't you smiling?'. She put her tray back on the food cart, looked him in the eye, and said, 'I'll tell you what. You smile first, then I'll smile'. The businessman smiled at her. 'Good,' she replied, 'now freeze and hold that for fifteen hours'.

Other accounts are real and Taylor and Bain (2003) describe the way that call centre workers used humour to strengthen their collective identity and undermine management. Through these stories the powerless triumph over the powerful and those who have to give respect but cannot expect it in return demonstrate their right to equal status.

Sometime this resistance can result in very real levels of autonomy for workers. Paules's (1991) account of women waitresses working in a small, downmarket restaurant chain in New Jersey shows workers who are poorly paid (wages start at $1.71 per hour, some 64¢ below the state minimum wage) and who rely mainly on tips for their income. Yet this wages structure (coupled with the extreme shortage of labour in the area) gives the waitresses a great deal of power. These are workers who 'don't take no junk' (p. 1). As entrepreneurs they can take steps to regulate their own earnings, varying the speed at which they clear and prepare tables to ensure a greater or lesser number of customers to serve in a shift (higher numbers means more tips means higher earnings) or even by diverting customers from other waitresses' tables. These waitresses are happy to flirt, if flirting gains them larger tips, but neither subordinate themselves nor allow others to subordinate them. According to one (pp. 150–1):

> This is my motto: 'You sit in my station at Route, I'll sell you the world. I'll tell you anything you want to hear.' Last night I had this guy, wanted my phone number. He was driving me nuts. And I wasn't interested . . . He goes, 'Well, how come you and your husband broke up?' I said, 'Well, he found out about my boyfriend and got mad. I don't know. I don't understand it myself.' And he started laughing. And I'm thinking, '*This is my money*. I'll tell you anything.' . . . I got five bucks out of him. He didn't get my phone number, but *I got my five dollar tip*. I'll sell you the world if you're in my station. (Emphasis added by Paules.)

Customers were not the masters of servants, they were a substance to be processed and waitresses could and did challenge or refuse to serve those who were rude, unpleasant or who left no tip. The detailed prescriptions that the company provided on the ways that staff should dress, the minutiae of the restaurant's appearance and the food preparation (including the amount of salt the chefs should put in the chicken gravy) were widely flouted in practice and waitresses enjoyed considerable autonomy in the ways that they worked, dressed and felt.

Discussion and conclusions

It seems that emotions at work are both complex and contradictory. In denying that the workplace is an arena for emotion, in moving towards the rational bureaucracy as the workplace ideal we wilfully misunderstand it. Equally, in claiming that emotions used by organisations are as innocent and pleasurable as those in social exchanges we are being naïve. The delights of engaging in activities that are intrinsically pleasurable need to be set against the lack of choice that employees have about which behaviours to display and which to conceal. Emotional engagements with colleagues, customers and employers need to be tempered by an understanding of the power relations that exist in the workplace. Emotion work is an unequal exchange that strips the worker of their right to consideration as a human being. They must tend to others, but cannot show when their own feelings are hurt; they must extend every courtesy, yet should not expect to be recipients of politeness. Moreover the courtesies extended may not be their own but their employer's, all of which must be scripted, learned and monitored.

This is not to understate the pleasures that many employees take in emotion work. A use-value does not end the moment an emotion comes to the attention of an employer and emotion work may bring great satisfaction to those who do it. Rather, it is to point out that, because emotions bring pleasure in private life, it does not necessarily follow that these pleasures can be transferred unalloyed to workplaces when emotions are appropriated, the line which most of the gurus follow.

Perhaps Bolton's (2000) work is useful here. Faced with the combating pleasures and pains of emotion work and emotional labour she attempts to classify emotions in work in a number of ways: as presentational, as philanthropic, as prescriptive and as pecuniary. *Presentational* emotional work is, following Goffman, a performance, but significantly the rules followed are general social norms rather than detailed corporate demands. So colleagues might extend courtesies to one another, act busy in front of their seniors and smile at their customers. *Philanthropic* acts are gifts rather than commodities, and people listen or smile out of friendship and concern. *Prescriptive* acts are demanded by the organisation, and the detailed lists provided by McDonald's, Delta Airlines and many call centres come under this heading. Finally, *pecuniary* emotion work is undertaken for gain just as the waitresses at 'Route', clear about where their financial interests lay, flirted or smiled in the hope of securing larger tips.

The divisions between these categories are blurred by both employees and employers. Organisations may devise sophisticated prescriptions, payment systems and professional ideals in pursuit of commitment. Selection practices are designed to find those who 'naturally' possess the attributes required so that controlled actions are genuine and work itself is a gift. Equally, workers may choose to switch between these various categories themselves. Callaghan and Thompson (2002) observed call centre workers, operating under the most prescriptive of managerial systems, chat to elderly, insomniac or lonely callers in acts of philanthropy.

Then too, the way that emotion work and emotional labour are experienced will also vary depending on the job a person holds and on its power and status. As Macdonald and Sirianni (1996) argue, the most demanding and degrading of 'feeling rules' are imposed on the 'emotional proletariat' of cleaners, call centre workers and carers. These jobs are the latter-day equivalent of the production line, with workers' feelings subjected to speed-up and slow-down. The alienation these workers experience is an alienation from their own feelings, which are increasingly appropriated by management (Hochschild 1983). Nor does this work attract material compensation. Many service workers are poorly paid and in jobs that offer little prospect of escape or advancement.

Professional workers have always had to inhabit their jobs in particular ways, demonstrating engagement, loyalty and commitment (Moss-Kanter 1977; Macdonald and Sirianni 1996). And they are expected to dress, act and feel 'properly' (Barnard 1962; Molloy 1977; McDowell 1997). But this is an expectation rather than a demand. Moreover traditionally such workers enjoy money, status and power in return for success in their profession. But here, apparent empowerment and psychic freedom to decide on emotional responses may simply be a more insidious, because more invasive, form of control (Biggart 1989). Workers left to decide for 'themselves' actually have heavy demands imposed on them since, 'acceptable' choices are predetermined. One of the key features of Richard Sennett's (1998) argument is that the emotional responses required by firms, which were demanded in environments characterised by insecurity and impermanence, made workers less able to express those emotions in ways that were genuine within their families and communities. Their intense emotional engagement may result in illness, burnout and alienation (Kidder 1981; Kunda 1992; Casey 1995).

When emotions become commodities it is difficult for any group of workers to emerge unscathed. Clearly, the 'emotional proletariat' are to be least envied. Professionals enjoy status and discretion and their commitment is generally rewarded with promotions. Freedom from detailed control certainly seems to increase the job satisfaction of those who work with their emotions (Wharton 1996) but this does not necessarily mean that the emotional elite escape the penalties, burnout and alienation of the emotional proletariat. McDowell's (1997) women bankers seem as subject to harassment as their less highly rewarded sisters in betting shops and call centres (Filby 1992; Taylor and Tyler 2000).

Nor is this as novel a phenomenon as many commentators assume. While factory work, with all its many disadvantages, often involved emotional freedom (see, for example, Burawoy 1979; Pollert 1981; Collinson 1992), servants and salespeople have always had emotional demands placed on them (Wright Mills 1956). These emotion rules are now more widespread, more sophisticated and more complete, but they are not new.

Emotions and aesthetics are now an integral part of the employment contract for many, if not most, of those in work. Such an inclusion brings both pleasure and pain to workers. The control systems designed to harness feelings are seldom as absolute in practice as they appear in theory and employees are not empty spaces to be moulded to managerial designs. Few workers may have sufficient labour market power or moral courage to say, with one of the wait-resses at 'Route', 'kiss my ass, and keep your two bucks' (Paules 1996:126). But many assert themselves through creating space in work, redefining what they do and the ways that they do it, misbehaving and resisting demands to secure their freedom in small ways. Yet these struggles to reclaim the managed heart are seldom totally successful, and the price of selling commodities in this particular market can be very high indeed.

7

Managing culture

Fellows, why aren't any of you asking about the total lack of correspondence between what we're preaching here and the way we run our company? (Jackall 1988:124)

I was very disappointed to discover 'The Vision' is mostly just the latest American Management Theory, re-hashed and re-packaged, not our creation at all. If some MIT or Harvard Guru rediscovers the virtues of hierarchical management structures in 3–4 years time, shall we have to put this all into reverse? (Weeks 2004:106–7)

Managing culture is remarkable in the faddish world of management initiatives and management writings for both its influence and its longevity. Ever since 1982 when Tom Peters and Robert Waterman captured the spirit of the times with *In Search of Excellence*, their account of the way successful American companies operated, culture has been seen as a recipe for success (Legge 1994:41). Strong performance is attributable to the 'right' culture and weak performance can be corrected through culture change.

In all of these accounts, it is the employees' beliefs, assumptions and norms that are subject to manipulation since it is the people who make the difference. Peters and Waterman dwell with enthusiasm on the way the concierge at the Four Seasons hotel remembers guests' names, the cleanliness of McDonald's, IBM's engagement with its customers, the rallies of the Tupperware sellers and the quality products of Procter and Gamble. It is 'the individual human being [who] still counts' (1982:8) and what that human being counts to do is feel enthusiasm, devotion and pride in their product or service.

Significantly, it is the managers of a company who decide what the culture should be and who actively shape it. Their task is to set out the myths, rituals, traditions and frames of reference that influence and direct the way people feel about their work (Pettigrew 1973, 1979, 1985; Mitchell 1985). Once these

115

have been defined and developed, they are cascaded down the organisation through newsletters, presentations, briefings and, of course, through the way the leaders themselves 'walk the talk'. Leaders are 'the ultimate change masters' (Kanter 1985:278) and 'the only thing of real importance that leaders do is to create and manage culture and . . . the unique talent of leaders is their ability to work with culture' (Schein 1985:2). Those who are successful at this are idolised. Colin Marshall of British Airways helped to serve breakfast to customers when a queue formed for a new service the company was offering (Höpfl and Linstead 1993), while Microsoft's Bill Gates and IBM's Tom Watson are legendary, both inside and outside their organisations (see, for example Peters and Waterman 1982; Kunda 1992; Coupland 1995).

For the individual employees, strong cultures hold out the prospect of a new way of being managed. Instead of securing compliance to bureaucratic order or obedience to regulation, the management of culture means that organisations can free employees from petty controls because all are genuinely committed to their firms. This is not *freedom from* control, but a different *type of* control. As Etzioni (1961:2) notes:

> Normative control is the attempt to elicit and direct the required efforts of members by controlling the underlying experiences, thoughts and feelings that guide their actions. Under normative control, members act in the best interest of the company not because they are physically coerced, nor purely from an instrumental concern with economic rewards and sanctions . . . Rather, they are driven by internal commitment, strong identification with company goals, intrinsic satisfaction from work . . . Thus, under normative control, membership is founded not on the behavioural or economic transaction traditionally associated with work organisations, but, more crucially, on an experiential transaction, one in which symbolic rewards are exchanged for a moral orientation to the organisation.

The rationale behind this is easy to see. Hiring someone to do a job does not guarantee that it will be done. Control mechanisms are less than perfect at ensuring that well-defined tasks are completed satisfactorily (Edwards and Scullion 1982; Doray 1988; Ackroyd and Thompson 1999). It is difficult to imagine that they could achieve less tangible outputs such as securing affective affiliation or inspiring creativity in employees. For these, the generation of normative control through the creation of strong cultures seems to offer an attractive solution. When people genuinely wish to work for an organisation, are enthusiastic about the product or service and are loyal to the company's leaders there is no need to make them conform to petty regulation and they can be free to be creative. This has the potential to be a genuinely new form of organisation with no middle managers, no bureaucratic regulations and the flexibility to cope with creativity, turbulence and technological innovation (Ouchi 1981; Deal and Kennedy 1982; Peters and Austin 1985; Graves 1986; Peters 1987).

There are, of course, problems with this organisational ideal. It is unitarist, equating the interests of employees with those of the organisation that employs them. No difficulties, either theoretically or practically, are anticipated in securing culture change and workers are considered infinitely malleable at management's behest. Such an approach and such omissions tell us more about the writings on culture than it does about its management. The material that praises culture change is evangelical and celebratory; designed to inspire and enthuse rather than assess the principal components of organisational performance. It is, like the human relations school of researchers from the 1930s and 1940s, a move away from the notion that organisations are necessarily impersonal and bureaucratic (Parker 2000). But the form it takes is far less scientific and lacks any historical perspective (Rowlinson and Procter 1999). In the populist books little attempt is made to give details of the research conducted. Prediction, prescription and anecdote are intertwined with references to serious studies and all are treated equally, with external influences on corporate success ignored (Guest 1992). This is not to argue that firms do not use normative control, nor that there are no examples of successful firms that use normative control. Rather, it questions the idea that culture management in the form it takes in the celebratory literature, is as positive for firms and employees or is as universally successful.

Strong cultures

As might be expected, accounts of strong, unifying cultures are much more prevalent in the celebratory literature. But they are not absent from the empirical work. In a detailed and ethnographic account of life in a self-consciously excellent high-tech company, Gideon Kunda (1992) shows how 'Tech' generated genuine devotion to the company. Car bumper stickers proclaimed 'I love Tech' and posters, stickers, slogans, newsletters, speeches, presentations and professionally produced corporate videos proclaimed company values, including the slogan, 'It's not work – it's a celebration.' Managers, corporate trainers and senior executives all urged employees to remember that it was up to them to take responsibility for their own careers, to take the initiative to develop products and services, to build teams, to secure funding from their seniors and to make the company great. The technical staff in particular were delighted at the freedom they had to develop products, one describing the company as an 'engineer's sandbox'. Devotion to the company went beyond the slogans, to the extent that many employees were reluctant to hear complaints about 'Tech' unless they were constructively phrased. Discontents were heckled or marginalised. Permanent employees (the elite at 'wage class 4') were guaranteed job security and their work was often genuinely fascinating.

In Britain Grugulis et al.'s (2000) study of a small consultancy firm shows a company set up by a group of friends, where senior management were determined not to let growth destroy its distinctive ethos. Workers were given a great deal of freedom in the jobs that they did but the culture was very actively managed. One longstanding employee was given the job of 'culture manager' and an annual budget of £250,000 a year, some 2% of turnover. With this she organised events, socials and get-togethers. 'ConsultancyCo' staff participated in 1970s discos, enjoyed football competitions in which the men competed while the women dressed as cheerleaders, had meals in restaurants and trips away on which families were invited. In the workplace, team-working both reinforced this message and ensured that all employees knew each other reasonably well. There were multiple teams, each linked to a different initiative. There were improvement teams, product teams, quality teams, senior management teams and (of course) a team for every business unit. Each team held regular team briefings with minutes posted on the company's intranet and everyone was actively encouraged to work on company procedures and improve them.

Attempts to control culture started at the recruitment stage. One of the workers had been hired when he shared a taxi with a director, and employees were urged to nominate suitable friends. Formal hiring processes were thought out with great care. Every year the firm's official graduate recruitment event coincided with Red Nose Day, a day dedicated to fundraising for charity when many people dress in costume to raise money. Candidates, dressed in their best suits and carrying briefcases, arrived in the office to find everyone there in fancy dress. French maids, cavaliers and teddy bears waved collecting buckets; interviews were conducted by Mickey Mouse; and the culture manager took careful note of interviewees' reactions.

For those who enjoyed this sort of environment, life in ConsultancyCo and Tech was very pleasant. Workers had freedom to focus on pet projects and to exercise and develop their skills. But this freedom came at a price and in ConsultancyCo it was at the cost of diversity, with recruitment focused on homosocial reproduction (Moore 1951). Of the 150 employees only 23 were women and all but 5 were confined to clerical and secretarial roles. Minority staff were even more poorly represented. The lists of workers boasted almost no names that were not of British origin and the only non-white employee observed was a board director of Chinese descent.

Non-participation in the social events was also penalised. 'ConsultancyCo' had few direct work controls and workers were trusted, but the key condition of this trust was being known (Fox 1974). Officially, attendance at company socials was neither demanded nor monitored. Yet because these events formed the axis of the system of cultural control, participation was only notionally voluntary and regular absence was taken seriously. This was something that was rather dramatically illustrated by the dismissal of 'Helen' the HR director, not because her work was of poor quality (indeed, her work was not mentioned at all) but because of her unwillingness to immerse herself in the company culture.

In 'Tech', the genuine orientation to the company and the fascination of projects meant that many employees worked long hours. According to one development manager (201–2):

> This is a real seductive organisation. You wanna do more and more. I work seventeen, eighteen hours a day. I get a few hours done in the early morning, then I take the kid to school, spend the day here, and work in the evening. It's family and work. That is it. It's hard. A lot of burnout . . . They say Tech encourages divorces. They promise you a lot, make it lucrative, give you more and more. It's not just Tech; it's the whole industry. People get addicted to work. I look around and I see weird things. I see screwed up marriages, I see fucked-up kids. I thought Ben had problems: alcoholism, a depressed wife. So I found him another job. But now his replacement has just left his wife and kids himself.

Divorces and burnouts were common. People spoke of nervous breakdowns, alcoholism, serious illness caused by overwork and physical collapse. Thanks to the well-funded employee assistance programme and the security of employment that all permanent staff enjoyed, such burnouts did not result in unemployment but they did lead to a great deal of ambiguity when employees discussed work, which was seen as both contaminated and attractive: 'shit', 'crap' and entirely engrossing. For many employees, it seemed as though *not* becoming obsessed by work was only achieved by a deliberate act of will. Workers had a great deal of freedom to choose how they operated but at the price of a sacrifice of self (see also Starbuck 1993).

In each of these organisations staff satisfaction was high, wage rates were above average and many employees were genuinely enthusiastic about their employers. Yet workers were also required to give their hearts, as well as their hands and minds (Warhurst and Thompson 1998). As Hochschild (1983) points out, one response to so much pressure to love the company is a genuine sublimation of self to the organisation. Under normative control it is the identity of the workers that is devoted to the organisation (Willmott 1993; du Gay 1996; du Gay *et al.* 1996; du Gay 2000; Weierter 2001). And individual employees become 'enterprising' subjects in the sense that they are persuaded to invest a key part of themselves in the organisation (Salaman 2001).

Desperately seeking culture

Both 'Tech' and 'ConsultancyCo' seem to match the celebratory accounts of corporate culture well. Staff are aware that the culture is being consciously and deliberately managed, but most accept this and many are enthusiastic. Their accounts of work clearly show the very negative impact it has had on their personal lives and health, but also reveal its fascination for them. The corporate good is accepted as a key goal to be achieved through the management of culture (Graves 1986).

But these are hardly typical organisations. Both employ largely well-paid, highly educated expert workers and 'Tech' targets its cultural interventions and its most prized employment conditions at these people. Moreover, 'Tech' has a long tradition of paternalistic management and positive industrial relations while 'ConsultancyCo' is a new organisation that has always sought to control its culture. Few firms have such positive legacies to build on, are prepared to treat and pay their employees so well, guaranteeing security in the face of persistent ill-health (often caused by persistent overwork), or are so consistent in the way that messages match employment practices.

Accounts of the effective management of culture are heavily outnumbered by evidence of failures. Keenoy and Anthony (1992) note that shortly after the TSB launched its cultural change programme (which aimed to construct an 'achievement-oriented culture') it announced that some 5000 staff were to be made redundant. Civil service attempts to change culture have been numerous, overlapping and deeply confusing. One middle manager interviewed by Driscoll and Morris (2001:816–17) protested that:

> Yes, there have been some changes in working practices, there have been some attempts to change values but the problem is that all these changes are not going in the same direction. Take my grade for instance, on the one hand [the latest initiative] is supposed to make me a facilitator of change, on the other we see delayering cutting back on management jobs. I've got nowhere to go from here,

no more promotion, I'm at the end of the line. This has made me very cynical of the organisation. Do cynics make the best leaders?

British Airways became one of the culture success stories of the 1980s and 1990s when it went from making losses of £200 a minute in 1981 (Blyton and Turnbull 2004) to become the world's most profitable carrier and the company that most graduates would like to work for in 1996 (*Financial Times* 9 July 1997); all, apparently, attributable to its new approach to culture and its 'putting people first'. Yet this much vaunted high regard for its staff was not apparent either in descriptions of the company's training programmes (Höpfl 1992, 1993) or in its behaviour through the industrial action of 1997 when workers contemplating strikes were threatened with dismissal, legal action, loss of pension rights, promotion prospects and travel discounts. Faced with this pressure from management, less than 300 of the cabin crew actually went on strike, but more than 2000 called in sick (Grugulis and Wilkinson 2002).

Often, initiatives fail because culture change is a means of altering the wage effort bargain, of intensifying work or gaining higher levels of commitment or flexibility from employees while firm commitment remains minimal. Coercion and insecurity can be highly effective tools for securing short-term changes in employee behaviour. Ogbonna and Harris's (2002) study of culture change in a major supermarket chain describes the way extensive redundancies and demotions among store managers meant that those who were left swiftly learned to put on an act in front of their peers, presenting the 'right' emotional orientation. At the same time half of these managers had to work more than eighty hours a week to safeguard their jobs or secure promotion. Unsurprisingly employees at almost every level were cynical about the programme. According to two respondents (Ogbonna and Wilkinson 2003:1165):

> It's a bit like communism, I'm telling you this is how it works – 'we want the masses to believe it, but I want to live in wealth and have millions in the bank, but you peasants – do as I say, not as I do'! (Regional manager)
> . . . most of the paternalism, if not all of the paternalism that we knew in the old company has gone and has been replaced by hard unfeeling and uncaring managers who compound that behaviour by actually putting the message out that they are the opposite, that they are in fact caring and solicitous employers which they are not. (Director)

One supermarket's emphasis on a new culture of customer focus resulted in 95 per cent of workers reporting changes in behaviour. But in these studies, such changes do not reflect an emotional orientation to the firm; rather they are compelled, calculative or resigned (Ogbonna 1992/1993; Ogbonna and Wilkinson 1988, 1990; Ogbonna and Harris 2002). Favourable reactions from managers seem to stem from the fact that promotions and job security

'What we have got is a guns and roses culture.'

'What the hell's that, Barry?', he was asked.

'It's a rock group or something isn't it?' added another.

'It is. And what a racket!' which was followed with:

'Do you reckon Barry's saying ZTC is a racket?' at which point Barry explained himself:

'We've got guns pointed at us. But they've got flowers sticking out of the barrels. "Watch it, else you'll get the bullet. But enjoy the sweet flowers – get some personal development in."'

'OK. OK.' Intervened the person chairing the meeting, which was about managers encouraging their 'team leaders' to implement the personal development scheme. 'Order, order. A rose by any other . . . Let's get down business,' whereupon the episode ended with one of the managers pointing two fingers, pistol like, at the chair person:

'Bang, bang'.

Watson (1994:123–4).

---

are dependent on their reactions either because this is coerced (Ogbonna and Wilkinson 2003; Weeks 2004) or because the managers and supervisors themselves see in the culture change programme an opportunity to get noticed (Storey 1992). Even in more positive accounts of culture management, where a series of small incremental changes genuinely make life better for employees, behavioural change is not the result of changing norms and values but a response to demands for behavioural change (Rosenthal *et al.* 1997).

In none of these accounts are employees 'passive recipients' (Keep 1989; Hill 1995), changing their attitudes, norms and beliefs because senior management tell them to do so. All were conscious of the process, all aware of the reasons for it and all had choices about the way they responded, responses which often included humour. In Weeks's (2004) study of 'BritArm' bank's repeated attempts to change its culture, one employee, after attending a presentation where increased profits were presented as bad news because costs were still too high, commented (p. 18): 'That's the culture. Everything is bad news. Otherwise they'd have to pay us more. Still, I don't suppose it's worse here than anywhere else.' As in Kunda's account of working life at 'Tech', workers at 'BritArm' were routinely shown glossy corporate videos, specially made to communicate with employees and provide a visual reminder of the culture. Although (pp. 14–15)

> [u]niformly of high polish the briefings and videos are routinely derided by management and staff alike. Any feelings of pride or gratitude in seeing CEO

Michael Cole explain the Bank's vision or hearing BBC newsreader Michael Buerk announce improvements to the Bank's systems are either absent or left unexpressed. Instead, mannerisms are mocked, clothing critiqued, errors highlighted, managerial claims loudly disbelieved and executive waffle snorted at. Those managers who choose to read the briefing notes verbatim rather than use them as guidelines for improvisation often have a hard time doing so with a straight face. Managers regularly preface the meetings with apologies for the material and typically join in the good-natured fun that follows.

Such mocking is widespread. The factory workers described by Collinson (1992) were unimpressed by their new, American management's attempt to change the culture from adversarial to cooperative industrial relations and the company newsletter was stigmatised as 'Goebbels's Gazette'. And employees of the American clothing store, The Gap, produced an alternative version of the company's 'words to live by' (see Box 7.3).

This wry consciousness that publicly acknowledges culture management as a euphemism for power is a far more accurate reflection of the cultures that exist in organisations than the rhetorical flourishes of senior management. Indeed, one of the problems with the celebratory literature is the view that culture is something that is unitary and homogeneous, designed and implemented by senior management. As ethnographic accounts of workplaces reveal, while management initiatives may influence cultures (as something to be responded to) they are neither the principal nor the only motive force (Roy 1958; Burawoy 1979; Beynon 1984; Collinson 1992; Hamper 1992; Watson 1994; Casey 1995).

Box 7.3

The Gap Words to Live By	**The Gap Words to Live By** *Staff contributions in italics*
Everyone counts	Everyone counts *the days until they leave*
Every difference makes a difference	Every difference makes a difference *apart from indifference*
Own it, do it, done it	Own it, do it, done it *EH?*
Less is more . . . simplify	*Our wages* Less is more . . . simplify
Take the smart risk	Take the smart risk *and quit*
Do it better every day	Do it better every day *and still feel shit*
Do the right thing	Do the right thing *and leave*

The Gap, 'Words to Live By'
British employees of the US-owned clothing store *The Gap* produced an alternative version of management's 'Words to Live By' (quoted in Grugulis and Wilkinson, 2002:182).

Weeks (2004) provides a fascinating example of this. 'BritArm' bank was not the most glamorous of research sites and the people who worked there were not high-fliers. One of the directors commented that (p. 25):

> You have to understand that BritArm UK does not attract top-notch people . . . The people we attract are steady, able performers who desire security and direction . . . Many of the people in the Bank really do want just to move paper from the left side of their desk to the right side all day. Those are the people being put in places like the [processing] centre. And they are better off there.

This was a bureaucratic organisation and many of the (male) staff were deeply loyal to their employer since they had been given status and opportunities beyond their early hopes. It could also serve as an example of both the sophisticated management of culture and corporate idiocy. The official 'vision' was supported by slick corporate videos, encouraging posters, staff teams and psychometric tests. But it was also an arena for internal rivalry when two separate head office departments, operations and personnel, each started their own initiative (with outside consultants) to measure and control the culture. Despite the expertise and effort put into the process, the vision made little impact on the shop floor other than as a target for humour. In defiance of management's best efforts, the most pervasive feature of the bank's culture was gentle, grumbling complaint. This was not a form of complaint that expected a response, rather it resembled chatting about the weather in the sense that grumbling provided a topic of conversation and united the speakers against a common enemy (usually another department of the bank). Similar comments from outsiders generally united staff in the bank's defence. This alternating loyalty and cynicism, an awareness of faults without their acceptance, is a far more human response to organisational life than the frenetic professionalism of 'Tech' or 'ConsultancyCo'.

Empowerment

One of the main ideas behind managing culture is that workers should be empowered, that they should be given the discretion and the resources to make decisions in the workplace themselves. This is a term borrowed from feminist and social movement writers (Fenton-O'Creevy 1995:154 cited in Edwards and Collinson, 2002:273). But in the process, its meaning has changed. Empowerment used

> to mean providing individuals (usually disadvantaged) with the tools and resources to further their own interests, *as they see them*. Within the field of management, empowerment is commonly used with a different meaning: providing employees with tools, resources and discretion to further the interests of the organisation (as seen by senior management).

This is a significant difference (Ramsay 1977a, 1977b, 1997; Sisson 1993) and it is further compounded by the elasticity of the term in use. Empowerment may mean responsibility for decisions or the power to discharge that responsibility (Hales 2000). This is an important distinction. Job autonomy (as discussed in Chapter 2) and the freedom to make decisions over work are important and have a positive impact on job satisfaction (Applebaum *et al.* 2000; Anderson-Connolly *et al.* 2002; Murray *et al.* 2002; Danford 2003; Rose 2003). It is not clear whether empowerment programmes provide these. McDonald's claimed to have empowered their staff when they allowed them to give any locally suitable initial and farewell greeting to customers (in place of the American 'have a nice day'). While Willmott (1993:526) cites the example of an enthusiastic Tupperware dealer, quoted in earnest by Peters and Waterman:

> The company gives me great freedom to develop my own approach. There are certain elements that need to be in every party to make it successful, but if those elements are coloured by you, a Tupperware dealer – purple, pink and polka dot, and I prefer it lavender and lace – that's okay. That freedom allows you to be the best that you are capable of being.

This is freedom over trivialities, a veneer of self-management and consultation that Willmott likens to Orwellian double-speak as a 'simultaneous affirmation and negation of the conditions of autonomy.'

Examples of such unempowering empowerment are numerous. People in non-managerial jobs are given managerial responsibility without the means to discharge it (Geary 1994; Ghoshal and Bartlett 1998; Wilkinson 1998) and even genuine attempts to introduce more autonomy for workers may be stymied by standard operating procedures (Rinehart *et al.* 1997); limited budgets (Foster and Hoggett 1999) or redundancies and delayering (Psoinois and Smithson 2002; Littler and Innes 2003).

So, in Smith's (1990) account of working life in an American bank, managers were told that they were empowered to solve staffing problems locally but what this meant in practice was being expected to defend work changes over which they had no control. Company trainers reinterpreted the politics and problems generated by the bank's restructuring as psychological maladjustment to be solved by the managers. When one manager protested (p. 73), 'How do you arbitrarily raise the bar for someone who has worked with the bank for 15 years?', the trainer replied, 'You know management isn't easy . . . You need to get involved in the process. *We* can't give you a cookbook.'

It is questionable whether empowerment increases the power of the workers (see, among others Hyman and Mason 1995; Cunningham *et al.* 1996; Benders 2005; Danford 2005; Harley *et al.* 2005) and when it does, this is at management's discretion rather than as of right (Ramsay 1977a; Sisson 1993;

Wilkinson 2001). At times the process has been criticised as abandonment (Ghoshal and Bartlett 1998) or served as a veneer for intensification (Legge 1995). One of Foster and Hoggett's respondents in their study of the benefits agency commented that (p. 31) 'because of the pressure some members of staff are turning on their weaker colleagues now, as pressure increases the problem of those who don't reciprocate becomes more acute.' Unsurprisingly, instances of genuine autonomy tend to rise with position in the hierarchy (Gallie 1996; Harley 1999).

Yet despite all these instances, the process of empowerment is not entirely one-way. Hales's (2000) study of a theme park shows that the senior managers were most enthusiastic about empowerment, which they used to reform the role of junior managers, reducing the number of posts and taking away responsibility for people management with the result that the new roles focused solely on the business side. Interestingly the junior managers then used the rhetoric of empowerment to fight back, creating a new function for themselves as coaches (see also Glover and Noon 2005).

Empowerment may be limited in scope (Harley 1999, 2001) or by type of worker (Sturdy and Korczynski 2005) but, as Edwards and Collinson (2002) argue, it may also make a difference. They are anxious not to lose the idea of empowerment to cynicism completely; acknowledging the gulf that can exist between rhetoric and reality, they also point out that there is little use in setting up an ideal that is unachievable and then criticising firms for not achieving it. Managers may be far more pragmatic and workers' hopes more mundane than the critics appreciate (Belanger *et al.* 2003). After all, in Rosenthal *et al.*'s study (1997:486) a trivial enlargement of discretion following what had been an almost total absence of freedom over work made a genuine difference to staff. Accordingly, Edwards and Collinson suggest a pragmatic, four-fold typology of empowerment: that employees should be given broad objectives rather than predefined tasks; that they should have the right of access to the means of achieving these; that they should have authority to make decisions on their own initiative; and that they should be able to debate and challenge the goals that are set. This is a useful typology. It is sufficiently ambitious to make a real difference to jobs but also realistic enough to be implemented.

Theoretical criticisms

It is not difficult to expose the practical problems involved in changing cultures. In no organisation does history start the moment management introduces a new change initiative, and the knowledge of what has gone before will influence the way such interventions are received. Mixed messages, as the enthusiastic rhetoric fails to match employment practice, and logistical idiocies such as rival programmes operating in the same company all mitigate against cultures being changed. But, while such disjunctions between theory and practice may well represent the way most of firms operate, there are dangers in focusing solely on these examples since they might imply that in a more ordered, more efficient environment culture change would succeed. There are some fundamental reasons to question this.

Most culture change programmes assume that workers are simply cultural vacuums ready to adopt whichever norms and beliefs their management prefers (Anthony 1994), an assumption that is extremely patronising. Every corporate culture programme is secondary, rather than primary, socialisation for the worker. An individual is first socialised as a child, by the family and carers who surround them, and this process may instil powerful lessons about the world. Later, or secondary, socialisations can never be as powerful since by definition those being socialised now know that this is *a* world, rather than *the* world (Berger and Luckmann 1967). That there are other frames of reference, points of interest and ways of responding to events. Corporate culture programmes are only one of a series of competing narratives.

Nor, in contrast to the small related groups of people among whom Malinowski (1922) conducted his research, are workplaces self-contained, homogeneous places. In consequence, it seems unlikely that they will have self-contained, homogeneous cultures. Rather, there are multiple cultures that are nested and overlapping and, since it is a natural human tendency to form groups, this multiplicity of cultures and subcultures is a consistent feature of society. Culture is not something that is perfectly shared but a complex pluralism (Hannerz 1992). Even within workplaces work organisation tends to focus on the differences between various groups of workers, rather than their similarities. As Alvesson (2002:49) argues:

> It would, in fact be odd if CEOs, typists, factory workers, salesmen, engineers and product designers shared norms and acted upon them in similar ways. Division of labour is a cornerstone of the modern corporation, and norms that opposed rather than reflected diversity would not necessarily make it more efficient.

As long as organisations and the people they employ are not sealed off from the rest of the world it is difficult to imagine corporate culture programmes succeeding entirely.

This is probably fortunate. As Willmott (1993), points out, while such programmes claim to be morally neutral, advantaging employees by enhancing their work and organisations by improving corporate performance their theoretical basis is totalitarian, eliminating any ambiguity about what employees should do or be and creating conformity even when they preach thriving on chaos. Managers have the task of telling employees how they should think and feel about what they produce and employees are encouraged to discipline themselves when they fall short. So self-direction is commended but its scope is dictated by the firm. There are worrying precedents for such a pursuit of conformity. As Anthony (1994:93) argues, '[t]he pursuit of one culture in substitution for the muddled complexity of subcultures and cultural segmentation is most familiar and visible in the political sphere', and the best-known examples include the old Soviet Union and Nazi Germany.

Culture and performance

Much of the allure of culture comes from its assumed link with organisational performance. The proponents argue that people work better, harder and more enthusiastically, to the extent that a 'company can gain as much as one or two hours of productive work per employee per day' (Deal and Kennedy 1982:15). Innovative, entrepreneurial and competitive companies are successful; bureaucratic, formal ones are not.

Yet although fact this belief is so prevalent that it has practically become a management truism, it is unproven. Originally, the link stemmed from the fact that the populist texts of the 1980s were written at a time when the Japanese economy was booming. Many argued that it was the strong cultures of the larger Japanese firms that facilitated this prosperity; ignoring both the numerous other contributory factors and the very different way that smaller employers in Japan operate (see, for example Kondo 1990). Interestingly, the economic problems subsequently experienced by those same firms and the Japanese economy as a whole have not prompted a rethink.

None of the writers on culture attempted to test the link between success and culture empirically. None established which organisations were most productive and then drew out the causal factors. Rather, they sought out particular cultures then eliminated unsuccessful companies from their enquiries (Peters and Waterman 1982), processes that simply serve to reinforce prejudice. Unsurprisingly, many of the firms praised in these accounts have gone on to perform poorly (Clayman 1987; Guest 1992; Ramanujam and Venkatraman 1988).

The idea of working in an unbureaucratic, entrepreneurial and innovative company, where workers are enthusiastic about their jobs and everyone is bound together by a strong and unifying culture, may be attractive, but there is nothing to show that such organisations perform better than their more bureaucratic competitors. The financial press has adopted the equation of 'good' and 'bad' cultures as enthusiastically as most of the gurus, but these tend to be used to legitimate success rather than cause it.

As Weeks argues (2004:39),

> It is not so much that entrepreneurial, innovative and risk-accepting cultures are thought to be good because they are the sorts of cultures that successful organisations have; rather, the credibility of a firm's success . . . is evaluated in part on the basis of how good the organisation's culture is judged to be.

In rich, complex and multifaceted organisations it is not difficult to find evidence of a range of different types of culture, so poor performers have their bureaucratic elements investigated while the innovative features of high performers are praised. This then leaves the problem of accounting for success in organisations that clearly do not correspond to the corporate ideal or explaining failure in ones that do. To do so, journalists tend to rely on linguistic sleight of hand. So McDonald's is praised for its military (rather than bureaucratic) aspects while Pepsi is condemned as being 'flashy' and 'out of control' (*Wall Street Journal* 1995, 1997; cited in Weeks, 2004).

Given the number and range of factors that can impact on organisational performance it is extremely unlikely that any single (internal) element can guarantee success or failure. Moreover, in their pursuit of a harmonious strong culture, introduced and supported by management, the journalists and gurus neglect a rich seam of evidence that points to a link between resistance to management and productivity. Ackroyd and Crowdy's (1990) study of a slaughterhouse shows a culture that was far from supportive. Harassment and degredations were common, while practical jokes often took the form of workers spraying their colleagues with excrement. These slaughtermen were engaged in work that was repetitive, physical, monotonous and deeply unpleasant. Yet they were also extremely productive. Casual absenteeism was almost unheard of and workers rarely took holidays (even when they did it was common for them to pop into the slaughterhouse for an hour or so or to stay in the pub that was local to their work). All took a very strong pride in their work, which was seen as the epitome of masculinity. Workers gained status within the group by being fast and accomplished at their tasks and those who were weakest or slowest on the line were generally the butt of the practical jokes. The workplace was characterised by a spirit of uncompromising competition. It is difficult to imagine anything less like the ideal presentations of organisations in the prescriptive literature yet the culture was a strong and cohesive one and the workers, both individually and collectively, very productive (see also Roy 1958; Burawoy 1979; Zhou and George 2001).

There are many ways of working, and many of succeeding. There is no guarantee that firms with strong cultures will perform well (Collinson 1992) or that those with unfashionable cultures will perform poorly (Weeks 2004). Moreover, as accounts of high performance reveal, strong cultures may unify workers against management rather than with them and this pride in their own capacity and agency may stimulate high levels of productivity (Burawoy 1979; Ackroyd and Crowdy 1990).

Discussion and conclusions

The alluring promises of the celebratory literature are not only illusory; they also project a highly distorted image of what culture is and why it is important. In these accounts culture is presented as a commodity, designed and implemented by senior management and accepted with a great deal of enthusiasm by the workers. There are problems with this. The literature itself exists to evangelise and prompt emotional responses rather than to assess the contribution of culture to organisational performance. Workers are not cultural vacuums, waiting passively for senior management to cascade beliefs down the organisation. It is morally difficult to approve of organisational initiatives that are fundamentally totalitarian and, even if such initiatives were approved, the evidence suggests that they are almost impossible to implement. Cultures may change over time (Ogbonna and Wilkinson 1990; Ogbonna 1992/1993) but this does not imply that such changes can be controlled. According to Legge (1995:207),

> Managing culture has sometimes be likened to 'riding a wave' (Morgan 1988). The best the surf-rider can do is to understand the pattern of currents and winds that shape and direct the waves. She may then use them to stay afloat and steer in the desired path. But this is not the same as changing the basic rhythms of the ocean.

Yet criticising the existing managerial accounts of culture is not the same as condemning the study of culture, for if we abandon that because of distortions in the management writings we are indeed throwing the baby out with the bathwater. As Anthony (1994:41) argues, there are three ways of looking at culture: the anthropological perspective, which sees culture as a complex analytical function, as a way of understanding societies and groups; the consultancy approach, in which culture is an ideal to aim at; and the corporate one in which culture is a unified, distinctive conception to prevent disaffection and promote unity. A distinction broadly between the idea of culture as something an organisation *has*, that can be altered, manipulated and managed (the managerial and consultancy view), and culture as something that an organisation *is*, which may be understood and engaged with but which is not necessarily amenable to control (Smircich 1983).

It is far more helpful, and more informative, to abandon the idea of culture as a homogeneous commodity that can be controlled, or as a reification of the social reality of organisational life, and return to the notion that it is a powerful analytical tool (Meek 1988). This has a number of advantages. Most notably, we escape from the idea of unified cultures shaped only by management an idea which, as Meek argues, flies in the face of most people's experiences of organisations. Ideas about what is good and desirable, about how hard to work or what constitutes acceptable play or attitudes to management are part of (a series of) relationships (Anthony 1994). They are certainly influenced by management; as Purcell (1979) points out in his notion of 'cumulation', everything managers do sends messages about the organisation to employees. But they are also influenced by fellow workers, trade unions, friends and colleagues and society as a whole. Indeed, in Galbraith's (1983) three different types of organisational power it is arguable that management has least control over conditioned power (belief). They may have the right to hire and discipline workers, an aspect of condign power (physical); they may have either relative freedom or strong negotiating power when pay levels are set for compensatory power (economic); but conditioned power, under which culture might be classified, is also heavily influenced by others, within and without the organisation.

Seen in this light, culture is naturally complex and multifaceted, constantly changing, fragmented and the subject of ongoing negotiation. One form of control does not completely replace others (Kunda 1992), so cultural control builds on bureaucratic and authority-driven structures, and different cultures respond to rather than replace one another. Management is involved in this process, since culture reconstitutes rather than dilutes managerial authority (Edwards 1995), but as one of the voices rather than the only one.

Such a perspective on culture also enables us to escape from the view that it is the organisational objectives that are rational or primary or neutral, while people's motives are irrational or secondary or less desirable (Gregory 1983). They are simply different perspectives or frames of reference which may compete or coincide with one another. Studying culture is analytically helpful. Through it we may more fully understand organisations and the people who work within them but, as with Legge's surfer, such understanding does not necessarily lead to control.

8

Management and leadership development

> Periodically, the subject of leadership attracts massive interest and attention. From time to time the amelioration if not the actual solution to humanity's various problems and challenges are perceived as best placed in the hands of exceptional individuals. (Storey 2005:89)

> [S]ome of the most effective leaders have been those who, merely through having more than their fair share of psychopathic traits, were able to release antisocial behaviour in others. (Dixon 1994:215 cited in Mole 2004:126)

The managers of an organisation are among its key staff. They wield more influence than non-managerial staff, direct strategy, control resources and monitor performance (Storey 1989). As a result, their qualifications and capabilities have a disproportionate effect on organisational performance (Bosworth 1999). Recently, if management texts are to be believed, this authority has increased as the people running organisations are needed to set out visions, to inspire those who work for them and to transform the workplace; in essence they are required not to manage, but to lead (Storey 2004a).

This chapter explores the nature of both management and leadership and the way that managers and leaders are developed. It starts by reviewing the nature of managerial work, an occupation that may appear 'surprisingly straightforward' (Salaman 1995:2) but is, in practice, remarkably wide-ranging and resistant to definition. It argues that attempts to construct a functionally-derived model of managerial work are misplaced since management is (and always has been) functionally broad. It then goes on to consider the extent to which management has been transformed into leadership. Numerous publications claim that this has been one of the most dramatic (and significant) shifts of recent years (Storey 2004a, 2005) and it is certainly true that 'leadership' has far more rhetorical appeal than the more mundane sounding management, but managerial texts are often better at making grand claims than at observing changes in practice and it is not clear whether the changes described extend beyond the aspirations of ambitious professionals.

What do managers do?

The traditional, 'classical' writings on managerial work present an image of management that is clear and unproblematic. The image of management that both Taylor and Fayol propounded was of an occupation that consisted of a generic set of functions and tasks, structured around a clear purpose, stable across all sectors of the economy and susceptible to clear definition. Fayol developed one of the best-known functional models of managerial work (Fayol 1949:5–6): 'to manage is to forecast and plan, to organise, to command, to co-ordinate and to control'.

Extrapolating management principles from the world of engineering has certain attractions. By imposing a positivist discipline on studies, complex areas could be reduced, simplified, generalised and (by implication) solved. Moreover, management itself could be (and was) unproblematically defined. While Taylor and Taylorism have been largely discredited (see, for example, Doray 1988), both the positivist research traditions and Fayol's definition of management retain their popularity, dominating current textbooks (Carroll and Gillen 1987).

Yet despite the consensus among the classical writers and their followers that management is an activity capable of accurate definition (and indeed that such definitions are readily available), the one 'correct' definition has managed to elude commentators for almost a century. Even those writers who agree that management is definitely generic disagree over exactly what its generic features consist of, and no task-based definition has, as yet, accurately described management as it is understood and practised across the economy. Each individual definition is problematic. Mary Parker Follett (Fox and Urwick 1973:55) maintained that management was the art of 'getting things done through people' and that, consequently, managers were those with staff reporting to them. While this aphorism was adopted by several generations of management writers it crucially neglects managers without line responsibilities and makes it difficult to differentiate between supervisors and managers. Decision-making, highlighted by Cyert and March (1963) as the key element of management, assumes that decisions are a managerial prerogative. Yet, as empirical studies of managerial work show, many of those involved do not spend most of their time making decisions. Rather they monitor performance, keep subordinates happy and act as a conduit between senior managers and front-line employees (see, for example Smith 1990; Watson 1994). According to 'Lisa', a first line manager herself (Cunliffe 2001:357),

> a lot of what I do at work is I have conversations with people and some days I feel I should be having more output. And they say to me, 'you tend to be in a job with a high degree of ambiguity and in those circumstances, talking things out with people and discussing them – that *is* your job, to help figure out where you are in those circumstances and what needs to get done.' And a lot of what I've been doing is calling together meetings that say we need to grapple with these issues, we need to confront this stuff.

Such realities sit ill with the optimal, mechanistic, decision-making models put forward by the theorists of the early twentieth century. Indeed, thus far, surprisingly little evidence has emerged to support the premise that there is a concrete (and, by implication, correct) definition of management 'out there' waiting to be discovered. It is possible that these universal templates of management are little more than the self-fulfilling prophecies of the writers who believe in them, since several *start* both their analysis and their research by clearly defining what is, and what is not, management. Salaman (1995) and Mintzberg (1973; 1975), following Mary Parker Follett (Fox and Urwick 1973), all restrict their work to managers who manage people. Mintzberg (1973), in his famous study of managerial work, took this reconceptualisation a stage further, restricting his study to people in charge of a defined area but extending it beyond the confines of titular managers: his work was based on diary studies of senior and middle managers in business; observations of street

---

Box 8.1

I. **Interpersonal roles:**
- figurehead
- leader
- liaison

II. **Informational roles:**
- monitor
- disseminator
- spokesman

III. **Decisional roles:**
- entrepreneur
- disturbance handler
- resource allocator
- negotiator

Mintzberg's managerial roles (Mintzberg 1973).

---

gang leaders, hospital administrators and production supervisors; analyses of the working records of US presidents; activity sampling of foremen's work; and structured observation of the work of chief executives.

So, in defence of a narrow definition of 'management', the definition of 'manager' was extended considerably beyond its traditional boundaries. A foreman or production supervisor, for instance, is generally classified as a 'supervisor', a role distinct from, and (in status terms) inferior to, that of a manager. And street gang leaders, relevant as they are to Mintzberg's conceptualisation, are not managers. Informative as Mintzberg's study may be on the work of those in charge of an occupational area, it does not necessarily contribute to our understanding of what *managers* do. It is difficult to justify a conceptual category that deliberately ignores a large section of the population it seeks to classify on the somewhat tautological grounds that they do not conform to the classification, are not 'real' managers and do not belong to the managerial population. Moreover, as Hales (1986) points out, these problems are compounded in the literature by a reluctance to identify what is specifically *managerial* in each of the models, either conceptually or through some form of empirical comparison with non-managerial jobs.

Managers and management

It seems that management is not a functionally coherent, readily identifiable set of tasks or roles but rather a diverse and heterogeneous range of activities and responsibilities which vary (in content, status and practice) from organisation to organisation and often individual to individual. Stewart (1963; 1976; 1988), who was one of the first to explore this broad, agnostic description, argued that a manager was 'anyone above a certain level, roughly above foreman whether . . . in control of people or not' (Stewart 1976:4). As Bamber (1986) points out, this (non-) definition produced an occupational group that was vertically narrow but horizontally broad, spanning engineers, scientists, accountants, personnel specialists, administrators and marketing experts.

Specifically, Stewart (1988) argued that diary studies of the way managers spent their time showed not one but five dfferent types of manager, with very distinct and incompatible work behaviours. The *emissaries* were the organisational ambassadors. They spent most of their time away from their own companies travelling, visiting others and entertaining. The *writers*, by contrast, spent more of their time in the office engaged in paperwork. Unlike other managers, writers spent little time in groups and most of their contact was on a one-to-one basis. *Discussers*, as their name suggests, spent far more time with colleagues and superiors, though little with subordinates, and Stewart described their activities as closest to the 'average' of the respondents in her study. *Trouble-shooters* were called in to deal with crises and run teams dealing with exceptional circumstances, so their work was far less predictable than many other managers; and finally the *committee-men*, as might be expected, spent a great deal of time in contact with other people, but unlike the emissaries their contacts were largely internal and they seldom met with representatives of other organisations. These categories described such a range of responsibilities, activities and priorities that Stewart concluded (p. 77): 'The variations were so great that it is misleading to talk, as much of the management literature does, about *the* managerial job, or about how the *average* manager spends his or her time.' (Emphasis in original)

This managerial heterogeneity is mirrored elsewhere. Pollard's (1965) historical study of eighteenth- and nineteenth-century managers reveals a highly diffuse, fragmented group with no distinctive identity, class, profession, occupation or body of knowledge (see also Bamber 1986; Whitley 1989). While Scase and Goffee point out (1989:20): 'It is self-evident that the duties

---

Box 8.2

Deciding at which point in the hierarchy managers are situated is contested and may vary from firm to firm, from department to department and over time. In Tony Watson's *In Search of Management* interviewees gave very different responses when asked whether they thought they were managers.

'Leonard Hilton' (p. 47):

> I used to be a manager. I've had quite large numbers of people working for me at times. I'm more senior in some ways now but I am really a sort of consultant. I am trying to change some of the management systems.

'Jane Trowell' (p. 56):

> Everybody knew I was managing, but it got to a point where if I was not called a manager it was a sort of slight on my ability. I was a section leader.

'Don Smalley' (p. 56):

> After four or five years I became a manager. That is a title, but as far as I was concerned the reality was as when I had joined; there were ninety people in industrial engineering and one manager. That was a manager. These days seventy out of the ninety would be called managers. They don't have section leaders any more. I was a section leader really.

Taken from Watson (1994).

and responsibilities of sales managers, for example, differ from those engaged in personnel, production, or market research.'

Watson's (1994) detailed ethnography of 'ZTC' reveals the differences between managers in personnel and production, between those who had degrees and those with 'zero qualifications', between the few at the top of the organisation devising strategy and those lower down whose task was to explain to others actions which they may have disagreed with and which have not been explained properly to them. All were concerned with shaping the organisation as a whole, but the activities, responsibilities and tasks they were given were very different. He notes that (p. 51) 'A managerial appointment is a stage in a person's hierarchical career in an organisation, rather than an entry into an immediately distinctive and clearly identifiable, occupational activity.' As Armstrong (1989) argues, management is not a technical activity, functionally derived and centrally defined; it is an agency relationship with managers acting as the agents of the firm owners, so managerial activities depend on the preferences and predilections of those owners, rather than any theoretical model of the managerial task (see also Willmott 1984). In consequence it cannot really be defined as a universal functional activity.

Management and politics

This has implications for the way we think about both management and organisations. If managers are agents of owners, rather than technical experts who act as a neutral 'third force' in employment relations (Störey 1980), then it is less likely that managerial work itself is rational and objective or that managerial decisions are always arrived at on reasoned, logical grounds (Anthony 1986; Alvesson and Willmott 1992).

Rather, management is a social and a political activity (Reed 1984) in which gaining advantage and making a show of strength are key contributors to survival and prosperity. As a result, managers are concerned not only with the greater good of the organisation but also with their own careers and with the success of their own departments; Dalton (1966) describes how supervisors tried to 'botch' running repairs to machinery to avoid maintenance being performed on their own shifts, where it would adversely affect their targets, and ensure that it was done on other supervisors' shifts. Useem and Gager (1996) take this to a more strategic level and point out that, as well as acting as the agents of owners, managers may themselves successfully challenge and replace those owners with ones they find more congenial.

In addition, the public rhetoric used by organisations often presents a very different view of management from that encouraged by the promotions

Box 8.3

Corporate ethics

In February 2000 *Fortune* magazine named Enron the most innovative company for the fifth year running as well as the firm with the highest-quality management. Its CEO, Ken Lay, was a prominent and regular speaker on business ethics and it was a household name. Less than twelve months later, Enron was even more of a household name, but not for high moral standards and excellent management. Instead it had gone down in history as a gigantic fraud. An organisation which, with the collusion of its accountants, Andersens, concealed debt and conflated assets and revenue streams. After the scale and nature of Enron's activities became apparent it was widely condemned and numerous senior staff confessed their guilt but while the company was successful none had gone on record saying that they considered there was anything wrong with the way the firm was run. Rather, like Jackall's (1988) managers, they viewed the firm as its own moral universe where standards were different because actions were 'just business'. Enron had a policy of hiring smart, ambitious and aggressive young professionals. At their twice yearly performance reviews the top 5 per cent of these were marked for preferment, the bottom 20 per cent for dismissal. Offices were large and open-plan, shouting, gesturing and loud telephone calls common and a culture of risk-taking and greed encouraged the most aggressive to compete with each other on the basis of short-term results.

Unsurprisingly, employees regularly sabotaged each other's work and corporate facades and con-tricks were common. In 1998 at the launch of Enron Energy Services when the dealing floor was not ready in time for the Wall Street analysts' walkabout an entire floor was stripped and computer equipment installed to convince the analysts that the business was up and running. Employees were rehearsed the day before and for the ten-minute visit gave a convincing performance of a successful business. This was a culture and a structure that encouraged moneymaking above all else. According to every sheet of Enron company paper the organisation's core values were respect, integrity, communication and excellence. In reality praise and promotions went to those who through innovative tax-avoidance schemes, confidence tricks and aggression made the most short-term profits.

Taken from Mangham (2004).

system. Managers operate in a high-trust environment (Moss-Kanter 1977) with few objective indicators of their performance, which means, in practice, that a key criterion influencing managerial assessments and careers is not an individual manager's performance but the *impression* of performance he or she conveys to others (Gowler and Legge 1983; Heller 1996:14):

There is no absolute criteria [*sic*] of managerial achievement. A manager is good and a company efficient only because others consider the results of their work good: their so-called goodness endures only as long as this good opinion holds.

Jackall (1988) draws a parallel between the managerial world of favour and privilege and the courtiers who served powerful monarchs. In both cases preferment could derive as easily from the gift of a more powerful courtier (or the monarch themselves) as through virtue and hard work (see also Lee and Piper 1988 for a study of promotions within a British clearing bank). Also, both Barnard (1962) and Moss Kanter (1977) suggest that physical attractiveness was a factor in managerial promotions. The rhetoric of organisational life emphasises the puritanical virtues, but the reality is more complicated.

Nor is this world of politically fraught impression management restricted to managerial promotions. As Sayles (1979, quoted in Willmott, 1984:391) argues, 'Only naïve managers assume that budgets get allocated and key decisions are made solely on the basis of rational decision making.'

And managers, accustomed to an official language which emphasises virtue, hard work and meeting objectives and a reality where actual performance has less meaning than perceived performance, grow adept at interpreting organisational symbols (Jackall (1988) calls his managers 'maze bright'). Most aspects

---

Box 8.4

It was more a rule than an exception that senior managers carefully listened to the CEO and then concurred with him. This strong orientation towards alignment often led to a lack of critical and constructive discussions, even when the CEO tried to encourage such discussions. The senior managers often did not want to stick their necks out by expressing a contradictory opinion to the CEO . . . [something well illustrated by their behaviour following a recruitment interview for an assistant project leader position] in a business development team. After the meeting the administrative manager, the project leader and an external consultant in hierarchical order attach their opinions to those of the CEO:

The candidate leaves the room. Silence (five to ten seconds).

CEO:	I think this will be good. And she is a structure fanatic.
Administrative manager:	I think this is going to be very good.
Project leader:	This will be good.
Administrative manager:	She had the right attitude, did you notice that?
External consultant:	She has straight hair. The straighter the hair is, the more structured one is.

Tengblad (2004:598).

of managerial life need to be considered in the light of these conclusions; budgets are not simply the resources necessary to achieve the corporate goals – they are symbols of individual power and occasionally individual empire-building; training courses do not only convey useful information and skills – they represent investment in, and confidence in, an individual, and are an expression of support; and written records are not only the factual narratives of events but also corporate propaganda and 'weaponry' in the managerial competition.

It also means that, bereft of objective indicators, managers may be measured and assessed only against the impression they convey of themselves, and norms established by other managers. Since managers can influence the direction their company takes (Watson 1977, 1994), employing them becomes an exercise in trust; to mitigate the risks the company might run, conformity and 'being known' become key conditions of entry (Moss-Kanter 1977; Dalton 1966) – criteria which result in the phenomenon that Moore (1951) termed homosocial reproduction, where like promotes like, because it is easier for people to trust those who are similar to them. This has important implications for the nature of management itself. Several authors have noted that, since managers tend to be male, managerial norms are male norms, which means that women have great difficulty winning admittance to the managerial ranks, and even greater difficulty securing appointment to those posts that carry the highest prestige (Marshall 1984; Root 1984; Collinson *et al.* 1990). Even in the service sector, which is dominated by part-time work and where twenty-four-hour opening often precludes consistent control by one person, few managers are part-time, not because the job could not be done by several part-time workers but because emotionally part-time workers are seen as having divided loyalties (Moss-Kanter 1977). Ironically, women who do gain senior positions tend to do so when their firms are going through turbulent times. When profits are high and activities going well promotions may be deeply conservative. When organisations are troubled and senior posts less desirable, recruitment committees may be prepared to take more risks to find a saviour (Ryan and Haslam 2005).

This is not to argue that management is devoid of technical expertise, nor that the sole task of managers is to cynically carry out whatever orders are given. Indeed, as detailed workplace studies reveal, many are very concerned with mitigating, ameliorating or changing orders with which they disagree or which they feel damage the firm or those who work for it (see, for example Smith 1990; Watson 1994). Rather it is a reminder, in the midst of a literature that emphasises the technical aspects of managerial work, that it is also a contingent and political process in which success may be measured by means other than technical triumphs.

Management as a universal practice

One of the key issues here is the extent to which all types of management resemble each other. At one level of abstraction it is certainly possible to generalise about the 'getting things done' of organisations; at another it is clear that running a prison camp requires a different set of knowledge and skills to running a baked bean factory, a university or a fast food restaurant (Keep 2001). Yet the generic image of management is a pervasive one and peculiarly Anglo-Saxon. In Germany, as Bamber (1986) points out, management is invariably management *of* something, so that gaining managerial rank and rising in the hierarchy necessarily involves experience and expertise in the activities being managed. This is often true elsewhere, with first-line managers in particular likely to supervise workers of the same gender and level of skill, so that male first-line managers predominate in construction, property services and printing while female ones may be found in health and education (Hales 2005).

Yet in tandem with this runs the idea that management is and should be divorced from the activities of the shop floor and that managers either need not be expert in those activities or, if promoted from inside the occupation, need to leave those experiences and interests behind. These differences are particularly apparent in the changes to the way the health services in a number of countries are being run. There the concerns of managers (budgets, markets, throughput and competitiveness) both contrast and clash with those of the healthcare professionals (care, appropriate treatment, the well-being of patients). Markets and quasi-markets, the introduction of competition and an increasing emphasis on managerial rather than professional norms create some interesting tensions (Ackroyd 1995; Ackroyd and Kirkpatrick 2003).

Empirical work reveals these differences vividly (Manley 2001). Managerial planners are seen to have aims so far removed from traditional medical ones that they are described as coming from 'Planet Zanussi' (Currie 1999:148); while managers criticise ward managers because they still 'think and act like nurses and are going through a grieving process of having to give up nursing' (Assistant Director of Nursing, cited in Brooks 1999:48). In some areas, management and front-line service are seen as so different that an absence of such experience is no bar to gaining managerial posts, in stark contrast to the old professional model in which medical staff gained knowledge and experience through socialisation, guided by their more expert colleagues and where senior posts were the almost exclusive preserve of the professionals themselves (Kitchener *et al.* 2000).

Yet in many instances this tension serves to change the nature of management as nurse managers resist, accommodate and devise ways of coping with change. As Bolton (2004b) argues, drawing on Strauss *et al.* (1973), management is a negotiated order, not an absolute set of values and practices imposed from above. In Bolton's study of gynaecology nurses, practice protocols were dismissed as 'dust gatherers' (p. 323), which few nurses bothered to read, and a central aspect of work was to mediate between patients and more senior management (p. 327):

> Their [management's] view of quality is two patients to a bed. They wouldn't know what quality care was if it jumped up and smacked them in the face. In fact that gives me an idea!
> We have to act as the patient's advocate and wade through all this quality stuff on their behalf. If it leads to better service provision then we'll do it but a lot of it's crap and I, for one, can't see the point.

There are tensions here. Management may be seen as an extension of front-line tasks, as a hierarchically senior way of 'getting things done', but it may also be cast in opposition to those activities, a form of discipline that contradicts lower-level values. This is a contradiction that may go some way towards explaining the low-trust relations that characterise many British and American firms (Fox 1974).

From management to leadership?

Management, it seems, is diverse and heterogeneous. Depending on the firm, 'manager' may be the title used by those who are comparatively junior in the hierarchy and who have just reached a particular point in the organisation structure, or it can be restricted to those who are extremely senior. Yet, just as the number of people working as managers rises, many of the pundits seem to have lost interest in the entire occupational group. From being the key elements for unlocking productivity in the workplace (Storey 1989), managers have become the cause of organisational sclerosis, an onerous and bureaucratic burden on firms and net subtractors of value (Littler *et al.* 2003). As Zaleznik (1992:127, cited in Storey 2004a: 2013) argues 'It takes neither genius nor heroism to be a manager, but rather persistence, tough-mindedness, hard work, intelligence, analytical ability and, perhaps most important, tolerance and good will.' He claims that leaders and leadership are the antithesis of managers and management. While managers follow organisational rules, leaders provide their followers with inspiration, vision and hope, urging them on to ever greater efforts. There might seem to be the potential for synergy here, with leaders providing flourishes to the mundane world of management, but, according to Zaleznik, the two groups cannot coexist since the entrepreneurial culture necessary for one group to flourish precludes the existence of the other.

Box 8.5

Managers versus leaders

Managers	Leaders
are transactional	are transformative
seek to operate and maintain current systems	seek to challenge and change systems
accept given objectives and meanings	create new visions and new meanings
control and monitor	empower
trade on exchange relationships	seek to inspire and transcend
have a short-term focus	have a long-term focus
focus on detail and procedure	focus on the strategic big picture

Storey (2004b:7).

This is a new direction for the literature. Academics have long been interested in people who are in charge of small groups; in whether their leadership skills were conferred by nature or developed by nurture; whether particular environments called for a particular type of person who might be overlooked under other conditions; whether a leader's style had an impact on their followers; and whether leadership could affect productivity (Vroom and Yetton 1973; Vroom and Jago 1988; Blake and Mouton 1964). But this latest outpouring of writings is, as Storey (2004a) notes, somewhat different. The focus is on the whole organisation rather than small work groups and on the individual qualities that leaders require.

Leadership qualities are generally sought from the (not particularly methodologically robust) source of lists of virtues that already successful leaders are assumed to possess (Storey 2004a). Given that adulatory biographies and autobiographies of business leaders (the 'with-one-bound-Jack-was-free' means of problem-solving literature; Harvey-Jones 1989) have become common as a fairytale version of organisational life, and that such texts are among the principal sources for accounts of suitable qualities, it is difficult to see how these provide genuine perspectives on organisational governance. The problems of defining skill and performance through personal qualities were discussed in Chapter 5 and to these might be added the difficulties of presenting a true picture through a celebratory lens. After all, it is not always virtue that carries people to the top of firms and helps them stay there (Armstrong 2001).

Accounts vary on what it is that leaders do and the ways they differ from managers. Alimo-Metcalfe and Alban-Metcalfe (2004; 2005) criticise traditional American studies for focusing exclusively on 'distant', male leaders, arguing that leadership should be a 'nearby' activity and that women's views (of leadership as transformational) should receive greater attention than men's (who see leadership as transactional). Wood (2005) takes their view of 'followership' one stage further by arguing that leadership is a process, enmeshed in social exchange, so as a result it is impossible to tell the difference between leaders and followers.

But these are exceptions. Most studies focus on the leader's soft skills, their capacity to inspire and the different way of organising that this implies (Storey 2004a). To a certain extent these accounts of leaders and leadership are linked to other proclamations and predictions on the nature of work and the way organisations are changing. As the emphasis shifts towards knowledge work and workers are empowered to take responsibility for their own jobs, organisations no longer require numerous layers of supervisory management to impose discipline and exert control. Rather, they need inspirational leaders with soft skills who can inspire their followers to new heights of creativity and unite them through and to a strong corporate culture.

The leadership rhetoric is certainly popular but it is not clear whether this change of language heralds genuine changes in the workplace or simply reflects new management fads and fashions. The contrasting accounts of management and leadership summarised in Box 8.5 offer little evidence either way since they simply ascribe all virtues to leadership and all vices to management. This is a familiar sight in the management literature, as switching labels enables empirical descriptions of one practice to be set against optimistic predictions of another. It tells us little about whether such changes are genuine (for discussion of the switch from 'personnel management' to 'human resource management' see, for example, Legge 1995; Storey 2001). It is unhelpful, if commonplace to acquire new buzz-words and assume that these will resolve all problems. And, as Storey (2004b) points out, this is often the way the word 'leadership' is used. He notes that, even in government documents, leadership is presented as a panacea that may cure the widespread and often long-term ills of the public sector (see also Alimo-Metcalfe and Alban-Metcalfe 2004). It is considered to be (p. 7) 'the answer to a host of hugely complex, large-scale and endemic problems: comparative lower pay than in the private sector, recruitment difficulties, low morale and so on.'

Clearly such hopes are unrealistic. It is extremely doubtful whether any organisational change, however worthwhile and substantive, could be such a cure-all. The issue is not whether this rhetoric is attractive: it is; it is rather whether it reflects any change in the way organisations are run, whether managers are disappearing and being replaced by leaders and whether higher-ranking jobs are being transformed.

Managers are certainly unpopular. According to Cappelli (2001) they are disproportionately affected by the 'new deal' of restructurings in the workplace while Littler *et al.* (2003) quote an Australian CEO as saying (p. 238): 'Middle managers have a negative impact on the business; they cost about $70,000 each and their main effect is to stuff up the business.' In their study of 2964 organisations in South Africa, Australia and New Zealand a high proportion of firms were delayering – with 30 per cent of these taking out two or more layers of management. Yet dramatic as these figures are, it is not clear that they signal the end of management. In Australia it was the largest firms which had delayered most dramatically and lost most managers, but many of these delayered managers had moved to smaller firms, often carrying out the same role for the same customer though with a different employer as risk was shifted through outsourcing (Littler and Innes 2004).

Nor has the demand for supervision lessened. Chapter 2 reviewed the (often limited) gains made from empowerment, and the corollary to this is the continuing involvement of first line managers in organising and overseeing work. Hales's (2005) research into working practices in London and the South-East of England reveals both changes and continuities in first-line managerial work, but little consistency in the direction these took. Job titles varied greatly and respondents rejoiced in various titles: manager, manager of a department or function, assistant manager, supervisor, foreman, team leader, senior professional, director, partner. Almost every post revolved around a performance-oriented supervisory core and most included additional responsibilities, though these varied from stewardship, translating strategy into operations, unit management and (exceptionally) business management. Restructuring was characterised by 'piecemeal opportunistic redistribution' (p. 473) rather than deliberate decentralisation.

Such findings can be replicated elsewhere. Studies of managerial work in Zimbabwe and Malaysia show the importance of administering staff, general work administration and managing routine information. As one British public sector manager noted, post-delayering (Hales 2002:59): '[T]he work I'm doing hasn't changed – I'm now further up a shorter totem pole, that's all.' Although, while the demand for middle management work has by no means reduced, the number of middle managers available to do the jobs has shrunk dramatically. Delayering has resulted in significant cuts to the numbers of management but has often occurred at the same time as pressures to improve customer service or raise quality levels. According to one hard-pressed respondent (Littler *et al.* 2003:241):

[Senior] Management seems to have no thought about how the organisation will run in the future, issuing employment equations that do not add up, such as 'less staff doing the same work better with emphasis on the customer'.

Studies vary on the managerial response to this. They may use the language of empowerment to confirm the need for their supervisory role (Hales 2000) or may welcome the changes in their work (Dopson and Stewart 1990; Thomas and Dunkerley 1999); increased workloads may widen managers' spans of control and responsibilities (although these are also reported independently of delayering), but restructuring and redundancies also result in increasing dissatisfaction, decreased motivation and decreased commitment (Littler *et al.* 2003).

Yet, while restructurings and reorganisations are now commonplace and while many layers of management have indeed been eliminated from organisational hierarchies, it is not clear whether either managers or middle managers are particularly endangered. First, despite the hype, bureaucratic forms of governance have not been abandoned. Indeed, audited, bureaucratic management is still going strong, particularly in the public sector (Power 1997; Protherough and Pick 2002). Hales's (2002) study of 'Parcelco', a delivery company, reveals that traditional forms of governance and data-gathering continue with a vengeance, with head office 'information hoovering' including the ironically named 'Vital Few' form which required 1000 separate data entries every month. As he argues, bureaucracies have always taken a range of forms and these latest organisational changes seem far more like a variation on a theme, a kind of 'bureaucracy-lite', than a genuinely new form of governance.

Second, there is still a strong and continuing demand for supervision, as opposed to inspiration or vision-building (Delbridge and Lowe 1997) and this demand may actually be strengthened by programmes of empowerment and customer focus (Hales 2000). In most workplaces, far from there being a shift towards self-managing teams, managers manage people and actively control performance, and this performance aspect of their work has risen in importance. Hales (2005) reports the way retail managers were 'named and shamed' if their store ranked bottom of the regional performance tables and sacked if performance did not improve, despite the fact that, according to one manager, 'there's actually not a lot they can do to affect the business' (p. 500). This increasing focus on performance resulted, not in greater discretion for the workers, but in higher levels of supervision and often micro-management. As Hales notes (p. 502), 'Rooted in supervision, staked to performance but here and there compelled to branch into management, the first line manager is the resilient, but put-upon survivor of organisational change.'

Finally, while many middle managers are the victims of corporate restructuring, they are not disproportionately affected. Indeed, as Littler and Innes (2004) demonstrate, managers are at a relatively low risk of being made redundant, with only professionals more secure. They also have the highest rate of re-employability (p. 1172), with 74 per cent of redundant managers succeeding in finding alternative employment compared with 43 per cent of labourers (although many may have accepted a lower-ranking job to keep in the labour market and only 57 per cent gained work as managers).

Managers are not disappearing and, compared with other occupational groups, they are relatively secure, but for a group who during the last twenty years suffered almost no risk of redundancy, the waves of job cuts, delayering and restructuring genuinely represents a dramatic change.

It seems that middle managers have neither disappeared nor been transformed into leaders. But what of those at the top of the organisation, the people who have the freedom to set out visions, inspire the workers and focus on the strategic? Here again, their transformative power has rather more limits than the celebratory literature suggests. Boyne *et al.*'s (2001) survey of public sector management and spending found that, in practice, chief executives had very limited influence over budget levels and priorities. They were not passive but had little power to fundamentally alter activities, so most changes of administration were characterised by continuity rather than change. Tengblad (2004), in a detailed study of eight Swedish chief executive officers, which sought to replicate Sune Carlson's (1951) classic work, found work patterns and a work environment that was far distant from many of the leadership accounts. These were unpretentious men (and all were men) who exercised regularly and drove Volvos. Much of their work involved participating in organisational ceremonies and disseminating information (see also Mintzberg 1973, 1975). They saw themselves not as untrammelled visionaries but as highly accountable, with most aspects of their performance open to public scrutiny. All felt dependent on investor confidence and all demanded long hours and an aggressive approach to work from those who worked for them. One said of an American manager (p. 595): 'He is a brute, not quite sane actually, but he is nevertheless my best manager.' Another, reacting with anger to an employee who hesitated about moving to Africa (p. 597), said: 'Haven't I the right to demand that you work your guts out?' People who worked 8 to 5 were seen as lacking in commitment. Nor were their positions particularly secure; two years after the study 4 of the 8 chief executives had stepped down or been forced to resign.

This does not necessarily mean that leaders have no impact but rather, particularly in large and complex organisations, that there is a limit to the influence one person can have. In small firms, where all are personally known to the leader, 'charisma' and personality may indeed dominate. However, as firms grow, such personal influence is less viable and systems and structures replace personal contact (Gerth and Mills 1948). This makes the firm less vulnerable to the whims of the leader and ensures an element of continuity when the leader changes, since the old systems and structures will still be in place (at least temporarily). As Storey (2005) argues, the influence of boards of directors, shareholders, bankers and auditors is rarely studied but does much to shape organisational activities. Strategy is, in practice, not an individual endeavour, but the collective product of the top management team (Storey and Salaman 2004). The person who heads an organisation does have a great deal of influence over the direction it takes, the people who are hired and the business it is in, but this is not unconstrained.

Interestingly, one of the most significant ways leaders affect their businesses is by the reputational capital they bring: the mystique of leadership is part of an organisation's brand, one of its intangible assets in the marketplace (Storey 2005). As with managers, this is generally the impression of performance, rather than performance itself, but the 'right' appointment can raise or depress a share price and attract enthusiastic or disparaging comment.

From this evidence, it is difficult to argue that managers, workplaces and organisations are being transformed either into or by leaders. The continuities of managers and in managerial work should not be surprising. After all, as Hales (1999) points out, despite restructuring, decentralisation and fragmented and fragmenting organisations, few changes have been made to the way managers are selected, developed, socialised or remunerated. Even the core elements of the managerial job are the same. Unless (p. 841) 'inside every bureaucratically strait-jacketed manager is an entrepreneur yearning for release', there is little incentive to change.

Moreover, most of the literature on leadership is bereft of any kind of detailed examination of the theories and practice it proclaims so proudly. Their value is simply asserted and their nature assumed (Storey 2004b). No evidence is brought forward to prove, for example, that downsized organisations need people leaders with soft skills or that visionary strategies succeed better than consensual ones. This is, as Weeks (2004) argued about culture, a way of legitimising and explaining success. There is nothing to prove that these activities are linked with success, nor that they are more likely to result in success than any other kind of activities (see Chapter 7).

Developing managers and leaders

What then are the implications of this discussion on the nature of management and leadership for the way managers and leaders are developed? The first, and perhaps clearest, conclusion we can reach about managers is that they are extremely diverse. As a result, activities that would be successful in one environment may fail in another (Scase and Goffee 1989). The experience and expertise required to harness the creative talents of a group of knowledge workers in a specialist consultancy company are likely to be very different from those demanded of the manager of a branch of McDonald's. As Storey argues (1990:5):

The implication of this variety for the study of management development is that, far from persisting with the overwhelmingly universalistic tenor of most of the conventional literature on management development, there is an urgent need to re-direct attention to different contexts.

Yet many of the most popular types of management development retain that universalistic approach. The MBA qualification boosts managers' career earnings significantly, aids progression from one sector of the economy to another and provides candidates with a grounding in the way that organisations work. But, with the exception of a few specialist qualifications targeted at particular sectors or occupations, it is a generic award subsuming different organisations, ways of working, industrial sectors and national cultures (Sturdy and Gabriel 2000). Nor is the qualification becoming more context-specific over time; rather the reverse as references to production are driven out of management syllabi (Armstrong 1987). This knowledge is not particularly advanced. Indeed, as Reed and Anthony (1992) note, in contradiction of the standard pyramid structure of academic qualifications (where candidates specialise in ever narrower fields of knowledge), the MBA may actually provide less material on accountancy or operations or law than a dedicated undergraduate degree.

It may be that many of the advantages an MBA confers come from the symbolic messages associated with it rather than from any specific knowledge acquired over the course of study. After all, candidates enrolled on these programmes are expected to work extremely hard, assimilating academic texts and linking lessons to their own industries, often while holding down demanding full-time jobs. And they, or their employers, must pay high fees. These are factors which might well be used as proxies by employers seeking bright, dedicated, ambitious workers who are prepared to invest in themselves (or whose previous employers considered them worthy of investment). Fellow students, alumni and members of various MBA associations might hold influential positions (or be likely to gain these in future), so constituting a useful professional network.

Other types of management development are equally generic (and often less easy to link to management practice). Outdoor activities and exercises; low-level, short courses which have roots in counselling and psychotherapy; and purposive games: all are stable features of the management training industry (see, for example Mole 1996). By no means all activities are developmental (Antonacopoulou 2001). It is hardly surprising that Grey and French (1996) question whether management education has a clear and functional relationship to management practice. Nor, perhaps, should it be wondered at that managers themselves tend to turn to gurus or that one best-selling book after another prescribes fads and fashions to cure all organisational ills. These

Box 8.6

[A joke] appeared in the . . . *Financial Times* some years ago about a fantasy management education establishment with no faculty. Participants, on arrival, were greeted by an automatically activated . . . message to this effect:

> Good evening gentlemen, welcome to the X management education establishment. You will have noted, perhaps with relief, the absence of faculty or curriculum. This is a regular feature of this programme and a closely-guarded secret of its alumni, present and past. If you should require any inducement to keep this secret you may be influenced by the £500 in crisp ten-pound notes which is to be found in a brown envelope in your bedroom. This represents half the fee paid by your employers and approximates expenditure what would otherwise have been incurred with respect to teaching staff salaries and related costs. In the meantime, meals and other services will be provided and the bar will remain open at normal opening times. You will have discovered that your colleagues are drawn from similar organisations to your own and contain amongst them a wealth of practical experience in all manner of managerial roles. There is also a first rate library at your disposal. How you decide to pass these six weeks is your own managerial decision; we trust you will enjoy it and find it beneficial.
> Thank you.

Mant (1977:104–5).

ambitious claims (often backed by authors who are successful orators) denounce previous principles of organisation but rarely succeed in transforming practice and performance themselves (Micklethwait and Wooldridge 1996; Clark and Salaman 1998).

The truth – that there is unlikely to be one universal panacea to resolve all the problems with which managers are beset; that organisations are contingent and any success in them is highly contingent; that in complex social systems improvements in one area may not have such favourable results elsewhere; and that management itself, an activity born of unequal power relations, is a problem – is nowhere near as palatable as the gurus' myths. There is no undisputed management knowledge (Whitley 1984; Reed 1989). In management, professional decisions are generally a matter of judgement rather than the application of rules and its practice is characterised by instrumentality, contingency and processuality (Squires 2001). This is the pursuit, not of transformation, but of a choice among alternatives when none is entirely satisfactory in search of the least-worst option (Hyman 1987).

Moreover, neither managers nor leaders are the sole influences on organisational performance. Chapter 3 revealed how different national employment and VET structures encouraged different types of competition and ways of working; the industry a firm is in; the expertise of the workers; the expectations of its investors and its legacy of employment relations all affect what decisions can be made and how effective they will be. This is not to argue that individual managers cannot make choices, that organisations cannot be changed or new strategies introduced, but rather that none of these activities occurs in a vacuum.

In many respects, the concerns about leadership development echo those of management development not least because, as Hales (1999) points out, these activities are the same. Here too, activities can be observed that bear little relationship to practice. There is, as Mole (2004) shows, little similarity between fording streams using only ropes, poles and oil drums, hunting for treasure, building paper towers or abseiling down cliff-faces and actual leadership challenges. Such activities seem to fit far more closely with the needs of the tutors than the demands of leadership itself. This is not to say that none of the training leaders receive is specific. Indeed, the British armed forces do not teach leadership at all: they train people how to perform as officers, a substantial amount of which is technical. Rather, it is that such training seems to be a minority of activities (and rarely figures under the heading 'leadership').

But leadership also raises some new issues, including problems with gaining enough good work experience. This is a leadership issue largely because it is leadership that is associated with (and supposed to emerge from) the delayering and fragmentation of organisations observed in many advanced economies (see, for example Cappelli 2001; Noon and Blyton 2002; Littler and Innes 2003). Since managers and leaders have traditionally risen through the hierarchy, gaining most of their expertise from work undertaken, projects led and any number of accidental and unstructured experiences (Mumford, Robinson and Stradling 1987), while organisations limited their risks and prepared people for high rank by promoting them through different jobs in the hierarchy, delayered organisations pose particular challenges. Individuals are deprived of many opportunities to hone their skills as their career progresses (Hirsch 2004) and appointment panels charged with recruiting leaders for flat structures face quite a challenge. In most call centres, for example, it is fairly straightforward to appoint team leaders to monitor the performance and activities of small groups of six to eight customer service representatives. But, given the gulf between these first-line managers and the general managers of the centre itself (who may well be next in the reporting line) it is extremely difficult to find suitable candidates for the top management posts. People with experience of call centre work are unlikely to have had management responsibilities, while those who have had management responsibilities are unlikely to have worked in a call centre.

The Strategic Leader Programme is about giving our senior leaders (many of whom do have a very similar profile, many of whom have been internally developed so they are home grown senior leaders) an exposure to a different world view, a different perspective. And it's also about how they take that and translate it into how they are and how they behave. How that affects them in the way they lead. So that's what it's about. And a good way of helping them challenge their perspectives on how they see the world is by getting them to experience bits of the world and to run up against things that challenge their values and challenge their perspectives. For example, we took a group out a few years ago to Bosnia, and we went to Mostar, we went to Sarajevo. We did everything from meet the Prime Minister and have discussions with him, through to talking with artists and musicians. You know, when they walk through the streets they see the devastation . . . each morning we ran a reflection session just about what's going on. For some people it has huge impacts, for some people it doesn't. When it was designed it was quite risky. It's not a 'tools and techniques' course – though there are some business-type inputs, so you've got some tangible parts. It's a programme that's been a bit of an investment of faith over the years. It's hard to measure. (Leadership Development Director, BAE Systems)

Quoted in Paton *et al.* (2004:121–2).

In place of this, there is a thriving leadership development industry. Books, courses, workshops, seminars and qualifications all offer something related to leadership (Storey 2004b, 2005). Leadership is also a staple of corporate universities where activities may involve observations of real-life tragedies (see Box 8.7). The Boeing Corporation's university focuses particularly on leadership; main board members contribute to programmes and a small troupe of actors is regularly flown in from New York to work with participants. All probably enjoy the site's five-star restaurant (Paton *et al.* 2004).

Such activities are also extremely popular among junior and middle managers since they have a particular cachet in the politicised world of organisational hierarchies. Their technical contribution to the way firms function may be questionable, but the advantage they confer seems to be clear. In Newell's (2004) survey of MBA students the majority preferred leadership skills for themselves, but suggested their colleagues might benefit most from operational and general management skills, leaving her to question, in an environment with so many leaders, where the followers might be found. Interestingly too, these formal development activities are generally restricted to middle and lower-level managers, with few top-level leaders participating, other than as exemplars (Storey 2005).

Discussion and conclusions

Managers and leaders are a heterogeneous group who possess no one specialism and no consistent place in the hierarchy. In consultancies the rank of manager is often a comparatively junior position, held by graduate trainees before they become fully fledged consultants; in one British offshoot of a Japanese investment bank the manager is the man at the top who runs the entire operation. Similarly a team leader in a call centre is a first-line supervisor who will have roles and responsibilities very different from those of the the much-lauded Jack Welch of General Electric or Richard Branson of Virgin.

This has implications for the study of management and the way managers are developed. Clearly it is possible to explore what happens in organisations (the financial aspects of operations, the way work is designed and controlled, the way products or services are marketed), but such subjects do not readily map onto what managers do and previous attempts to set managerial competences centrally have not been successful (Grugulis 1997, 2000). It is easy to understand why, in labour markets where professional skills are highly valued, managers might want their own body of knowledge, but such attempts, by seeking generalisable 'truths' and ignoring organisational realities, have rarely been wholeheartedly accepted by most practising managers. As Child (1969:225) argues:

> Management's claim to professionalism . . . was only plausible if it could be shown to possess some uniform and generalised system of knowledge upon which its practitioners could draw. The so-called 'principles of management' could be presented as the theoretical base upon which the subject of 'management' rested. Furthermore, by ignoring problems of conflict, change and uncertainty within administrative organisation, the principle gave management an appearance of cohesion and rationality which it did not often possess in practice.

Non-managers perform managerial functions (Grey 1999), while real managers do jobs which barely resemble the theoretical models of their work. And national differences, resulting from differences in production systems as well as in cultures, are rarely given the prominence they deserve (though see Whitley 2003; Ray et al. 2004 for important exceptions to this).

It may be that, given this diversity, it is more appropriate for management development to focus on the differences between managers rather than seeking to emphasise what they share. From the perspective of securing productivity this would be a useful exercise since clearly competitive pressures, labour market factors and internal drivers vary significantly from sector to sector. It may well be more expensive than current activities (since the advantage of generic programmes, of all kinds, is that they need not be rewritten for each cohort), and an orientation towards specific rather than generic qualifications may impede those who use existing certificates to switch sectors, but the advantages are easy to see.

Then too it should be remembered that management development is not simply a pragmatic problem-solving exercise and that organisations, as complex social systems, contain within them many different interest groups. Juggling these is unlikely to result in the much-hyped win:win:win scenarios of the management gurus. Indeed, as Hales (2005) points out, a large aspect of many front-line managers' jobs is reconciling the divergent expectations of more senior managers and workers. It would be nice to hope that future management and leadership development initiatives would focus, not on the fantasy of organisational life, but on its reality – an emphasis that is more difficult, less glamorous and less coloured by unsullied optimism, but far more likely to result in better-run firms.

9

Knowledge work and knowledgeable workers

Gone are the days when companies were seen only as physical entities that converted raw materials into tangible products. Today, physical capital is of less relative importance for creating and sustaining competitive advantage than intellectual capital. For many companies the market value of intellectual capital is now too large to be categorised as goodwill. The emerging recognition of knowledge and intellectual capital has laid the groundwork for new, knowledge-based concepts, theories and practices of management. (Roos and von Krogh 1996:333)

Knowledge *worked*, then, does not necessarily require certificated knowledge *workers*. (Brown and Hesketh 2004:55)

Put bluntly, the more management, the less knowledge to 'manage', and the more 'knowledge' matters, the less space there is for management to make a difference. (Alvesson and Karreman 2001:996)

So far this book has dealt with the ideas underlying human resource development primarily by drawing on the notion of skill, but there is also another key aspect, that of knowledge. According to some commentators work itself is becoming more knowledgeable. Because of the shift from manufacturing to the service sector, workers are now engaged in manipulating symbols and people rather than physical products. Since these are less predictable than physical products, work itself is more complex (Bell 1973, 1974). And since knowledge is required to deal with people or ideas or symbols, it becomes the key resource on which organisations compete and the source of the highest quality power (Nonaka and Teece 2001; Nonaka *et al.* 2001). A firm's competitive advantage now depends not on land or labour or capital but on its ability to create, transfer, utilise and protect knowledge assets (Drucker 1993; Spender and Grant 1996; Teece 2001, 1998). There certainly seems to be a premium for effectively managing knowledge. In Bierly and Chakrabarti's (1996) study of US pharmaceuticals companies it was the firms that put most effort into learning (through research and development as well as through learning from other companies) that were most likely to make high profits.

Different types of knowledge management can lead to competitive success. 'Knowledge capture' centralises or systematises an organisation's stock of knowledge (and often raises issues of ownership; Leadbeater 2001). Dow Chemicals' knowledge management programme catalogued their (highly disorganised) data archive and, as a result, the company now earns a significant income from licensing its technologies (Scarbrough and Swan 2001). Knowledge management interventions can also seek to provide a supportive environment in which people can be creative or bring people with different specialisms together to produce innovations. Matsushita's bread-making machine was the result of extensive collaborations between engineers and bakers (Nonaka and Takeuchi 1995).

Such a dramatic shift also has implications for organisational structures. When the emphasis is on the knowledge possessed by individuals then the systems of managerial control need to change; while bureaucracies were designed to minimise the skill required in each job and produce standardised goods efficiently, 'knowledge-creating companies' need to provide the space and incentives to ensure that highly skilled workers collaborate, share ideas and develop new customised innovations (Karreman and Alvesson 2004). Internal management structures must also change. Randle and Rainnie (1997) report on the way that Glaxo, a major pharmaceuticals manufacturer, managed their highly qualified R&D workers and tried to encourage creativity while maintaining control. According to one senior manager (pp. 37–8):

> Most of our management is done through science. You don't want a heavily structured or heavily organised environment if you want people to be creative. I always say it's like running an opera house ... You've got to make sure that the toilets are clean, the tickets are sold, the ice creams are there in the interval, your gin and tonics are available, but if the fat lady doesn't sing, it's all a waste of time. And it's generating an environment where ultimately the prima donnas perform, because it's the prima donnas who actually make the invention, who take you to places you couldn't otherwise go ... But there are a few people out there who are really a bit special, who put things together in a different way ... What we've got to create is something that allows them to perform, not something that necessarily satisfies the aspirations of the masses, because you can do that by making it run very smoothly. Everyone will enjoy coming to work and say it's a fantastic place to work, but you never make inventions. What the hell good's that?

Knowledge work shares many elements with the traditional professions of accounting, medicine and the law. In all there is a focus on individual expertise and the key function of professional firms is to harness this. Members of these traditional professions, can be and are described as 'knowledge workers' (see for example Starbuck 1993; Winch and Schneider 1993; Robertson *et al.* 2003). But the term 'knowledge work' also encompasses newer occupational groups such as consultants, IT experts and researchers (Knights *et al.* 1993; Scarbrough 1993; Sturdy 1997; Ram 2000b; Robertson and Swan 2004). Reed (1996) argues that these knowledge workers adopt a 'marketisation' strategy to build up their expert power, gaining status and funds by packaging and selling their knowledge rather than by providing long apprenticeships, restricting entry to the occupation and monitoring professional expertise. Consultants and IT professionals do not gain and maintain their positions because they hold a particular qualification but because they can convince others of their expertise. While members of the traditional professions formed partnerships, many of these new-style knowledge workers are employed, enjoying power *within* organisations not power *over* organisations (Scarbrough 1993; May *et al.* 2002).

The interest in knowledge management is significant and it is certainly a welcome and dramatic shift to have knowledge treated as a public good rather than as something to be nullified (McKinlay 2005). But, as with every management initiative and every new way of organising, there is a great deal of difference between the enthusiastic hype that captures imaginations and the realities of organisational practice. It would be nice to believe that most work is intrinsically interesting and is undertaken by enthusiastic and motivated knowledge workers, employed on 'at will' contracts and earning high financial rewards for their expertise. However, it is not clear whether this description of the workplace is really an accurate one. This chapter attempts to sift the reality from the rhetoric to observe both the changes and continuities underlying this increasing interest in knowledge management. Drawing on Thompson and Warhurst's work, it also seeks to distinguish between *knowledge work* and *knowledgeability in work* (Warhurst and Thompson 1998; Thompson *et al.* 2001; Thompson 2004).

What is knowledge management?

In practice, knowledge and knowledge management cover such a diverse range of activities that the terms are almost meaningless (Hull 2000). It is not clear whether 'knowledge' in the work process refers to inputs (expert workers, attempts to harness creativity, well-designed work processes) or outputs (innovative products, customisation) (Noon and Blyton 2002). Nor is it clear whether knowledge is the exclusive property of a minority or whether everyone in the workplace is knowledgeable in different ways (see, for example Blackler 1995).

Different types of knowledge

Embrained knowledge. Abstract or conceptual knowledge, 'knowledge that' or 'knowledge about'.

Embodied knowledge. Action oriented and probably only partly explicit, 'knowledge how', acquired by doing and rooted in specific contexts. This may also include certain types of problem solving and a tacit understanding of machines.

Encultured knowledge. The process of achieving shared understandings gained through socialisation and acculturation and likely to be socially constructed and open to negotiation.

Embedded knowledge. Knowledge which resides in systemic routines, combinations of physical, mental, inter-personal, technical and socio-structural factors.

Encoded knowledge. Information conveyed by signs and symbols such as books, manuals, codes of practice and (increasingly) various electronic means. Because this information is encoded through decontextualised, abstract symbols it is inevitably highly selective in the representations it can convey.

Blackler (1995:1023–6).

Knowledge management takes a range of different forms and each of these has different implications for workers and for the type of work being conducted. The first variety is an extended library (Alvesson and Karreman 2001). Here firms attempt to 'capture' all available knowledge so that it reposes with the organisation rather than the individual worker; knowledge can then be harnessed more effectively and the firm is no longer at risk if a particularly knowledgeable worker quits. Hence Dow Chemicals' successful cataloguing exercise and the way many sales companies attempt to use the technological opportunities offered by laptop computers and mobile phones to keep central records of their salesforce's contacts (Hayes and Walsham 2000; Hodgson 2001). However, some of these initiatives resemble managing ignorance far more than managing knowledge. Davenport and Klahr (1998), in an article extolling the virtues of knowledge management for customer support activities, assert that (p. 198):

Many firms have already achieved measurable benefits through the management of support knowledge. They have captured, distributed and applied knowledge in order to reduce call times, resolve customer problems without dispatching a field service person, use less expert (and expensive) support personnel and reduce the need for support personnel completely through customer self-service. Hewlett-Packard, for example, reduced its average call time by two-thirds, from 15 minutes down to 5 minutes, while employing support analysts with a lower level of technical skills. London Electricity reduced its call volume by 40 per cent. New support employees at Dun & Bradstreet Software (now part of Geac Computer Corporation) could resolve 70 per cent of customer issues the very first day in the job.

Such an approach may be efficient but it does not seem particularly knowledgeable; systems are designed to minimise human input to the extent that customer service representatives can deal with most queries on their first day and most can be dealt with quickly. This resembles the deskilling and tight managerial control described in Chapter 2 far more closely than distinctive new forms of organisation.

The second focus of the knowledge management literature is rather more 'knowledgeable'; it is on 'knowledge-intensive firms' where "most work can be said to be of an intellectual nature and where well-educated, qualified employees form the major part of the workforce." (Alvesson 2000:1101); or on knowledge-intensive departments in larger firms (Randle and Rainnie 1997; McKinlay 2000; Alvesson and Sveningsson 2003). While a minority of writers report on knowledgeable ways of working in more mundane settings (Orr 1996; Tsoukas and Vladimirou 2001; Rothenberg 2003).

These organisations are distributed knowledge systems (Tsoukas 1996), and in them structures and systems are designed to help the prima donnas to perform (Randle and Rainnie 1997). Hierarchical relations are minimal, and often resisted (Starbuck 1993; Robertson and Swan 2004); matrix structures, project teams and flexible networks help to support collaborations and learning communities (Teece 2001); and strong cultures provide a unifying force that allows a high level of tolerance for ambiguity (Hackley 2000; Robertson and Swan 2003). Robertson *et al.* (2003) describe 'ScienceCo', a company that specialised in scientific innovations and patenting new work where 116 of the 140 employees were scientists (most with PhDs), where project teams were unstructured with leaders, who were often relatively inexperienced consultants, 'emerging' for each project. Personal and divisional revenue targets were set and employees described as both competitive and combative, but there was no onus on them to account rigorously for their time, so they could, if they choose, work through weekends and take extended holidays of two or three months or work for 24 hours solid and take a couple of days off. Work was documented so that the firm could gain patents but most learning took place through experimentation (see also Robertson and Swan 1998; Newell *et al.* 2002; Robertson and Swan 2004).

In these organisations management practices and processes are expected to differ from those deployed in 'standard' firms (Alvesson and Sveningsson 2003). While conducting research in an award-winning advertising agency Hackley (2000) found that the senior management intervened so little and so subtly that he dubbed the process 'silent running' after the way that wartime submarines would operate without speaking for fear of attack. In this agency creativity and knowledge were harnessed through strong systems of normative control. Employees were young, bright graduates, mainly from Oxbridge. They were free to work what hours they chose, provided with an endless supply of free food, snacks and fruit, given generous travel and lunch expenses and expected to work hard to meet deadlines. Here consent, motivation and a desire to participate in the goals of the organisation were assumed. These systems of normative control to harness knowledge are new forms of managing culture, as described in more detail in Chapter 7. There too could be found instances of motivated expert workers who embraced the organisational culture (Kunda 1992; Grugulis *et al.* 2000).

Social knowledge

In all of the accounts of knowledge-intensive working where experts are brought together to share their ideas the process of exchanging, passing on, developing and challenging knowledge is a social one (McInerney and LeFevre 2000). Starbuck's (1993) account of working life at Wachtell Lipton, an exceptional New York law firm which recruited only the most able and agreed to take only the most challenging specialist legal cases, describes the way every lawyer working for the firm operated an open-door policy, to the extent that their colleagues would walk in (always bearing cookies or coffee or soda from the small kitchen) and distract attention from the telephone call or the meeting that had been taking place before their arrival. This was (p. 898) 'a congenial home for people who can't function in a hierarchy'. Such vignettes provide a fascinating and amusing glimpse of a very distinctive work process but they also reveal the way knowledge was exchanged.

Nonaka and Takeuchi (1995) argue that there are two types of knowledge, tacit and explicit. Tacit knowledge is personal and not easily codifiable; it is the subjective and intuitive aspect of judgement, the complex interplay of knowledge, experience and gut feel. Explicit knowledge by contrast is formally set out in manuals, procedures and recommended 'best practices'. It is easily codified and often generic. It is also dynamic. Knowledge may move from tacit to tacit, as in a traditional craft apprenticeship; from explicit to explicit, as when existing but unrelated bodies of information are brought together; from tacit to explicit, as in the study of craft skills; or from explicit to tacit, when new knowledge is internalised (Blackler 1995:1033). This dynamism changes both the knowledge and the knowers (see Box 9.2).

This distinction between tacit and explicit knowledge is a simplification. As Tsoukas and Vladimirou (2001) point out, Polanyi (1962, 1975), from whom

Box 9.2

Different modes of knowledge and the type of knowledge created within each mode

	Tacit knowledge *to* Explicit knowledge	
Tacit knowledge from	(Socialisation) Sympathised knowledge	(Externalisation) Conceptual knowledge
Explicit knowledge	(Internalisation) Operational knowledge	(Combination) Systemic knowledge

Taken from Nonaka and Takeuchi (1995:72).

Nonaka and Takeuchi took their theories of knowledge, argued that it was never possible to strip knowledge of its ownership. All knowledge is contextual, situated in a particular place and time, and all knowledge gains meaning because it is personal (see Tsoukas 1996, 2002 for a more detailed discussion). Blacker (1993) links this approach to the work of Russian psychologists, including Vygotsky, who attempted to synthesise ideas on thought and action, avoiding the dichotomies which characterised Western theory.

As a result of these beliefs about the nature of knowledge, a great deal of effort in knowledge management initiatives has been put into developing 'communities of practice' (Lave and Wenger 1991); groups of experts who will provide social conduits for knowledge (Brown and Duguid 2002). These processes are very different from the attempts to 'capture' and control workers' knowledge in the way Davenport and Klahr (1998) describe. Randle and Rainnie's (1997) account of the way pharmaceutical innovations were introduced in collaborations between marketing staff (who tried to estimate what would sell) and scientists (who knew what was possible), and Orr's (1996) detailed study of how photocopier technicians acquired knowledge and skills through conversation as colleagues discussed difficult cases or shared triumphs and disasters, show the way that workers use discretionary spaces to develop their skills. The nature of the knowledge 'managed' is also different. Tacit knowledge is inherently individual.

Werr and Stjernberg's (2003) research into the way major management consultancies work illustrates this well. Every firm they studied had extensive databases of past projects, ways of working and consulting templates. But these served to provide a shared language and a set of commonly known principles that could act as a point of departure for consultants, not a mechanistic strait-jacket they were expected to follow rigidly. The junior consultants, who tended to be the ones actually carrying out the work, would always refer to their company's records but often the most valuable information they gleaned was the contact details of colleagues who had run similar projects and might be suitable sources of information. According to one junior Ernst Young consultant (p. 890):

> When thinking of the method, you mainly think of the overall working steps, rather than the detailed list of activities. I see the method more as a thought model, with certain recurring steps and basic building blocks one can learn. Once learned, you can build more freely with them.

This is the type of knowledge that is learned only from personal contacts, so meetings, intranets and social events become integral parts of knowledge management (Tsoukas 2002). McKinlay's (2000) research into 'Pharma', a US-owned pharmaceutical company, shows the extensive efforts put into both the technical and the social side of knowledge management. 'Lessons Learned' was a $12 million database of 'tips', which would enable workers engaged in particular projects to see what had gone on before and gain from their experience. But virtual exchanges were also encouraged so that the transatlantic development teams would learn to collaborate. When one project coordinator had US participants open birthday cards or boxes of European biscuits during videoconferences to encourage a virtual version of a sociable research laboratory, the company quickly insisted that this become standard practice on all projects. A chat room was set up for workers on lower-level tasks to meet for virtual coffee-breaks. According to one of the employees, such activity went beyond team-working (p. 114): 'Teams are last year's thing – been there, done that, got the T-shirt. It's all about going beyond teams – way beyond teams – it's all about creating communities. Communities are larger, looser, more inclusive, more transient.'

But these social aspects of work are the hardest for management to control. After all, as Alvesson and Karreman (2001) point out, there is a tension between knowledge and management (see also Alvesson 1993). Many of the social processes described here appear to be almost the antithesis of management and exist to obscure power relations, to encourage a gift exchange rather than an economic exchange between workers and to foster normative control (see Chapters 6 and 7). They can be pleasant forms of control but they are forms of control and they are not inevitably effective. It is a short step between acknowledging the importance of social interaction and tacit knowledge and accepting problems with knowledge management processes. Thompson and Walsham (2004) describe the way that, following a takeover, a large US software company attempted to capture the knowledge of a small British software house. This smaller company had never had any tradition of documenting procedures; rather, expertise was shared through the 'Bardic tradition'. According to one practice manager (p. 730): 'Before there was writing . . . the bard would hold all the knowledge . . . it would be passed on, one to one.' The larger company introduced a whole range of knowledge management practices to document and pass on best practice but none was felt to be particularly successful. Client databases documented the technical side of work but not the qualitative issues such as relationships with clients or previous successes and failures, which would have been far more useful. More worryingly, since client information was recorded in an abstract form project teams actually lost any sense of context and often went to set up projects having entirely misunderstood what the client wanted.

The aspects of the formal knowledge management practices that worked best were, ironically, those that mirrored and assisted the old Bardic tradition. Communities of practice indices gave the names and job titles of everyone in the organisation (the 'corporate yellow pages'), special interest groups brought people together and email kept them in touch. It was the face-to-face activity that was the most enduring and effective at passing on knowledge. Ineffective knowledge management here did not mean that employees ceased to be expert or to pass on knowledge, rather that the formal systems devised for them to do so and the templates on which they were to record their work simply distorted that expertise. The knowledge transferred through the official systems was very different, and far less useful, than the knowledge passed from person to person.

Knowledge work and knowledgeable workers

So knowledge can take a number of forms and be demonstrated in a range of ways (Blackler 1993, 1995; Nonaka and Takeuchi 1995; van den Bosch and Volberda 1999), and knowledge creation or transfer or development is often a social process because much if not all knowledge is personal and gains meaning or value from the context in which it is situated (Tsoukas 1996, 2002; Tsoukas and Vladimirou 2001). There are advantages in acknowledging these aspects of knowledge. They help illustrate its fragility (von Krogh 1998), prevent organisations taking knowledge creation systems for granted (McNulty 2002) and successfully convey its complexity (McKinlay 2005). But once such an inclusive definition of knowledge has been accepted, it then becomes extremely difficult to distinguish between types of work that demand high (or extensive or in-depth or detailed) levels of knowledge and those that demand little, since, as Blacker (1995) points out, all workers are knowledgeable.

There is no one objective set of criteria to define knowledge work, the most expert jobs are more mundane then they first appear, while the most routinised offer hidden spaces for decision-making. One example of this is the knowledge work occupations which Reed (1996) labels the entrepreneurial professions; these are occupations founded in higher education and with a strong case for being named professions. As Alvesson (1993:998) argues:

> It does not seem reasonable to see law and accounting firms – the most commonly recognised professional companies – as distinct from architectural, management or computer consultancy firms or advertising agencies in terms of most organisational aspects.

There are strong similarities between these workers and the professions, just as there are disparities between the realities of professional work and the accepted definition of professionals (Abbott 1988; Freidson 1988, 1994). Yet the knowledge claims of these groups are often extremely vulnerable. Software development is not an absolute science but a negotiated order in which innovations may be developed with service-users and rely on the latter's readiness to cope with bugs and errors (Kidder 1981; Baxter 2000; Darr 2004; Barrett 2005a). While, within organisations, the lines between managerial and technical work are blurred (Scarbrough 1993). Consultants' professionalism is even more contentious and since, here, it is more important to be seen to be an expert than actually to be one, more effort is put into regulating impressions, rhetoric and language games to convince others of the existence of expertise than into developing any actual skills (Alvesson 1993; Sturdy 1997; Ram 2000b). The trick is always to offer a product that is sufficiently intangible not to become a commodity yet standardised enough to be distinguishable from the services provided by others (Winch and Schneider 1993). Knowledge management programmes may help to brand and legitimise this knowledge. They may also help to deskill it, as Alvesson and Karreman's (2001:1008) interview with a consultant revealed. Discussing his colleagues he commented that: 'Many are here directly from school. So it is necessary to support them, with an easily accessible knowledge capital. It is a competitive advantage as well. A 27 year old consultant is cheaper than a 45 year old one.' This expertise does not rely on any formal qualifications, nor is it easy to tell whether work has been completed well, so creating the impression of being knowledgeable is key (Craig 2005). Such knowledge is not necessarily virtuous (Alvesson and Karreman 2001).

The expert base of the entrepreneurial professions is a fragile and varied one. But most claims to knowledge are socially constructed, a fact neglected by enthusiastic accounts of the social nature of knowledge creation (Alvesson and Karreman 2001). Perceptions of knowledge, expertise and skill may vary depending on the labour-market power of the worker, their gender, race, age, appearance or status (see Chapter 2 for a fuller discussion of this). Shorn of these trappings, skill may be difficult to label definitively (Alvesson 1993:1001):

> If one does not define knowledge as the number of years of education and formal training – which appears mechanical and reductionistic – it is rather difficult to compare different workers and sort out who is the most knowledgeable. Can one compare a heart surgeon to a bus driver in terms of who needs or has 'most' knowledge? One could say the surgeon only has to know about a rather limited area of work, while a good bus driver must know the geography of the city, the vehicle, how to cope with passengers in a variety of situations, etc. and that comparisons are impossible or meaningless.

Certainly detailed accounts of even apparently routinised jobs reveal hidden depths of variety and complexity. Tsoukas and Vladimirou's (2001) account of call centre work shows how customer service representatives often consulted one another on issues that were new, that they would tap into each other's accumulated experience, narrate work related episodes about awkward customers and uncommon questions and, in work, respond to the way a customer spoke as well as to what they said. The authors argue that (p. 976):

> Put simply, data require minimal human judgement, whereas knowledge requires maximum judgement. Knowledge is the capacity to exercise judgement on the part of an individual which is either based on an appreciation of context or is derived from theory, or both.

The real world of work is far more messy, imperfect and complex than any of the abstract formulations used to describe it and, no matter how apparently routinised the job, people learn to use their judgement to mediate between these rules and what actually happens (see also Leidner 1993; Wray-Bliss 2001).

This is a useful discussion but it is also a dangerous one. Knowledge and skills are contested, they are socially constructed and the success of many of the weapons used to defend them bears little relationship to the quality or quantity of expertise on offer. Yet acknowledging both this and the diversity of ways workers can be knowledgeable does not mean all types of work are knowledge work. This label is useful when it describes a particular type of labour. If it simply becomes a courteous synonym for work it becomes meaningless. Moreover, such a term may distort our understanding of the nature of work, distracting attention from what are often routinised and scripted tasks, poorly paid workers and tight supervisory controls.

Warhurst and Thompson distinguish between *knowledge work* and *knowledgeable workers* (Warhurst and Thompson 1998; Thompson *et al.* 2001; Thompson 2004). Even Frederick Taylor (1949) acknowledged that people employed in almost any job, no matter how narrowly defined the tasks, will become knowledgeable about their work. So the employees of the catering company observed by Rainbird and Munro (2003) became adept at putting portions that were the exact number of grams required into plastic serving trays; workers at McDonald's proved surprisingly capable of fixing the machinery when it broke down (Sennett 1998); and few workers follow the guidelines offered by Scientific Management work studies (Doray 1988). Even where tasks are tightly specified, where workers have little or no discretion over what they do, how they do it for and how long doing it takes, they can become proficient. Often the quality and pace of others' work will depend on this proficiency (Pollert 1981; Delbridge 1998; Rainbird and Munro 2003) and expertise may be highly prized (Burawoy 1979; Ackroyd and Crowdy 1990). But observing that workers become knowledgeable about the tasks they have to do is not the same as claiming that every worker is engaged in knowledge work.

Even among the entrepreneurial professions the label 'knowledge work' may focus attention away from routine, mundane or deskilled aspects of work (Thompson 2004), but at least these are occupations where workers are granted considerable discretion and where tasks are not routine (McKinlay 2000; Robertson and Swan 2003). Using these criteria as a basis for judgement it is harder to argue that knowledge work is now all-pervasive and accounts for the majority of those in work; indeed Stewart's (1997) figure of 59 per cent of the workforce looks barely credible (cited in Storey and Quintas 2001). Thompson et al. (2000) challenge the assumption that all service sector work is knowledge work. Admittedly, the service sector includes growing numbers of consultants, psychologists, computer experts and advertising workers who might come under the heading knowledge workers, but it also includes, and in far greater numbers, cleaners, carers, security guards, waitresses and receptionists, the personal service workers whom Reich (1993) predicted would be disadvantaged by the growing power of the 'symbolic analysts'. Their work often involves person-to-person contact, and human beings require more complex forms of interaction than inanimate objects (Bell 1973), but these interactions may be, and are often, deskilled. As Warhurst and Thompson (1998:5) argue:

> [T]here is a contradiction at the heart of the service encounter. The very uncertainty that inevitably accompanies the human element, in itself often provided by relatively unqualified labour, drives management to try and *standardise* the encounter as a means of ensuring 'quality' or at least consistency. (Thompson et al. 1996)

As a result, many of these jobs demand little more than data-processing of their holders. Few would dispute the fact that knowledge workers exist or that it is distinctive, but attempting to apply the label to everyone in the workplace in the mistaken belief that it is a compliment will do little to help our analysis or ameliorate their working conditions. Call centre workers may engage with complex social situations, those employed on the factory line may develop alternative, and more effective, ways of working and counter staff in fast food restaurants may know far more about the machinery they use than their employers ever suspect. But this does not alter the fact that the skill levels demanded by these jobs are minimal. Cockburn's (1983) definition of different types of skill (see Chapter 2) and Warhurst and Thompson's (1998) distinction between knowledge work and knowledgeability in work help us acknowledge the skills that exist without losing a sense of proportion.

Politics and problems

Knowledge management, then, is concerned with both knowledge work and knowledgeability in work. Organisational systems can seek to routinise and control this or facilitate and support it. There is certainly a great deal of activity to be observed. According to one KPMG survey, 43 per cent of respondents were undertaking some kind of knowledge management initiative (cited in Scarbrough and Swan 2001). Yet the majority of these fail (Storey and Quintas 2001; Beech et al. 2002).

Part of the reason for this is simple. It is not possible to solve the much quoted lament of Lew Platt, the chairman of Hewlett-Packard that: 'I wish we knew what we knew at HP', nor the comment of Jerry Junkins, the CEO of Texas Instruments – 'If TI only knew what TI knows' (cited in Storey and Quintas 2001:340) – since tacit knowledge is difficult to capture and knowledge management systems may end up recording only the trivial, which is codifiable (Storey and Barnett 2000). Moreover many workers are already more than overloaded with information so reports recording old projects go unread; as one engineer protested (Rothenberg 2003:1795), 'I don't need more information. I need to figure out how to use all the information I am getting now!'

But there is a more fundamental reason for failure. Neutral as the phrase 'knowledge transfer' sounds, it is in fact a deeply political process (Knights et al. 1993; Hull 1999; Contu and Willmott 2000). And when the most precious competitive asset the firm has is knowledge, knowledge is also what employees will gain promotion or payment or praise for. When knowledge confers competitive advantage, it needs to be safeguarded rather than shared (Tregaskis 2003). One NUMMI worker said that, when the plant first opened (Rothenberg 2003:1796),

[t]here was this great fear of management knowing too much about what actually occurred. Whatever knowledge you had needed to be kept segregated from anyone else. Don't document anything, don't write anything, don't standardise anything because the minute you do you will become instantly replaceable.

Small wonder then that Scarbrough (1996a) reports the way different units of the same business would rather call in a consultant than cooperate with one another, and O'Dell and Grayson (1998:155) quote an award-winning businessman as saying, 'We can have two plants right across the street from one another, and it's the damnedest thing to get them to transfer best practices.'

Consultants are accustomed to defending their knowledge in this way. Dyerson and Mueller's (1999) account of unsuccessful computerisation in the Department of Social Security shows how, when consultants were brought in to supply expertise and keep the project to deadline, they realised that transferring their know-how to the in-house staff would effectively make them unemployed. Accordingly, they passed on only sporadic and partial pieces of information and ensured that the system was developed in such a way as to demand their continued employment. They are also accustomed to accusing others of similar activities. In McKinlay's (2000) study of pharmaceutical workers, when the experts reported that tacit knowledge was twice as important as technical or explicit knowledge, the consultants engaged to manage the knowledge management practices argued that the scientists were simply reluctant to formally record their expertise. Small wonder then that in Newell *et al.*'s (2000; 2001) accounts of the way a bank sought to harmonise its fragmented internal system of more than 150 different intranets, local users reshaped the project to create electronic fences around their own areas of knowledge and reinforce their own local identity rather than forming part of a global, networked bank (see also Storey and Barnett 2000). Nor are these defensive barriers one-way. As Zahra and Filatotchev (2004) point out, directors are wary of passing their knowledge on, for fear that any beneficiaries may leave the company.

Workers who already enjoy high levels of power and status are best placed to defend themselves against attempts to limit their knowledge base or their span of control, as accounts of attempted changes to the health professions reveal (Ashburner and Fitzgerald 1996; Manley 2001; Swan *et al.* 2002). Some organisations have responded to this by attempting to restructure employees' incentives (Marsden 2004; Un and Cuervo-Cazurra 2004), but such activities are generally minor and unsuccessful, One firm even protested to its employees that 'hoarding' knowledge went against the principles of diversity management and its knowledge management scheme simply aimed to level the playing-field (Hull 1999).

When knowledge management systems are introduced their effects may be very different from the ones anticipated for them, since workers will not be slow to realise how to reveal themselves to best advantage. Medical sales agents, on being told that they would be rated on the number of contacts they made in any given month, promptly started to include everyone they met on their databases (nurses, doctors, accountants) whether or not these people were relevant to securing sales. When qualitative information was added so that sales staff could share good practice and information about clients, sales staff quickly learned that management monitored records of meetings. They responded by learning the 'right' comments to record and putting them down. The system effectively became a means of sending political messages to top management rather than recording any useful information about work processes. One database, which survived this politicisation process, ceased to be useful when it came under managerial control. According to a medical liaison manager (Hayes and Walsham 2000:79):

> The [name] database was really well used but has petered out now. This happened soon after our boss, the medical director, asked if he could be included in it because he had heard how successful it was. No-one felt that they could comfortably share views in the knowledge that he was reviewing the database.

Given these issues, it is small wonder that the 'IT optimism' of many knowledge management experts, that there would be a technical, software-based solution to every organisational problem, proved unfulfilled (Hull 1999; Chumer *et al.* 2000; Adair 2004).

Knowledge itself may also be political, partial or simply plain wrong. The discussion above noted that consultants' claim to expertise was a fragile one and that it was often difficult to tell whether a project had been done well. Equally, it might also be difficult to tell (until afterwards) whether a project was being done badly or whether the 'knowledge claim' was simply a marketing device. This might explain Szulanski's (1996) finding that two of the principal barriers to knowledge transfer were not motivation and commitment but mistrust of the knowledge itself or of its source. Dyerson and Mueller's (1999) account of the Department of Social Security's politically motivated computer consultants also reveals how poorly designed the new system was (effectively superimposing a software programme onto an outdated clerical system). Since the consultants wished to keep themselves in work they revealed very little of their expertise to the department's internal staff, who were required to simply accept the consultants' generalised prescriptions – a process Dyerson and Mueller condemn as 'superstitious learning'. By contrast, when the Inland Revenue reviewed its systems it started small, kept most of the work in-house and, when it hired consultants, ensured they knew more about the systems than anyone internally and were prepared to pass on that knowledge as part of their contract.

In liberal market economies the remedy for such self-serving forms of consultancy seems, broadly, to be *caveat emptor*. Professional associations are important networks for knowledge workers to share expertise and learn about new products and processes (Swan 1996), and in Sweden, the Netherlands and Finland this does indeed seem to be the way they are used. However, in Britain, associations were particularly likely to fall victim to the latest fad or fashion in the industry (Swan *et al.* 1999). And consultants would become association activists as a form of advertising, to promote their own product or process. Yet few other members seemed to appreciate this. When recommendations came from members of their professional association (even when these members were known to be consultants), many firms considered them 'unbiased' (Robertson *et al.* 1996).

In these instances, knowledge is not a universally accepted truth but a highly contentious, political and politicised concept (Spender 1996; Spender and Grant 1996). So knowledge management can be a way of asserting managerial control over the workforce (Hayes and Walsham 2000), shifting established spans of control (Ashburner and Fitzgerald 1996) or intensifying work (Knights *et al.* 1993). But while there is evidence that knowledge management initiatives can be (and are) all of these things, there is also a positive aspect to knowledge-sharing. Where power is contested and knowledge is one of the means of asserting power then passing on knowledge will confer disadvantage. However, where power is not contested and trust relations are high, sharing knowledge is not a zero-sum game (Scarbrough 1996b). In Werr and Stjernberg's (2003) account of the way consultants work, codifying practices conferred advantage because it provided them with a shared language through which to share experiences and on which to build. As the account of knowledge creation and development showed, increasing knowledge is often a social process, so joint developments with colleagues, clients and customers confer advantage on all. This, after all, is the principle behind most university departments and several of the more innovative knowledge-intensive firms (Robertson *et al.* 2003; Newell *et al.* 2002).

Organisational networks

Because knowledge work is assumed to be qualitatively distinct from other types of work, a great deal of discussion has been devoted to the type of organisation that best supports it. Knowledge work demands the freedom to be creative and organisational mechanisms that coordinate this creativity, so that the knowledge worker is put in proximity to others who are similarly creative to ensure that their talents are harnessed to innovations. Work groups need to be small enough to foster social exchange and make sure that tacit

Box 9.3

Knowledge and organisation structure

Knowledge agent
(autonomy and control)

		Individual	Organisation
Standardisation of knowledge and work	High	Professional bureaucracy	Machine bureaucracy
	Low	Operating adhocracy	J-form (Japanese) organisation

Lam (2000:494).

knowledge is shared, developed and passed on, but they also need to be large enough to gain from economies of scale. The type of organisation required is a structure somewhere between market and hierarchy, which captures the flexibility of the former with the capacity to coordinate of the latter. So, knowledge work is situated in 'networked' organisations (Castells 1996). It is a shift, according to Brown and Duguid (2001), from structure to spontaneity through inter-firm networks (Thompson 2005), professional associations, regional groupings, outsourcing, joint ventures, strategic alliances, partnerships and spinoffs (Storey 2002), where the central task of the firm is to coordinate knowledge (Grant 1996, 2001) and where networks are the locus of innovation (Powell 1998).

Some large organisations attempt to mimic the advantages of networks and small firms internally by setting up 'learning networks' (Tregaskis 2003); one high-tech engineering company organised itself as a group of decentralised business units which worked independently, and to some extent competitively (Blackler *et al.* 2000); Hewlett-Packard's British operations keep small and knowledge-intensive by automatically splitting into separate subdivisions when the firm reaches a certain size (Storey and Quintas 2001); while Microsoft assigns new software developers to teams of 3 to 7 people (Quinn *et al.* 2002). The number of firms that outsource services is rising dramatically (Cully *et al.* 1999) and this includes knowledge work. In 2003, 16 IT outsourcing contracts, each worth more than $1 billion, were announced (Grimshaw and Miozzo 2005:9). Alternatively knowledge may be accessed through inter-firm alliances (Grant and Baden-Fuller 2004) or acquisitions (Thompson and Walsham 2004) which offer the dual advantage of market presence and specialist knowledge (Castro and Neira 2005).

The economic success of Italy's Emilia-Romagna district shows how networks of small firms can provide support, expertise and encourage innovative and competitive industries (Piore and Sabel 1984). Here community-based industrial districts mean that groups of small firms collaborate to develop products, support skills and compete effectively in international markets. The fact that such firms are regionally based means that high-trust relations can be established and that security at work is supported (since, if a small firm makes an employee redundant, others in the community may take them on). Traditionally such local ties have been associated with economic backwardness, but since the 1970s Emilia-Romagna, Tuscany and the Veneto had both the highest concentrations of workers in manufacturing industry and of small firms. Cooperative relations with trade unions and extensive skill-building networks (in which regional and national governments have only just started to become involved) support a range of businesses including high-fashion clothes and shoe labels and food (Crouch *et al.* 1999).

An alternative network model can be observed in Japan, where large and small firms collaborate (Appleyard 1996). Fruin (1997) describes the way Toshiba's Yanagicho factory outsources production of 80 per cent of its goods to supplier firms and has 232 key suppliers for between 700 and 800 different products. These small firms are socialised into the Toshiba way of working and have their expertise enhanced through Toshiba's supplier association (Ray 2002), which engages in knowledge-sharing, engineer exchanges and an

---

Box 9.4

Cooperation and inter-firm knowledge sharing may make innovations possible. Grugulis *et al.* (2003) draw on research in Scotchem, a chemicals company, that fostered special links with a small number of organisations which it did not consider to be competitors. Joint problem-solving groups, use of each other's facilities and joint ventures harnessed each other's expertise. These inter-organisational collaborations produced tangible innovations including a complex automated loading facility for part of the Scotchem site, changes to the quality of goods produced (to the benefit of a supplier) and larger and tougher bags for powdered chemicals. Extensive collaboration with one preferred supplier in producing bag specifications had maximised benefits for both parties by significantly reducing leakage which might foul the loading equipment.

Taken from Grugulis *et al.* (2003).

extensive calendar of social events as well as providing a system of governance for these companies (though see also Chikudate 1999). In Britain close links between large car manufacturers and the SMEs that supplied them with parts provided the economies of scale to develop employees' skills and also meant that best practice in work design could be passed on (Brown 2001). While Hunter *et al.* (1996) observing a range of different forms of 'partnership' between firms, comment particularly on the exchange of expertise. Because such networks are flexible they can combine different types of expertise and different modes of organisational governance, avoiding standardisation and fostering inter-company learning (Lam 2000; Miles *et al.* 2002).

According to the knowledge management writers, this fragmentation and marketisation of firms' activities is mirrored by individuals (Kunda and Ailon-Souday 2005), who are increasingly opting for project work, self-employment, agency work and portfolio careers, combining a range of different activities to keep interesting and fulfilling work (Handy 1990; Garvey and Williamson 2002) – to the extent that, by the mid 1990s, Manpower, the temporary employment agency, had displaced General Motors as the largest employer in the USA (Storey 2002:350). Albert and Bradley (1997) argue that this will change organisational structures from the grass roots. They draw on studies of the Hollywood film industry, where actors and agents are setting up their own companies, AT&T's expert network of 'internal temps' and a London temporary employment agency specialising in accountants to argue that such 'at will' employment contracts are the choice of the knowledge workers themselves, to gain (p. 153) 'discretion, variety, enhanced networks and increased knowledge'. They contend that (p. 98):

> Experts are the catalysts, elements and structure of specific new organisations. Their opportunities, choices and lifestyles are particular. The power that they wield in both the labour and product markets suggest that they will impact on others as well. Organisational theory has tended to emphasise the importance of demand side influences on organisations. This has generally led to an under-appreciation of the influences of individuals on organisations and change. In contrast, our theory emphasises individual preferences, networks and agencies which constitute the essence of the emerging structure for organisations.

Certainly the evidence suggests that self-employed consultants enjoy their employment status and, given the choice, would not return to full-time, permanent work (Harvey and Kanwal 2000; Kunda *et al.* 2002; Mallon and Duberley 2002).

This image, of a liberated labour market in which professionals choose to work on projects that interest them and organisations seek to harness creativity and make working life pleasant for workers, is an attractive one. It is also a welcome challenge to the tradition in employment that secure work is good and insecure work bad or that only the employer has agency in negotiating contractual status. However, this shift in truisms may simply exchange one universal generalisation (that all contingent work is bad) with another (that all contingent work is good), with neither close to reality.

The literature on networks of organisations and workers covers a wide variety of alliances, including: 'flexible firms' (Atkinson 1984), 'shamrock organisations' (Handy 1990), 'network firms' (Castells 1996) 'boundaryless organisations' (Ashkenas *et al.* 1995), 'flexible specialisation' (Piore and Sabel 1984) and 'flexible capitalism' (Sennett 1998). These labels are as wide-ranging as the practices involved and it is naïve to assume that all such networks are centred upon exchanges of knowledge or are particularly new. Indeed, ironically, the professional partnership, an enduring and successful means of organising small groups of expert workers (Greenwood and Empson 2003), is seldom mentioned in the new knowledge management literature, perhaps because such a model of organising also confers power on the expert workers.

Yet on closer scrutiny, many of these networks are neither as loose nor as novel as they first appear. The public sector reforms in Britain, justified by attacks on bureaucracy, have simply exchanged a professional bureaucracy for a managerial one with increasing power devolved to administrators (Alvesson and Thompson 2005). Even when firms are liberal adhocracies, designed to encourage learning and the free exchange of information, such structures may not be sustainable over time (Robertson and Swan 1998, 2004). Networks and new forms of organisation are neither necessary nor sufficient preconditions to organisational or individual learning. Grimshaw and Miozzo's (2005) cross-national study of large-scale computer outsourcings shows how most were staffed by workers who had been transferred over from the client companies, rather than from the specialist IT firm. One senior manager in Argentina commented that (p. 14):

> It was bad, because everyone was anxious to see what EDS would be like. I always remember during the first six months [of EDS in Argentina], I asked the president of EDS, 'Where is EDS? Where are the people from EDS?' And he told me 'You are EDS'.

Such transfers were often approved of by the workers because they gave them more attractive career development opportunities (though see also Grimshaw *et al.* 2002; Vincent and Grugulis 2005) and the client firms had access to the wider skills and experience of the large computer firms, but most often these networks involved the same workers who had been employed when the service was in-house and the only change was that they were now employed on a different basis.

Networks of organisations may collaborate, but the members of these networks are discrete entities with their own separate interests which may not fully coincide (Rubery *et al.* 2002). Changing from internal to external provision of services in particular may create new problems as well as opening up new opportunities (see, for example Brusoni and Prencipe 2001), and knowledge is not necessarily best served by 'spontaneous organisation' (Brown and Duguid 2001). In one study of a housing benefit office, outsourcing work to a private sector provider actually resulted in a massive rise in the monitoring of work. Since forms were not completed internally and no other agency had the authority to approve benefit claims, council staff were required to check every section of every claim before authorising payment, and errors resulted in forms being returned to the claimants (via several departments in the firm to which the work had been outsourced). Caseworkers who previously had had the discretion to waive through minor errors were required to mechanistically follow procedures. Worker autonomy was reduced and compliance costs rose dramatically (Grugulis *et al.* 2003). Moreover, the existence of a network may distract attention from the core task, rather than focus it. Lampel and Shamsie (2003) argue that Hollywood was far more creative in the Golden Era of the industry when production was dominated by major studios and the majority of workers were contracted to them. In modern productions the creative effort is diverted into bringing together a fragmented amalgam of small firms and independent workers, with each project being staffed from scratch.

Inter-firm alliances may also be exploitative. Rainnie's (1988) work has clearly shown not only how small firms may gain from finding niche areas in which to compete but also how their large customers and suppliers may take advantage of superior negotiating power. Blyton and Turnbull's (2004) account of work outsourced to 'Sew and Son' by Marks & Spencer shows, not knowledge-sharing, but total control of the work processes. Inspectors ensured that everything was done to M&S specifications and quality controllers rejected whole batches of garments when flaws were found, effectively reducing the larger company's risk. Scarbrough's (2000) research into supply chains highlights the double-edged impact that external influences had on employment practices, encouraging new skills while simultaneously putting pressure on work and work organisation. The existence of supply chains does not alter the fact that most of the power reposes with the large organisations (Alvesson and Thompson 2005). Such asymmetric exchanges may be accepted by the less-powerful partners because, although returns are unequal, they can still gain from the process (Hunter *et al.* 1996), but this is far from the optimistic accounts of the proponents of networks. It seems that inter-firm alliances may confer disadvantage on those who participate in them as much as they offer advantage.

Nor are individual knowledge workers any better placed. Indeed, while networks of firms can and do exchange knowledge, the experience of individuals on 'at will' contracts is rather more erratic. In the USA strong alumni associations and professional bodies provide freelance computer consultants with opportunities to develop, update and add to their skills (Finegold 1999; Kunda *et al.* 2002). In Britain, where university alumni associations are less well organised, outside the traditional professions there are fewer formal networks to access for support and skills and knowledge development. Detailed research into the careers of self-employed consultants reveals that individuals were concerned primarily with winning the next contract, and few had time to keep up to date with developments in their profession. Indeed, it was the consultants themselves who expressed concern that they were still relying on knowledge and expertise gained at the start of their careers (Mallon and Duberley 2002). There were instances of collaborations between contractors and contracting firms, in which training was included as part of the fee (see also Harvey and Kanwal 2000) but these were isolated, and often resisted by the contracting firms. In media production, where much work is done by small firms and only a small minority of production workers undertake recognised training schemes or qualifications, social networks and being known are the principal factors that secure offers of work (Blair 2001; Baumann 2002; Culkin *et al.* 2005). Some networks offer support for skill development (Saundry *et al.* 2005). But it is not clear how effective 'jobbing labour' is at fostering individual or sectoral capacity.

Despite the claims of the literature that flexible and insecure forms of employment confer freedom on the individual workers, many find themselves more tightly monitored than in-house employees, working on a contract rather than a trust basis (Fox 1974; Streeck 1987). One frustrated teacher, who found that working for a temp agency meant that she could no longer plan her own teaching, commented that (Grugulis *et al.* 2003:51):

> I thought I would have more freedom to [do] certain things. I thought, I will be able to decide I am here for a day and we will do a project on that and at the end of the day we would have produced a book about so-and-so and they would go home thinking, right it has been a whole day with a different person who has been really nice to us because you can afford to be friendly with them and you decided what they are going to do and you have got their co-operation, they are excited about the topic and they go home with a piece of work that they have done and finished and you cannot do that. So that is a bit disappointing. (Janet, supply teacher)

Not only do workers lose access to internal labour markets and the possibility of promotion (Rainbird and Munro 2003); they may also lose access to the most skilful and challenging aspects of their work.

Finally, and most fundamentally, knowledge workers are underrepresented in flexible work arrangements (Cully *et al.* 1999; Storey *et al.* 2002). Most of the work that is outsourced is peripheral to the organisation and undertaken by poorly paid and low-skilled workers who are often further disadvantaged by the fact that work is outsourced. According to the Workplace Employee Relations Survey some 90 per cent of organisations subcontract one or more services and about three-fifths use both contractors and one other form of non-standard labour (Cully *et al.* 1999:35). But the services most often outsourced are cleaning, catering and security. Forde and Slater's (2005) detailed analysis of the Labour Force Survey reveals that agency work is disproportionately concerned with clerical, secretarial and routine operative jobs. Few knowledge work occupations, associate professionals or managers appear as temporary workers and knowledge workers are no more likely to take agency work on voluntary basis than their less-skilled peers.

Discussion and conclusions

The term knowledge work covers a diverse range of organisational practices. At one level it describes the creativity of an elite within systems of normative control. These are the symbolic analysts whose employers provide them with innumerable perks, from lavish expense accounts (Hackley 2000) to biscuits from Harrods or Fortnum & Mason, weekend shooting parties and a chauffeur-driven Mercedes (Robertson *et al.* 2003). They are given freedom at work and expected to be productive and creative within it (McKinlay 2000). These are the people with impeccable academic credentials, recruited against almost impossibly demanding selection criteria from top institutions (Starbuck 1993; Blackler *et al.* 1993). Studying the way such a knowledge elite operates is an interesting and worthwhile task but this group is, by definition, not typical of the majority of the workforce (Hinings and Leblebici 2003), and the management practices used to inspire the elite to creativity do not necessarily bear any relationship to the ones deployed elsewhere.

This is a key point. Accounts of knowledge work focus on small groups of experts: consultants, computer professionals, lawyers, architects, research and development staff, scientists and stock market traders (Winch and Schneider 1993; Scarbrough 1996b; Randle and Rainnie 1997; McKinlay 2000; Alvesson and Karreman 2001; May *et al.* 2002; Robertson and Swan 2003; Werr and Stjernberg 2003). Such workers are a distinctive subset of employees and managing them raises important questions, not the least of which is whether it is possible to manage knowledge (Swan and Scarbrough 2001) and whether management and creativity are mutually incompatible (Alvesson 2000). Few would deny the importance of this or question the evidence such studies are based on. It is less easy to understand the leap of faith (powered largely by optimism) that goes on to assume that, because *some* jobs are knowledge work, *all* or *most* will be in the future (Stewart 1997). As Thompson (2004:3) argues:

[W]hile there are knowledge-intensive firms and knowledge-based work, attempts to characterise the pursuit and utilisation of knowledge as the defining feature of the contemporary economy does nothing to help us understand how it operates; and that while knowledge workers undoubtedly exist, their extent is exaggerated and their nature misunderstood.

Sharing knowledge is a core problem (Prichard 2000; Becker 2001; Murray 2001), but not all firms that compete on the basis of knowledge subscribe to knowledge management (Harrison and Leitch 2000) and by no means all (or even most) organisations compete on the basis of knowledge. It is entirely possible to compete on the basis of low-skill, low-cost goods and there is little to suggest that firms that compete on this basis are in any way more vulnerable than those which compete on 'knowledge' (see particularly chapters two and three). Even in firms where knowledge work forms a key element of organisational success, the term 'knowledge-intensive' may distort as much as it informs (Thompson 2004). Pharmaceutical companies will rely on their R&D departments to discover and innovate but these innovations are likely to be produced in bulk by factories where work is Taylorised and discretion limited. Retailers, where the majority of the workforce are hired on the basis of 'soft skills' and flexibility, may gain part of their competitive advantage from sophisticated systems of transport. It may require a great deal of expertise to calculate the actuarial risk premia for particular behaviours, but most of the front-line staff in insurance companies are clerks required to follow procedures. As McKinlay (2005) notes, the focus of knowledge management writings is on the organisation rather than the individual. This can help offer a systematic view of the way certain firms operate but it provides only an impoverished perspective of the employees and may demand that the firm is labelled in a digital fashion (as knowledge-intensive or not knowledge-intensive). Rather than devising a schedule of the proportion of work, or workers, or turnover, or profits that needs to be knowledge-intensive before a firm can be labelled knowledge-intensive it might be more realistic to acknowledge that most forms of work and organisation involve restricting skills and knowledge as well as managing them. Such an appreciation should help ground more realistic understandings of organisations and the way they operate.

10
Developments and developing in the new economy

The goal of decent work is best expressed through the eyes of people. It is about your job and future prospects; about your working conditions; about balancing work and family life, putting your kids through school or getting them out of child labour. It is about gender equality, equal recognition, and enabling women to make choices and take control of their lives. It is about personal abilities to compete in the marketplace, keep up with new technological skills and remain healthy. It is about developing your entrepreneurial skills, about receiving a fair share of the wealth that you have helped to create and not being discriminated against; it is about having a voice in your workplace and your community ... For everybody, decent work is about securing human dignity. (International Labour Office 2001:7–8 cited in Green, 2006:19–20)

On the one hand, it is emphasised that modern work, as a result of the scientific-technical revolution and 'automation', requires ever higher levels of education, training, the greater exercise of intelligence and mental effort in general. At the same time, a mounting dissatisfaction with the conditions of industrial and office labour appears to contradict this view. For it is also said – sometimes even by the same people who at other times support the first view – that work has become increasingly subdivided into petty operations that fail to sustain the interest or engage the capacities of humans with current levels of education; that these petty operations demand ever less skill and training; and that the modern trend of work by its 'mindlessness' and 'bureaucratisation' is 'alienating' ever larger sections of the working population. (Braverman 1974:3–4)

This book started with a quotation from Noon and Blyton's (1997) text *The Realities of Work* that describes, with tongue firmly in cheek, what the workplace of the future might look like. It has dealt with some of the most significant ideas, practices, predictions and changes that underlie human resource development and has attempted to link them to empirical accounts of what is really happening in organisations, why things change and why they stay the same. Clearly such evidence-based accounts cannot support global conclusions. The work practices observed in research laboratories in Singapore may not resemble those in Australian family restaurants, New York sweatshops, German retail banks or African mining corporations. The skills that organisations harness may be assisted by national or occupational development activities, the management styles by socially acceptable norms, and the firm structures by management fashions.

Then too, we should not underestimate the importance of continuities, as well as changes in work. Novelty may attract the attention of writers and researchers but not many workplaces change dramatically every few years and few of the interventions described here are as novel as the claims made for them. Workers' moral character is a matter of enduring interest to their employers and was a precondition of advantageous wages in the Ford motor company's brief trial of the $5 day (Beynon 1975). Harnessing the willing cooperation of skilled and knowledgeable workers is a perennial tension in capitalist organisations (Warhurst and Thompson 1998), and Storey and Quintas (2001) provide a history of the importance of knowledge to economies dating from the writings of Alfred Marshall in the nineteenth century (see also Collins 1997).

With that in mind, this chapter attempts to draw together some of the arguments made in the book and to consider what is happening to jobs. In particular, it explores the presence of and possibilities for good jobs. After all, as many of the earlier chapters have demonstrated, there are still many jobs that are narrow and alienating where developmental activities fit people only

---

Box 10.1

Opportunities to expand low-skilled jobs
A maintenance operative in a home for the elderly explained that he had started working in maintenance and repairs, having worked in a factory for most of his working life. He took a test to drive a minibus and would take residents to a do-it-yourself shop to choose wallpaper to decorate their bedrooms. He started working as a 'floater', covering for staff on holiday leave by working alongside care staff. He called bingo, played games with the residents and had bought his own Father Christmas outfit to distribute gifts at Christmas. He was clearly putting enormous emotional energy into this work, claiming: 'I love life and I love serving people. If you can bring a smile to someone's face you have achieved something . . . Tomorrow's promised to nobody.'

Rainbird and Munro (2003:39).

for the current task or serve to distract them from the nature of the work. Skills relevant for employers are not necessarily enriching for employees (Rainbird and Munro 2003). Yet there is enormous potential to broaden the skill content in these jobs, and such changes might have far-reaching social consequences (Lloyd and Payne 2003).

The shift to services

One of the main changes, highlighted repeatedly here, has been the shift from manufacturing to service-based employment. An advertisement currently getting a great deal of airtime both reflects and pastiches this change. It is marketing a reduced sugar variant of an alcoholic drink and starts with a shot of muscled and grimy manual male labourers harvesting sugar cane in the heat of the sun. Thanks to the popularity of this new drink they have lost their original, traditional, blue-collar jobs, an event that must strike a chord with many viewers, but they are retrained and shown, still sweaty and dressed in dirt-covered overalls, shampooing women's hair, engaged in synchronised swimming, and smiling at the media as they cut the ribbon to open a new building. The old economy of manual work is replaced by the new one of person-to-person services, public entertainments and emotion work.

This shift is a dramatic one. Some of the figures are exaggerated, as outsourcing services such as cleaning, security or support departments means that staff who would have counted as employees engaged in manufacturing now appear as service workers, but most of the change comes from the decline, automation and off-shoring of manufacturing industry coupled with changing social mores which raise the demand for different services. And service sector work requires very different skills of those who carry it out. While much of the attention in manufacturing was focused on the product (though see Garrahan and Stewart 1992; Thompson *et al.* 1995; Shibata 200), in service sector work the process of being served is as important as the product being served, so the way workers look and feel, the feelings they provoke in others and the personal qualities they display attract more organisational attention.

Service sector work is also female-dominated, but while participation in paid work gives women more economic power this is not an unalloyed good, nor does it herald equal treatment in the workplace. Full-time women workers still earn less than their male colleagues, progress more slowly through the organisational hierarchy and are likely to find that motherhood may severely limit that progression. Part-time women workers (and many service sector workers are part-time) are even less well paid, are generally cut off from career ladders and perform work that is almost automatically classified as low-skilled because it is done part-time by women. At the other end of the organisational hierarchy, while women are now very evident in the professions and junior management, few are visible in the top echelons of either. In Britain only 1 in 10 company directors is a woman, while in the USA women make up just under 16 per cent of corporate officers (Edwards and Wajcman 2005:76).

Much of the move to service sector work has meant a shift from full-time, male, unionised and often skilled employment to part-time, female, non-unionised and unskilled work. Moreover the 'new' skills that employers say workers require are so intangible and so subjective that they are likely to confer far less labour market power on their holders than traditional technical skills, which were often formally certified and protected by union agreements. This is not to argue that the service sector is necessarily the locus of labour market disadvantage, and many of the growing number of well-paid 'knowledge worker' jobs are located in the service sector. Rather, it is to note that while more people are taking on such challenging work (Green 2006), the low-skill, low-wage tasks that cannot readily be automated are unlikely to disappear.

Box 10.2

The term 'training' covers a multitude of activities from low-level, short courses to in-depth, educational ones and, as Wallis and Stuart's (2005) study of low-skilled council workers reveals, participants strongly prefer relevant courses that teach them something new. NVQs were generally unpopular with workers since these focused only on existing competences and reactions to other activities varied (pp. 14–15):

> It was psychobabble! It was thinking outside the box and all that. I thought, 'right, yeah' and at the end of it . . . the chance of taking anything back was . . . It was a waste of time. (Merseyton Council employee)

> I mean . . . I certainly take into account more the political climate and that kind of thing. What we can and can't do . . . Now I take into account what we're liable for as a borough where beforehand I probably wouldn't have done. (Merseyton Council employee)

> I did the bereavement training. That was very interesting. I learned a lot about how to help people in that situation . . . It made me think about how to support people in that situation . . . I helped a carer when his wife died, and helped him to move on. I got some information for a [support] group that runs to help him. (Aireton Council employee)

Taken from Wallis and Stuart (2005).

Knowledge workers

What then of the knowledge workers, the members of global communities who earn money from their ideas (Reich 1993)? Knowledge work and knowledge workers exist, but their influence in the literature is not matched by any numerical strength in the workplace and there is little evidence to suggest that all or most of the employees of the future will be hired for their expertise. It may be, too, that the knowledge workers themselves may be more vulnerable since the communities of practice organised (by employers) to facilitate creative endeavour are pale shadows of the social and knowledge-based ties formed through traditional craft work which often covered a person's whole working life (McKinlay 2005). Relying on individual negotiation can mean that the entrepreneurial professions lack many of the power bases of their predecessors. Knowledge is an important aspect of work and people, associations or organisations who control it have power, but it is not the only nor the most significant source of power.

It is also useful to distinguish between *knowledge work* and *knowledgeable workers* (Warhurst and Thompson 1998; Thompson *et al.* 2001). Most workers are knowledgeable about their jobs and even the most ostensibly routinised tasks leave spaces for expertise (in putting the requisite number of grams of food in the container or inserting components into their allocated slots with speed). But saying that workers know about or are proficient in a task is not the same as calling them knowledge workers. Skill reposes in the job and in the social setting as much as in the individual. McDonald's employees may be adept at their tasks or unexpectedly able to fix equipment when it breaks down (Royle 2000; Leidner 1993; Sennett 1998), but they are not knowledge workers and calling them that may blind us to the way that organisational structures and routines rely on the presence of ignorance.

Knowing that knowledge workers are a (self-conscious) elite may also help us to understand their response to various human resource interventions. Managerial initiatives which may be extremely successful when practised on small, well-paid and trusted enclaves of employees rarely achieve such positive results when extended to the majority of the workforce; largely because one of the principal reasons for their success is the fact that they are practised on small, well-paid enclaves of employees. For the majority the fashionable rhetorics (of empowerment or learning communities or motivation) often sit ill with low pay, tightly regulated jobs, a lack of security and poor career prospects. The workplace is an arena where order is negotiated and if, as part of their contribution to the negotiations, management offer poor terms and conditions it is not really surprising that employees may not respond to requests with enthusiasm (although small workplace changes may also mean a great deal to workers who are generally not involved in human resource practices) (Rosenthal *et*

Rainbird, Munro and Holly's (2004) study of a council cook–freeze centre illustrates some of the problems of increasing skill levels and making work more interesting. The centre prepared 15,000 meals and 11,000 sweets each week and 14 staff were employed in food production and packaging. Much of the work was repetitive and women became 'experts at putting 80 grams of meat into the containers'. Despite the fact that their jobs were far from glamorous, staff took pride in doing work that was socially valuable. One catering assistant attended a course in Afro-Caribbean cookery in his own time. He had hoped to use this knowledge in the cook–freeze centre but the cost of providing meals was too high. Undeterred he continued to study, at his own expense, for an NVQ in cookery and another in intermediate food hygiene. Though to put these new skills into practice he would probably have to seek work elsewhere.

Taken from Rainbird, Munro and Holly (2004).

al. 1997; Edwards and Wajcman 2005). For human resource development activities to be judged effectively they need to be set against the context of the workplace as a whole, not the individual intervention.

Skills, jobs and societies

Assessing the direction of skill change is never straightforward. Writing in 1974 Harry Braverman noted the tensions between rising levels of education, a rhetoric that emphasised increasing skills and the constant, petty subdivision of work. His conclusion, that there is a natural tendency within capitalism to deskill as workers and managers vie with one another for control, are too dramatic. Skill levels overall seem to be rising, workers may resist managerial changes as well as comply with them, and capital generally seeks profit rather than control. But many of his observations on the difference between organisational claims and tightly controlled jobs still have resonance today and they certainly provide a welcome corrective to more optimistic predictions on the future world of work (see, for example Trist 1974).

Green (2006) in an impressively detailed study deals with some of the incongruities that beset jobs in the developed world today. Most significantly he points out that people are far better off than they were thirty years ago. With the exception of the USA (where a reduction in minimum wages and anti-trade-union legislation in the 1980s has meant that average real wages have actually declined), real wages in most developed economies have doubled and workers are far more affluent now than ever before. For many, skills are rising (though substantial numbers of low-skill jobs still exist) and the risk of accidents and injury at work has substantially reduced.

Yet at the same time, work effort has been dramatically intensified. A process that is often linked to technological developments, a call centre for example, by creating a national or international centre for queries, overcomes the inefficiencies caused by a queue in Birmingham or Sydney when staff are sitting idle in Melbourne or Milton Keynes. Discretion too has reduced (except in Austria and Germany, where employees now have *higher* levels of control over work tasks and Finland where levels are static). Workers have less choice about how, when, and how quickly tasks are done and professionals are particularly dramatically affected by this.

This is a paradox. We would expect work to intensify and autonomy to decline when workers have less bargaining power, but this would also be linked to a fall in real wages, as happened in the British public sector between 1992 and 1997 when wages declined but effort levels intensified. At a time of rising real wages it is surprising that workers do not try to negotiate for better-quality jobs, effectively spending their money on more interesting, or more liberating work, just as they might purchase a washing machine or a new car. Yet this does not seem to be happening. Indeed, it is those workers with most education and skill (and, in theory, most negotiating power) whose working hours are rising (Bosch 2005). It may be that job design, in economies in which consultation is not embedded and where involvement often takes the form of top-down communication, is held to fall within the managerial prerogative; or that declining trade union influence means that bargaining power and topics are restricted. Yet it is not that workers are power-less.

Developing resourceful humans?

Perhaps the question should be, not what *is* happening, but what should happen. As Edwards and Wajcman (2005) point out, capitalism is indeed the dominant system but it is not a fixed frame of reference, unchanging from place to place. As Chapter 3 showed, there are many different types of market economy and the structures that support employment, skill development systems and consultation arrangements can dramatically affect the way organisations compete and the skills their employees can gain and exercise.

Encouragingly, some international institutions have started to focus not simply on job creation (which may rely on low pay, low skill and insecurity) but on the generation of decent jobs. Brown's (2001) model, discussed in Chapter 3, which argued for consensus, competitive capacity, capability, coordination, circulation, cooperation and closure, is of help here. As too is the work of Lloyd and Payne (2003; 2005), who point out that while many governments espouse the high-skills society and the need for better jobs, few of these debates enjoy any sort of precision in their aims or objectives. Eschewing a simple recommendation to look to other economies for a model that can be transplanted, each nation should attempt to introduce its own type of skills society. They suggest a wide-ranging model in which skills are an important component, but not the most important one (2005:167):

- a relatively high proportion of intermediate and high-skilled jobs, alongside greater levels of autonomy and participation at work;
- a more equal distribution of income;
- better provision and more equal access to welfare, health and education;
- strong labour and social rights;
- relatively high-waged.

These criteria reach not only into most aspects of workplace organisation but also into the way societies are structured, a debate that would be considered natural in a text on education but which is rarely referred to in works on human resource development. Yet building or restricting workplace skills can dramatically affect workers' life chances, so it is difficult to claim that living standards, citizenship or the impact of skills and work structures on communities are irrelevant here.

What then of the future? It should come as no surprise to learn that there is no automatic answer. Neither technology, nor organisational structures, nor knowledge work, nor human resource management, nor any of the other elements of work discussed here exert a deterministic force that is sufficient to pull an economy into knowledge-intensive work or push it into deskilling. Employees, firms, sectors and national governments all make choices of which some increase workplace skills and some decrease them. The optimistic message may be that there are still choices to be made. The skill and knowledge an individual possesses has an influence that extends beyond the economic success or otherwise of the organisation that employs them. Health, life expectancy, status and earnings may all depend, at least in part on education, and skill levels. This is too important an issue to leave to individual firms or workers in the hope that whatever decision is economically rational for them at the time will also benefit society as a whole. It would be nice to believe that, in future, such choices will seek to improve working lives, to support citizenship and to pursue social justice as well as to protect profits.

Bibliography

Abbott, A. (1988) *The System of Professions*. University of Chicago Press.

Ackers, P. and D. Preston (1997) 'Born again? The ethics and efficacy of the conversion experience in contemporary management development', *Journal of Management Studies* 34(5):677–702.

Ackroyd, S. (1995) 'From public administration to public sector management: a consideration of public policy in the United Kingdom.' *International Journal of Public Sector Management* 8(2):4–24.

Ackroyd, S. and P.A. Crowdy (1990) 'Can culture be managed? Working with "raw" material: the case of the English slaughterman', *Personnel Review* 19(5):3–13.

Ackroyd, S. and I. Kirkpatrick (2003) 'Transforming the professional archetype: the new managerialism in the UK public services.' *Public Management Review* 5(4):509–9.

Ackroyd, S. and S. Procter (1998) 'British manufacturing organisations and workplace relations – some attributes of the new flexible firm', *British Journal of Industrial Relations* 36(2):163–83.

Ackroyd, S. and P. Thompson (1999) *Organizational Misbehaviour*. London: Sage.

Adair, K. (2004) 'Knowledge management: a misjudged instrument of strategic change?' *Organization* 11(4):565–74.

Adkins, L. (1992) 'Sexual work and the employment of women in the service industries', in *Gender and Bureaucracy*, edited by A. Witz and M. Savage. Oxford: Blackwell.

Adler, P. (1992) 'Introduction', in *Technology and the Future of Work*, edited by P. Adler. New York and Oxford: Oxford University Press.

Ainley, P. (1993) *Class and Skill: Changing divisions of Knowledge and Labour*. London and New York: Cassell.

Ainley, P. (1994) *Degrees of Difference*. London: Lawrence & Wishart.

Ainley, P. and M. Corney (1990) *Training for the Future: The Rise and Fall of the Manpower Services Commission*. London: Cassell.

Alasoimi, T. (2003) 'Promotion of workplace innovation – reflections on the Finnish workplace development', presented at the Future of Work/SKOPE/Centre for Organisation and Innovation Conference on Skills, Innovation and Performance, 31st March–1st April, Cumberland Lodge, Windsor Great Park.

Alberga, T., S. Tyson and D. Parsons (1997) 'An evaluation of the investors in people standard', *Human Resource Management Journal* 7(2):47–60.

Albert, S. and K. Bradley (1997) *Managing Knowledge: Experts, Agencies and Organisations*. Cambridge University Press.

Alimo-Metcalfe, B. and J. Alban-Metcalfe (2004) 'Leadership in public sector organisations', in *Leadership in Organizations: Current Issues and Future Trends*, edited by J. Storey. London and New York: Routledge.

Alimo-Metcalfe, B. and J. Alban-Metcalfe (2005) 'Leadership: time for a new direction?' *Leadership* 1(1):51–71.

Allen, S. (1997) 'What is work for? The right to work and the right to be idle', in *The Changing Shape of Work*, edited by R.K. Brown. Basingstoke: Macmillan.

Alvesson, M. (1993) 'Organisations as rhetoric: knowledge intensive firms and the struggle with ambiguity', *Journal of Management Studies* 30(6):997–1015.

Alvesson, M. (2000) 'Social identity and the problem of loyalty in knowledge-intensive companies', *Journal of Management Studies* 37(8):1101–23.

Alvesson, M. (2002) *Understanding Organizational Culture*. London: Sage.

Alvesson, M. and D. Karreman (2001) 'Odd couple: making sense of the curious concept of knowledge management', *Journal of Management Studies* 38(7):995–1018.

Alvesson, M. and S. Sveningsson (2003) 'Good visions, bad micro-management and ugly ambiguity: contradictions of (non-)leadership in a knowledge-intensive organization', *Organization Studies* (after 1 January 2003) 24(6):961–88.

Alvesson, M. and P. Thompson (2005) 'Post-bureaucracy?', in *Oxford Handbook of Work and Organization*, edited by S. Ackroyd, R. Batt, P. Thompson and P.S. Tolbert. Oxford and New York: Oxford University Press.

Alvesson, M. and H. Willmott (1992) *Critical Management Studies*. London: Sage.

Anderson-Connolly, R., L. Grunberg, E.S. Greenberg and S. Moore (2002) 'Is lean mean? workplace transformation and employee well-being', *Work, Employment and Society* 16(3):389–413.

Anderson-Gough, F., C. Grey and K. Robson (2000) 'In the name of the client: the service ethic in two professional service firms', *Human Relations* 53(9):1151–74.

Andrews, C.K., C.D. Lair and B. Landry (2005) 'The labour process in software start-ups: production on a virtual assembly line?', in *Management, Labour Process and Software Development: Reality Bytes*, edited by R. Barrett. Abingdon: Routledge.

Anthony, P.D. (1986) *The Foundation of Management*. London: Tavistock.

Anthony, P.D. (1994) *Managing Culture*. Buckingham: Open University Press.

Antonacopoulou, E.P. (2001) 'The paradoxical nature of the relationship between training and learning.' *Journal of Management Studies* 38(3).

Applebaum, E., T. Bailey, P. Berg and A.L. Kalleberg (2000) *Manufacturing Advantage: Why High Performance Work Systems Pay Off*. Ithaca, NY and London: Cornell University Press.

Appleyard, M.A. (1996) 'How does knowledge flow? Interfirm patterns in the semi-conductor industry', *Management Learning* 17 (Winter special issue):137–54.

Armstrong, P. (1987) 'The abandonment of productive intervention in management teaching syllabi: an historical analysis', in *Warwick Papers in Industrial Relations*. Coventry: University of Warwick.

Armstrong, P. (1989) 'Management, Labour Process and Agency.' *Work, Employment and Society* 3(3):307–22.

Armstrong, P. (2001) 'Entrepreneurship.' Presented at ESRC Seminar on the Changing Nature of Skills and Knowledge, 3rd–4th September, Manchester.

Arthur, J.B. (1999) 'Explaining variation in human resource practices in US steel mini-mills', in *Employment Practices and Business Strategy*, edited by P. Cappelli. Oxford and New York: Oxford University Press.

Ashburner, L. and L. Fitzgerald (1996) 'Beleaguered professionals: clinicians and institutional change in the NHS', in *The Management of Expertise*, edited by H. Scarborough. Basingstoke: Macmillan.

Ashkenas, R., D. Ulrich, T. Jick and S. Kerr (1995) *The Boundaryless Organisation*. San Francisco, CA: Jossey-Bass.

Ashton, D. (2004) 'The political economy of workplace learning', in *Workplace Learning in Context*, edited by H. Rainbird, A. Fuller and A. Munro. London and New York: Routledge.

Ashton, D. and A. Felstead (1995, 1st edn) 'Training and Development', in *Human Resource Management: A Critical Text*, edited by J. Storey. London and New York: Routledge.

Ashton, D. and F. Green (1996) *Education, Training and the Global Economy*. Cheltenham: Elgar.

Ashton, D. and J. Sung (1994) 'The State, Economic Development and Skill Formation: A New Asian Model?', *Working Paper 3*. Leicester: Centre for Labour Market Studies, University of Leicester.

Atkinson, J. (1984) 'Manpower strategies for flexible organisations', *Personnel Management*.

Attewell, P. (1990) 'What is skill?', *Work and Occupations* 17(4):422–448.

Attewell, P. (1992) 'Skill and occupational change in US manufacturing', in *Technology and the Future of Work*, edited by P. Adler. Oxford University Press.

Baccaro, L. (2003) 'What is alive and what is dead in the theory of corporatism', *British Journal of Industrial Relations* 41(4):683–706.

Bach, S. (2005) 'Personnel management in transition', in *Managing Human Resources: Personnel Management in Transition*, edited by S. Bach. Oxford: Blackwell.

Bach, S. and K. Sisson (2000) 'Personnel Management in Perspective', in *Personnel Management*, edited by S. Bach and K. Sisson. Oxford: Blackwell.

Backes-Gellner, U., B. Frick and D. Sadowski (1997) 'Codetermination and personnel policies of German firms: the influence of works councils on turnover and further training', *International Journal of Human Resource Management* 8(3):328–47.

Bacon, N. (1999) 'Union de-recognition and the new human relations: a steel industry case study', *Work, Employment and Society* 13(1):1–17.

Bacon, N. and P. Blyton (2000) 'The diffusion of teamworking and new working practices: what role do industrial relations factors play?' in *Teamworking*, edited by S. Procter and F. Mueller. Basingstoke: Macmillan.

Bacon, N. and P. Blyton (2003) 'Teamwork and skill trajectories: a longitudinal study of who wins, who loses', *Human Resource Management Journal* 13(2):13–29.

Bamber, G. (1986) *Militant Managers*. Aldershot: Gower.

Barnard, C. (1962) *The Functions of the Executive*. Cambridge, MA: Harvard University Press.

Barrett, R. (2004) 'Working at Webboyz: an analysis of control over the software development labour process', *Sociology* 38(4):777–94.

Barrett, R. (2005a) 'Introduction: myth and reality', in *Management, Labour Process and Software Development: Reality Bytes*, edited by R. Barrett. Abingdon: Routledge.

Barrett, R. (2005b) 'Managing the software development labour process: direct control, time and technical autonomy', in *Management, Labour Process and Software Development: Reality Bytes*, edited by R. Barrett. Abingdon: Routledge.

Batt, R. (2000) 'Strategic segmentation in front-line services: matching customers, employees and human resource systems', *International Journal of Human Resource Management* 11(3):540–61.

Batt, R. and V. Doellgast (2005) 'Groups, teams and the division of labour: interdisciplinary perspectives on the organization of work', in *Oxford Handbook of Work and Organization*, edited by S. Ackroyd, R. Batt, P. Thompson and P.S. Tolbert. Oxford and New York: Oxford University Press.

Batt, R. and J. Keefe (1999) 'Human resource and employment practices in telecommunications services', in *Employment Practices and Business Strategy*, edited by P. Cappelli. Oxford University Press.

Baumann, A. (2002) 'Informal labour market governance: the case of the British and German media production industries', *Work, Employment and Society* 16(1):27–46.

Baxter, L. (2000) 'Bugged: the software development process', in *Managing Knowledge: Critical Investigations of Work and Learning*, edited by C. Prichard, R. Hull, M. Chumer and H. Willmott. Basingstoke: Macmillan.

Beaumont, G. (1995) *Review of 100 NVQs and SVQs*. London: NCVQ/SCOTVEC.

Becker, G.S. (1964) *Human Capital: A Theoretical Analysis with Special Reference to Education*. New York: Columbia University Press.

Becker, M.C. (2001) 'Managing dispersed knowledge: organisational problems, managerial strategies and their effectiveness', *Journal of Management Studies* 38(7):1037–51.

Beech, N., R. MacIntosh, D. MacLean, J. Shepherd and J. Stokes (2002) 'Exploring constraints on developing knowledge: on the need for conflict', *Management Learning* 33(4):459–75.

Belanger, J., P.K. Edwards and M. Wright (2003) 'Commitment at work and independence from management: a study of advanced teamwork', *Work and Occupations* 30(2):234–52.

Bell, D. (1973) *The Coming of Post-Industrial Society*. New York: Basic Books.

Bell, D. (1974) 'Notes on the post-industrial society', in *Man-Made Futures*, edited by N. Cross, D. Elliott and R. Roy. London: Hutchinson.

Benders, J. (2005) 'Team working: a tale of partial participation', in *Participation and Democracy at Work: Essays in Honour of Harvie Ramsay*, edited by B. Harley, J. Hyman and P. Thompson. Basingstoke: Palgrave Macmillan.

Bennett, R., H. Glennerster and D. Nevison (1992) *Learning Should Pay*. Poole: British Petroleum.

Berger, P. and T. Luckmann (1967) *The Social Construction of Reality: A Treatise in the Sociology of Knowledge*. London: Penguin.

Beynon, H. (1975) *Working for Ford*. Wakefield: EP Publishing.

Biddle, J.E. and D.S. Hamermesh (1998) 'Beauty, productivity and discrimination: lawyers' looks and lucre', *Journal of Labour Economics* 16(1):172–201.

Bierly, P. and A. Chakrabarti (1996) 'Generic knowledge strategies in the US pharmaceutical industry', *Strategic Management Journal* 17 (Winter special issue): 123–35.

Biggart, N.W. (1989) *Charismatic Capitalism: Direct Selling Organisations in America*. University of Chicago Press.

Blackler, F. (1993) 'Knowledge and the theory of organisations: organisation as activity systems and the reframing of management', *Journal of Management Studies* 30(6):863–84.

Blackler, F. (1995) 'Knowledge, knowledge work and organisations: an overview an interpretation', *Organization Studies* 16(6):1021–46.

Blackler, F., N. Crump and S. McDonald (2000) 'Organising processes in complex activity networks', *Organization* 7(2):277–300.

Blackler, F., M. Reed and A. Whitaker (1993) 'Editorial introduction: knowledge workers and contemporary organisations', *Journal of Management Studies* 30(6):851–62.

Blair, H. (2001) 'You're only as good as your last job: the labour process and labour market in the British film industry', *Work, Employment and Society* 15(1):149–69.

Blake, R.R. and J.S. Mouton (1964) *The Managerial Grid*. Houston, TX: Gulf Publishing.

Block, F. (1990) *Post-Industrial Possibilities: A Critique of Economic Discourse*. Berkeley: University of California Press.

Bluhm, K. (2001) 'Exporting or abandoning the "German Model"? Labour policies of German manufacturing firms in Central Europe', *European Journal of Industrial Relations* 7(2):153–73.

Blyton, P. and P. Turnbull (2004) *The Dynamics of Employee Relations*. Basingstoke: Palgrave Macmillan.

Bolton, S.C. (2000) 'Emotion here, emotion there, emotional organisations everywhere', *Critical Perspectives on Accounting* 11:155–71.

Bolton, S.C. (2004a) 'Conceptual confusions: emotion work as skilled work', in *The Skills that Matter*, edited by C. Warhurst, I. Grugulis and E. Keep. Basingstoke: Palgrave Macmillan.

Bolton, S.C. (2004b) 'A Simple Matter of Control? NHS Hospital Nurses and New Management.' *Journal of Management Studies* 41(2):317–33.

Bolton, S.C. (2005a) *Emotion Management in the Workplace*. Basingstoke: Palgrave Macmillan.

Bolton, S.C. (2005b) '"Making up" managers: the case of NHS nurses', *Work, Employment and Society* 19(1):5–23.

Booth, A. and D.J. Snower (1996) 'Does the free market produce enough skills?' in *Acquiring Skills*, edited by A. Booth and D.J. Snower. Cambridge University Press.

Bosch, G. (2003) 'Skills and innovation – a German perspective', presented at the Future of Work/SKOPE/Centre for Organisation and Innovation Conference on Skills, Innovation and Performance, 31st March–1st April, Cumberland Lodge, Windsor Great Park.

Bosch, G. (2004) 'Towards a new standard employment relationship in Western Europe', *British Journal of Industrial Relations* 42(4):617–36.

Bosch, G. (2005) 'Employability, innovation and lifelong learning', Presented at Second International Conference on Training, Employability and Employment, 21st–23rd September, Prato.

Bosworth, D. (1999) 'Empirical Evidence of Management Skills in the UK', *DfEE Working Paper*. Sheffield.

Bowles, S. and H. Gintis (1976) *Schooling in Capitalist America: Educational Reform and the Contradictions of Economic Life*. New York: Basic Books.

Boxall, P. and J. Purcell (2003) *Strategy and Human Resource Management*. London: Palgrave.

Boyatzis, R.E. (1982) *The Competent Manager*. New York: Wiley.

Boyne, G.A. (2003) 'What is public service improvement?', *Public Administration* 81(2):211–27.

Boyne, G., R. Ashworth and M. Powell (2001) 'Environmental change, leadership succession and incrementalism in local government.' *Journal of Management Studies* 38(6):859–78.

Bradley, H., M. Erickson, C. Stephenson and S. Williams (2000) *Myths at Work*. Cambridge: Polity Press.

Braverman, H. (1974) *Labour and Monopoly Capital*. New York: Monthly Review Press.

Brewis, J. and J. Sinclair (2000) 'Exploring embodiment: women, biology and work', in *Body and Organisation*, edited by J. Hassard, R. Holliday and H. Willmott. London: Sage.

Brockington, D. (2002) 'Key skills within the National Qualifications Framework 14–19', *SKOPE Research Paper*. Universities of Oxford and Warwick.

Brodo, S. (1989) 'The body and the reproduction of femininity', in *Gender, Body, Knowledge*, edited by A. Jaggar and S. Brodo. New Brunswick: Rutgers University Press.

Brooks, I. (1999) 'Managerialist professionalism: the destruction of a non-conforming subculture.' *British Journal of Management* 10(1):41–52.

Brown, A. (2001) 'Supporting learning in advanced supply systems in automotive and aerospace industries', presented at Joint Network/SKOPE/ TLPRP international workshop, 8th–10th November, University College Northampton.

Brown, A. and S. Kirpal (2004) 'Old nurses with new qualifications are best: competing ideas about the skills that matter in nursing in Estonia, France, Germany and the UK', in *The Skills That Matter*, edited by C. Warhurst, I. Grugulis and E. Keep. Basingstoke: Palgrave Macmillan.

Brown, J.S. and P. Duguid (2001) 'Structure and spontaneity: knowledge and organisation', in *Managing Industrial Knowledge*, edited by I. Nonaka and D. Teece. London: Sage.

Brown, J.S. and P. Duguid (2002) 'Local knowledge: innovation in the Networked Age', *Management Learning* 33(4):427–37.

Brown, P. (2001) 'Skill formation in the twenty-first century', in *High Skills: Globalization, Competitiveness and Skill Formation*, edited by P. Brown, A. Green and H. Lauder. Oxford University Press.

Brown, P. and A. Hesketh (2004) *The Mismanagement of Talent: Employability and Jobs in the Knowledge Economy*. Oxford University Press.

Brown, P., A. Green and H. Lauder (2001) *High Skills: Globalization, Competitiveness and Skill Formation*. Oxford University Press.

Brown, R. (1997) 'Introduction: work and employment in the 1990s', *The Changing Shape of Work*, edited by R.K. Brown. Basingstoke: Macmillan.

Brusoni, S. and A. Prencipe (2001) 'Managing knowledge in loosely coupled networks, exploring the links between product and knowledge dynamics', *Journal of Management Studies* 38(7):1019–35.

Buchanan, J. and J. Evesson (2004a) 'Creating markets or decent jobs? Group training and the future of work', in *Australia National Training Authority, NCVER*. Adelaide.

Buchanan, J. and J. Evesson (2004b) 'Redefining skill and solidarity at work: insights from Group Training Arrangements in Australia', Presented at 22nd International Labour Process Conference, 5th–7th April, Amsterdam.

Buechtemann, C. (1993) 'Introduction: employment security and labour markets', in *Employment Security and Labor Market Behavior*, edited by C. Buechtemann. Ithaca, NY: ILR Press.

Bunting, M. (2004) *Willing Slaves: How the Overwork Culture Is Ruling Our Lives*. London: HarperCollins.

Burawoy, M. (1979) *Manufacturing Consent*. London: University of Chicago Press.

Burchell, B., J. Elliot, J. Rubery and F. Wilkinson (1994) 'Management and employee perceptions of skill', in *Skill and Occupational Change*, edited by R. Penn, M. Rose and J. Rubery. Oxford University Press.

Burke, J.W. (1989) 'Introduction', in *Competency Based Education and Training*, edited by J.W. Burke. London: Falmer.

Butterwick, S. (2003) 'Life skills training: "open for discussion"', in *Training the excluded for Work*, edited by M.G. Cohen. Vancouver and Toronto: UBC Press.

Buyens, D. and A. De Vos (2001) 'Perceptions of the value of the HR function', *Human Resource Management Journal* 11(3):70–89.

Callaghan, G. and P. Thompson (2002) 'We recruit attitude: the selection and shaping of routine call centre labour', *Journal of Management Studies* 39(2):233–54.

Callendar, C. (1992) *Will NVQs work? Evidence from the construction industry*, Sussex: University of Sussex/Institute of Manpower Studies.

Cappelli, P. (1995a) 'Is the "skills gap" really about attitudes?' *California Management Review* 37(4):108–24.

Cappelli, P. (1995b) 'Rethinking employment', *British Journal of Industrial Relations* 33(4):563–602.

Cappelli, P. (2001) 'The new deal with employees and its implications for business strategy', in *Strategy, Organisations and the Changing Nature of Work*, edited by J. Gual and J.E. Ricart. Cheltenham: Elgar.

Carlson, S. (1951) *Executive Behaviour*. Stockholm: Strombergs.

Carlzon, J. (1987) *The Moment of Truth*. Cambridge, MA: Ballinger.

Carroll, S.J. and D.J. Gillen (1987) 'Are the classical managerial functions useful in describing managerial work?' *Academy of Management Review* 12(1):38–51.

Carroll, M., F.L. Cooke, I. Grugulis, J. Rubery and J. Earnshaw (2001) 'Analysing diversity in the management of human resources in call centres', Presented at the Human Resource Management Journal conference Call Centres and Beyond: the HRM implications, 6th November, Kings College London.

Casciaro, T. and M.S. Lobo (2005) 'Competent jerks, lovable fools and the formation of social networks', *Harvard Business Review* 83(6):92–9.

Casey, C. (1995) *Work, Self and Society: After Industrialism*. London and New York: Routledge.

Castells, M. (1996) *The Rise of the Network Society*. Oxford: Blackwell.

Castro, C. and E. Neira (2005) 'Knowledge transfer: analysis of three internet acquisitions', *International Journal of Human Resource Management* 16(1):120–35.

Caulkin, S. (2005) 'The red herring of red tape', *Observer*. London, 29 May p. 10.

CEML (2002) *Managers and Leaders: Raising our Game*. Council for Education in Management and Leadership. http://www.managementandleadershipcouncil.org

Chikudate, N. (1999) 'The state of collective myopia in Japanese business communities: a phenomenological study for exploring blocking mechanisms for change', *Journal of Management Studies* 36(1):69–86.

Child, J. (1969) *British Management Thought: A Critical Analysis*. London: Allen & Unwin.

Chumer, M., R. Hull and C. Prichard (2000) 'Introduction: situating discussions about "knowledge"', in *Managing Knowledge: Critical Investigations of Work and Learning*, edited by C. Pritchard, R. Hull, M. Chumer and H. Willmott. Basingstoke: Macmillan.

Clark, J. (1993) 'Full flexibility and self supervision in an automated factory', in *Human Resource Management and Technical Change*, edited by J. Clark. London: Sage.

Clark, T. and G. Salaman (1998) 'Telling Tales: Management Gurus' Narratives and the Construction of Managerial Identity.' *Journal of Management Studies* 35(2):137–61.

Clarke, L. and C. Wall (1996) *Skills and the Construction Process: A Comparative Study of Vocational Training and Quality in Social Housebuilding*. Bristol: Policy Press.

Clarke, L. and C. Wall (1998) 'UK construction skills in the context of European developments', *Construction Management and Economics* 16:553–67.

Clarke, L. and C. Wall (2000) 'Craft versus industry: the division of labour in European housing construction', *Construction Management and Economics* 18:689–98.

Clarke, S. and T. Metalina (2000) 'Training in the new private sector in Russia', *International Journal of Human Resource Management* 11(1):19–36.

Clayman, M. (1987) 'In search of excellence: the investor's viewpoint', *Financial Analysts Journal* 33:54–63.

Cockburn, C. (1983) *Brothers: Male Dominance and Technological Change*. London: Pluto Press.

Cockburn, C. (1987) *Two-Track Training: Sex Inequalities and the YTS*. Basingstoke: Macmillan.

Coffield, F. (2002) *A New Strategy for Learning and Skills: Beyond 101 Initiatives*. Newcastle: University of Newcastle, Department of Education.

Cohen, M.G. (2003) *Training the Excluded for Work*. Vancouver and Toronto: UBC Press.

Cole, R.E. (1992) 'Issues in skill formation in Japanese approaches to automation', in *Technology and the Future of Work*, edited by P. Adler. New York and Oxford University Press.

Collins, D. (1997) 'Knowledge work or working knowledge? Ambiguity and confusion in the analysis of the "knowledge age"', *Employee Relations* 19(1):38–50.

Collinson, D. (1992) *Managing the Shopfloor*. Berlin: de Gruyter.

Collinson, D., D. Knights and M. Collinson (1990) *Managing to Discriminate*. London and New York: Routledge.

Conniff, R. (1994) 'Big bad welfare: welfare reform politics and children', *Progressive* 58(8):18–21.

Contu, A. and H. Willmott (2000) 'Comment on Wenger and Yarrow. Knowing in practice, a delicate flower in the organisational learning field', *Organization* 7(2):269–76.

Cook, E. (1997) 'Fattism: a hard act to swallow', *Independent on Sunday*, 17 August.

Coopers and Lybrand Associates (1985) *A Challenge to Complacency: Changing Attitudes to Training*. London: Manpower Services Commission and National Economic Development Office.

Corbett, J.M. (1996) 'Designing jobs with advanced manufacturing technology: the negotiation of expertise', in *The Management of Expertise*, edited by H. Scarborough. Basingstoke: Macmillan.

Corby, S. and G. White (1999) 'From the New Right to New Labour', in *Employee Relations in the Public Sector: Themes and Issues*, edited by S. Corby and G. White. London and New York: Routledge and Cardiff University.

Coupland, D. (1995) *Micro-serfs*. London: Harper Perennial.

Craig, D. (2005) *Rip-Off! The Scandalous Inside Story of the Management Consulting Money Machine*. London: Original Book Company.

Crenin, C.S. (2003) 'Self-starters, can do-ers and mobile phoneys: situations vacant columns and the personality culture in employment', *Sociological Review*:109–28.

Crompton, R. and G. Jones (1984) *White Collar Proletariat: Deskilling and Gender in the Clerical Labour Process*. London: Macmillan.

Crouch, C. (2005) 'Skill formation systems', in *Oxford Handbook of Work and Organization*, edited by S. Ackroyd, R. Batt, P. Thompson and P.S. Tolbert. Oxford and New York: Oxford University Press.

Crouch, C., D. Finegold and M. Sako (1999) *Are Skills the Answer? The Political Economy of Skill Creation in Advanced Industrialised Countries*. Oxford University Press.

Culkin, N., K. Randle and P. von Sychowski (2005) *Facing the Digital Future: The Implications of Digital Technology for the Film Industry*. Hatfield: University of Hertfordshire.

Cully, M., S. Woodland, A. O'Reilly and G. Dix (1999) *Britain at Work: As Depicted by the 1998 Workplace Employee Relations Survey*. London: Routledge.

Culpepper, P.D. (1999) 'The future of the high-skill equilibrium in Germany', *Oxford Review of Economic Policy* 15(1):43–59.

Cunliffe, A.L. (2001) 'Managers as practical authors: reconstructing our understanding of management practice.' *Journal of Management Studies* 38(3):351–71.

Cunningham, I., J. Hyman and C. Baldry (1996) 'Empowerment: the power to do what?' *Industrial Relations Journal* 27(2):143–54.

Currie, G. (1999) 'The influence of middle managers in the business planning process: a case study in the UK NHS.' *British Journal of Management* 10(2):141–55.

Cyert, R.M. and J.G. March (1963) *A Behavioural Theory of the Firm*. Englewood Cliffs, NJ: Prentice-Hall.

Dalton, M. (1966) *Men Who Manage*. New York and London: Wiley.

Danford, A. (1997) 'Teamworking and labour regulation: a case study of shop floor disempowerment', Presented at 15th International Labour Process Conference, Edinburgh.

Danford, A. (2003) 'Workers, unions and the high performance workplace', *Work, Employment and Society* 17(3):569–73.

Danford, A. (2005) 'New union strategies and forms of work organisation in UK manufacturing', in *Participation and Democracy at Work: Essays in Honour of Harvie Ramsay*, edited by B. Harley, J. Hyman and P. Thompson. Basingstoke: Palgrave Macmillan.

Darr, A. (2002) 'The technicization of sales work: an ethnographic study in the US electronics industry', *Work, Employment and Society* 16(1):47–65.

Darr, A. (2004) 'The interdependence of social and technical skills in the sale of emergent technology', in *The Skills that Matter*, edited by C. Warhurst, I. Grugulis and E. Keep. Basingstoke: Palgrave Macmillan.

Davenport, T.H. and P. Klahr (1998) 'Managing customer support knowledge', *California Management Review* 40(3):195–208.

de Wolff, A. and M. Hynes (2003) 'Snakes and ladders: coherence in training for office workers', in *Training the Excluded for Work: Access and Equity for Women, Immigrants and First Nations, Youth and People with Low Income*, edited by M.G. Cohen. Vancouver and Toronto: UBC Press.

Deal, T. and A. Kennedy (1982) *Corporate Cultures*. Harmondsworth: Penguin.

Dearden, L., S. McIntosh, M. Myck and A. Vignoles (2000) *The Returns to Academic, Vocational and Basic Skills in Britain*. Sheffield: DfEE.

Debrah, Y.A. and G. Ofori (2001) 'The state, skill formation and productivity enhancement in the construction industry: the case of Singapore', *International Journal of Human Resource Management* 12(2):184–202.

Del Bono, E. and K. Mayhew (2001) 'The specification and quality of British products', *SKOPE Research Paper*. Universities of Oxford and Warwick.

Delbridge, R. (1998) *Life on the Line in Contemporary Manufacturing*. Oxford University Press.

Delbridge, R. and J. Lowe (1997) 'Manufacturing control: supervisory systems on the "new" shopfloor.' *Sociology* 31(3):409–26.

Delbridge, R., J. Lowe and N. Oliver (2000) 'Worker autonomy in lean teams: evidence from the world automotive components industry', in *Teamworking*, edited by S. Procter and F. Mueller. Basingstoke: Macmillan.

Dench, S., S. Perryman and L. Giles (1999) 'Employers' perceptions of key skills', in *IES Report*. Sussex: Institute of Manpower Studies.

Department for Education and Skills (2001) *Modern Apprenticeships: The Way to Work.* Sudbury: DfES.

Department for Education and Skills (2003) *Statistics of Education: Education and Training Statistics for the United Kingdom.* London: TSO.

Department for Education and Skills (2004a) 'First Release: Participation in Education, Training and Employment by 16–18 year olds in England: 2002 and 2003', London.

Department for Education and Skills (2004b) *Skills Alliance: Skills Strategy Progress Report.* Nottingham: DfES.

Department for Education and Skills/DTI/HM Treasury/Department for Work and Pensions (2003) *21st Century Skills, Realising our Potential: Individuals, Employers, Nation.* Norwich: HMSO.

Dickerson, A. and F. Green (2002) 'The growth and valuation of generic skills', *SKOPE Research Paper.* Universities of Oxford and Warwick.

DiNardo, J. and J.S. Pische (1997) 'The returns to computer use revisited: have pencils changed the wage structure too?' *Quarterly Journal of Economics* 112:291–303.

Diprete, T.A. (2005) 'Labour markets, inequality and change: a European perspective', *Work and Occupations* 32(2):119–39.

Dispatches (1993) 'All our futures?' Channel 4, 15 December.

Dixon, N.F. (1994) *On the Psychology of Military Incompetence.* London: Pimlico.

Domagalski, T.A. (1999) 'Emotion in organisations: main currents', *Human Relations* 52(6):833–852.

Dopson, S. and R. Stewart (1990) 'What is happening to middle management?', *British Journal of Management* 1(1):3–16.

Doray, B. (1988) *From Taylorism to Fordism: A Rational Madness.* London: Free Association.

Dore, R. and M. Sako (1989) *How the Japanese Learn to Work*: Nissan Institute/Routledge.

Driscoll, A. and J. Morris (2001) 'Stepping out: rhetorical devices and culture change management in the UK civil service', *Public Administration* 79(4):803–824.

Drucker, P.F. (1993) *Post Capitalist Society.* Oxford: Butterworth-Heinemann.

DTZ Pieda Consulting (1999) *Evaluation of the IiP Small Firms Development Projects* (No. RR135) Nottingham: DfEE.

du Gay, P. (1996) *Consumption and Identity at Work.* London: Sage.

du Gay, P. (2000) *In Praise of Bureaucracy.* London: Sage.

du Gay, P., G. Salaman and B. Rees (1996) 'The conduct of management and the management of conduct: contemporary managerial discourse and the constitution of the "competent" manager', *Journal of Management Studies* 33(3):263–82.

Dundon, T., I. Grugulis and A. Wilkinson (2001) 'New management techniques in small and medium-sized enterprises', in *Contemporary Human Resource Management,* edited by T. Redman and A. Wilkinson. London: Financial Times Prentice-Hall.

Dyerson, R. and F.U. Mueller (1999) 'Learning, teamwork and appropriability: managing technological change in the department of social security', *Journal of Management Studies* 36(5):629–52.

Eaton, S.C. (1996) '"The customer is always interesting": unionised Harvard clericals renegotiate work relationships', in *Working in the Service Society*, edited by C.L. Macdonald and C. Sirianni. Philadelphia, PA: Temple University Press.

Ebbinghaus, B. and B. Kittel (2005) 'European rigidity versus American flexibility? The institutional adaptability of collective bargaining', *Work and Occupations* 32(2):163–95.

Edwards, P. (1995) 'The employment relationship', in *Industrial Relations: Theory and Practice in Britain*, edited by P. Edwards. Oxford: Blackwell.

Edwards, P. (2001) 'The puzzle of work: autonomy and commitment plus discipline and insecurity' Skope Research Paper. Universities of Oxford and Warwick.

Edwards, P. (2003) 'The employment relationship and the field of industrial relations', *Industrial Relations: Theory and Practice*, edited by P. Edwards. Oxford: Blackwell.

Edwards, P. and M. Collinson (2002) 'Empowerment and managerial labour strategies: pragmatism regained', *Work and Occupations* 29(3):272–99.

Edwards, P. and H. Scullion (1982) *The Social Organisation of Industrial Conflict*. Oxford: Blackwell.

Edwards, P. and J. Wajcman (2005) *The Politics of Working Life*. Oxford University Press.

Edwards, P., M. Collinson and C. Rees (1998) 'The determinants of employee responses to total quality management: six case studies', *Organization Studies* 19(3):449–75.

Edwards, P., M. Gilman, M. Ram and J. Arrowsmith (2002) 'Public policy, the performance of firms and the "missing middle": the case of the employment regulations and a role for local business networks', *Policy Studies* 23(1):5–20.

Edwards, R. (1979) *Contested Terrain*. London: Heinemann.

Edwards, T. (1998) 'Multinationals, labour management and the process of reverse diffusion: a case study', *International Journal of Human Resource Management* 9(4):696–709.

Edwards, T. and A. Ferner (2002) 'The renewed "American Challenge": a review of employment practices in US multinationals', *Industrial Relations Journal* 33(2):94–111.

Elias, P. and K. Purcell (2003) 'Measuring Change in the Graduate Labour Market', in *Researching Graduate Careers Seven Years On*. Bristol and Warwick: Employment Studies Research Unit, University of the West of England and Warwick Institute for Employment Research.

Employment and Productivity Gazette (1968) Statistics. 60–1.

Employment Department (1992) 'Clerical and secretarial skills: a neglected resource?' in *Skills and Enterprise Briefing*.

Eraut, M. and G. Cole (1993) 'Assessing Competence in the Professions', in *Technical Report*. Sheffield: Employment Department, Methods Strategy Unit.

Eraut, M., S. Steadman, J. Trill and J. Parkes (1996) 'The Assessment of NVQs', in *Research Report*. Brighton: University of Sussex.

Erickson, B.H., P. Albanese and S. Drakulic (2000) 'Gender on a jagged edge: the security industry, its clients and the reproduction and revision of gender', *Work and Occupations* 27(3):294–318.

Esping-Andersen, G. (1999) *Social Foundations of Postindustrial Economies*. Oxford University Press.

Etzioni, A. (1961) *A Comparative Analysis of Complex Organisations*. New York: Free Press.

Evetts, J. (2002) 'New directions in state and international professional occupations: discretionary decision making and acquired regulation', *Work, Employment and Society* 16(2):341–53.

Fayol, H. (1949) *General and Industrial Management*. London: Pitman.

Federal Statistical Office, G (2005) 'Press Release',

Felstead, A. and D. Ashton (2000) 'Tracing the link: organisational structures and skill demands', *Human Resource Management Journal* 10(3):5–21.

Felstead, A., D. Ashton and F. Green (2000) 'Are Britain's workplace skills becoming more unequal?' *Cambridge Journal of Education* 24(6):709–27.

Felstead, A., D. Gallie and F. Green (2002) *Work Skills in Britain 1986–2002*. Nottingham: DfES.

Felstead, A., D. Gallie and F. Green (2004) 'Job complexity and task discretion: tracking the direction of skills at work in Britain', in *The Skills that Matter*, edited by C. Warhurst, I. Grugulis and E. Keep. Basingstoke: Palgrave Macmillan.

Fenton-O'Creevy, M. (1995) 'Empowerment', in *Blackwell Encyclopaedic Dictionary of Organizational Behaviour*, edited by N. Nicholson. Cambridge, MA: Blackwell.

Fernandez, R.M., S. Taylor and E. Bell (2005) 'How long until we get there? A survival analysis of the Investors in People initiative 1991–2001', *SKOPE Research Paper*. Universities of Oxford and Warwick.

Ferner, A. (1997) 'Country of origin effects and HRM in multinational companies', *Human Resource Management Journal* 7(1):19–37.

Ferner, A. and J. Quintanilla (1998) 'Multinationals, national business systems and HRM: the enduring influence of national identity or a process of "Anglo-Saxonisation"', *International Journal of Human Resource Management* 9(4):710–31.

Ferner, A. and M.Z. Varul (2000a) 'Internationalisation of the personnel function in German multinationals', *Human Resource Management Journal* 10(3):79–96.

Ferner, A. and M.Z. Varul (2000b) '"Vanguard" subsidiaries and the diffusion of new practices: a case study of German multinationals', *British Journal of Industrial Relations* 38(1):115–140.

Filby, M.P. (1992) 'The figures, the personality and the bums: service work and sexuality', *Work, Employment and Society* 6(1):23–42.

Findlay, P., A. McKinlay, A. Marks and P. Thompson (2000) '"Flexible when it suits them": the use and abuse of teamwork skills', in *Teamworking*, edited by S. Procter and F. Mueller. Basingstoke: Macmillan.

Finegold, D. (1991)' The implications of training in Britain for the analysis of Britain's skill problem: how much do employers spend on training?' *Human Resource Management Journal*, 2(1), 110–15.

Finegold, D. (1999) 'Creating self-sustaining, high-skill ecosystems', *Oxford Review of Economic Policy* 15(1):60–81.

Finegold, D. and D. Soskice (1988) 'The failure of training in Britain: analysis and prescription', *Oxford Review of Economic Policy* 4(3):21–43.

Finegold, D. and K. Wagner (1997) 'When lean production meets the German model: innovation responses in the US and German pump industries', *Industry and Innovation* 4(2):207–32.

Finegold, D. and K. Wagner (1998) 'The search for flexibility: skills and workplace innovation in the German pump industry', *British Journal of Industrial Relations* 36(3):469–87.

Finegold, D., K. Wagner and G. Mason (2000) 'National skill-creation systems and career paths for service workers: hotels in the United States, Germany and the United Kingdom', *International Journal of Human Resource Management* 11(3):497–516.

Fineman, S. (1993) 'Organisations as emotional arenas', in *Emotion in Organisations*, edited by S. Fineman. London: Sage.

Fineman, S. and Y. Gabriel (1996) *Experiencing Organisations*. London: Sage.

Fennell, E. (1993) 'As others will see us: the UK's qualifications system', *Competence and Assessment* 23:20–1.

Fischer, E., B. Gainer and J. Bristor (1997) 'The sex of the service provider: does it influence perceptions of service quality?' *Journal of Retailing* 73:361–82.

FitzRoy, F. and K. Kraft (2005) 'Co-determination, efficiency and productivity', *British Journal of Industrial Relations* 43(2):233–47.

Forde, C. and G. Slater (2005) 'Agency working in Britain: character, consequences and regulation', *British Journal of Industrial Relations* 43(2):249–71.

Foster, D. and P. Hoggett (1999) 'Change in the benefits agency: empowering the exhausted worker?', *Work, Employment and Society* 13(1):19–39.

Fountain, J.E. (2001) 'Paradoxes of public sector customer service', *Governance* 14(1):55–73.

Fox, A. (1966) *Industrial Sociology and Industrial Relations*. London: HMSO.

Fox, A. (1974) *Beyond Contract: Work, Power and Trust Relations*. London: Faber.

Fox, E.M. and L. Urwick (1973) *Dynamic Administration: The Collected Papers of Mary Parker Follett*. London: Pitman.

Francis, B. and R. Penn (1994) 'Towards a phenomenology of skill', in *Skill and Occupational Change*, edited by R. Penn, M. Rose and J. Rubery. Oxford University Press.

Freeman, R. (2005) 'What are the implications of globalization for worker well-being and trade unions?' presented at British Universities Industrial Relations Association, 7th–9th July, Northumbria University.

Freidson, E. (1988) *Professional Powers*. Chicago and London: University of Chicago Press.

Freidson, E. (1994) *Professionalism Reborn, Theory, Prophecy and Policy*. Cambridge: Polity Press.

French, S. (2001) 'Works councils in Germany. Still loyal to the trade unions?', *International Journal of Manpower* 22(6):560–78.

Frenkel, S., M. Korczynski, K.A. Shire and M. Tam (1999) *On the Front Line: organisation of work in the information economy*. Ithaca and London: Cornell University Press.

Friedman, A.L. (1977) *Industry and Labour: Class Struggle at Work and Monopoly Capitalism*. London: Macmillan.

Fruin, W.M. (1997) *Knowledge Works: Managing Intellectual Capital at Toshiba*. New York and Oxford University Press.

Fuller, A. and L. Unwin (2001) *From Cordwainers to Customer Service: the Changing Relationship between Apprentices, Employers and Communities in England*. Oxford and Warwick Universities, ESRC funded Centre on Skills, Knowledge and Organisational Performance.

Fuller, A. and L. Unwin (2004a) 'Expansive learning environments: integrating organisational and personal development', in *Workplace Learning in Context*, edited by H. Rainbird, A. Fuller and A. Munro. London and New York: Routledge.

Fuller, A. and L. Unwin (2004b) 'Does apprenticeship still have meaning in the UK? The consequences of voluntarism and sectoral change', in *Balancing the Skills Equation: Key Issues and Challenges for Policy and Practice*, edited by G. Hayward and S. James. Bristol: Policy Press.

Fuller, L. and V. Smith (1996) 'Consumers' reports: management by customers in a changing economy', in *Working in the Service Society*, edited by C.L. Macdonald and C. Sirianni. Philadelphia, PA: Temple University Press.

Gadrey, J. (2000) 'Working time configurations: theory, methods and assumptions for an international comparison', *Flexible Working in Food Retailing: A Comparison Between France, Germany, the UK and Japan*, edited by C. Baret, S. Lehndorff & L. Sparks. London and New York: Routledge.

Galbraith, J.K. (1983) *The Anatomy of Power*. London: Corgi Books.

Gallie, D. (1991) 'Patterns of skill change: upskilling, deskilling or the polarization of skills?' *Work, Employment and Society* 5(3):319–51.

Gallie, D. (1994) 'Patterns of skill change: upskilling, deskilling or polarisation?' in *Skill and Occupational Change*, edited by R. Penn, M. Rose and J. Rubery. Oxford University Press.

Gallie, D. (1996) 'Skill, gender and the quality of employment', in *Changing Forms of Employment: Organisations, Skills and Gender*, edited by R. Crompton, D. Gallie and K. Purcell. London: Routledge.

Gangl, M. (2005) 'Income inequality, permanent incomes and income dynamics: comparing Europe to the United States', *Work and Occupations* 32(2):140–62.

Garrahan, P. and P. Stewart (1992) *The Nissan Enigma: Flexibility at Work in a Local Economy*. London: Mansett.

Garvey, B. and B. Williamson (2002) *Beyond Knowledge Management*. Harlow: Financial Times Prentice-Hall.

Geary, J. (1994) 'Task participation: employees' participation enabled or constrained?' in *Personnel Management: A Comprehensive Guide to Theory and Practice in Britain*, edited by K. Sisson. Oxford: Blackwell.

Geary, J. (1995) 'Work practices: the structure of work', in *Industrial Relations: Theory and Practice in Britain*, edited by P.K. Edwards. Oxford: Blackwell.

Gerth, H. and C. Wright Mills (1948) *From Max Weber: Essays in Sociology*. London: Routledge & Kegan Paul.

Ghosal, S. and C. Bartlett (1998) *The Individualized Corporation.* London: Heinemann.

Glass, J.L. (1999) 'The tangled web we weave: editorial introduction to the special issue on ethnicity, race and gender in the workplace', *Work and Occupations* 26(4):415–21.

Glover, L. and M. Noon (2005) 'Shopfloor workers perceptions of the impact of quality management upon the quality of working life: some case study evidence', Presented at British Universities Industrial Relations Association, 7th–9th July, University of Northumbria.

Goffman, E. (1959) *The Presentation of Self in Everyday Life.* Harmondsworth: Penguin.

Gospel, H. (1998) 'The revival of apprenticeship training in Britain?', *British Journal of Industrial Relations* 36(3):435–57.

Gowler, D. and K. Legge (1983) 'The meaning of management and management of meaning: a view from social anthropology', in *Perspectives on Management,* edited by M.J. Earl. Oxford University Press.

Grant, R.M. (1996) 'Toward a knowledge-based theory of the firm', *Strategic Management Journal* 17 (Winter special issue):109–22.

Grant, R.M. (2001) 'Knowledge and organisation', in *Managing Industrial Knowledge,* edited by I. Nonaka and D. Teece. London: Sage.

Grant, R.M. and C. Baden-Fuller (2004) 'A knowledge accessing theory of strategic alliances', *Journal of Management Studies* 41(1):61–4.

Graves, D. (1986) *Corporate Culture – Diagnosis and Change.* London: Pinter.

Green, A. and A. Sakamoto (2001) 'Models of high skills in national competition strategies', in *High Skills: Globalisation, Competitiveness and Skill Formation,* edited by P. Brown, A. Green and H. Lauder. Oxford University Press.

Green, F. (2006) *Demanding Work: The Paradox of Job Quality in the Affluent Economy.* Princeton and Oxford: Princeton University Press.

Green, F. and D. Gallie (2002) 'High Skills and high anxiety: skills, hard work and mental well being', *SKOPE Research Paper.* Universities of Oxford and Warwick.

Green, F., D. Ashton, D. James and J. Sung (1999a) 'The role of the state in skill formation: evidence from the republic of Korea, Singapore and Taiwan', *Oxford Review of Economic Policy* 15(1):82–96.

Green, F., K. Mayhew and E. Molloy (2003) 'Employer Perspectives Survey', *SKOPE Research Papers.* Universities of Oxford and Warwick.

Greenwood, R. and L. Empson (2003) 'The professional partnership: relic or exemplary form of governance?' *Organization Studies* (after 1 Janusry 2003) 24(6):909–33.

Greenwood, W. [1933] (1993) *Love on the Dole.* London: Vintage.

Gregory, K.L (1983) 'Native view paradigms: multiple cultures and culture conflicts in organisations', *Administrative Science Quarterly* 28:359–77.

Grey, C. (1999) '"We are all managers now"; "we always were": on the development and demise of management.' *Journal of Management Studies* 36(5):561–85.

Grey, C. and R. French (1996) 'Rethinking management education: an introduction', in *Rethinking Management Education,* edited by R. French and C. Grey. London: Sage.

Grimshaw, D., F.L. Cooke, I. Grugulis and S. Vincent (2002) 'New technology and work practices', *New Technology, Work and Employment* 17(3):45–59.

Grimshaw, D. and M. Miozzo (2005) 'Host country and network effects: the case of US multinational computer service firms in Argentina, Brazil, Germany and the UK', Presented at 23rd International Labour Process Conference, 21st–23rd March, University of Strathclyde.

Grubb, W.N. (2003) 'What's right and what's wrong with the education gospel: vocationalism in the US (and elsewhere)', Presented at SKOPE Seminar, 30th April, University of Oxford.

Grugulis, I. (1997) 'The consequences of competence: a critical assessment of the Management NVQ', *Personnel Review* 26(6):428–44.

Grugulis, I. (2000) 'The management NVQ: a critique of the myth of relevance', *Journal of Vocational Education and Training* 52(1):79–99.

Grugulis, I. (2002) 'Emotions and aesthetics for work and labour: the pleasures and pains of the changing nature of work', in *School of Management, Salford University Working Paper*.

Grugulis, I. (2003) 'The contribution of NVQs to the growth of skills in the UK', *British Journal of Industrial Relations* 41(3):457–75.

Grugulis, I. and S. Bevitt (2002) 'The impact of Investors in People on employees: a case study of a hospital trust', *Human Resource Management Journal* 12(3):44–60.

Grugulis, I. and D. Stoyanova (2005) 'Skill and performance', Presented at 23rd International Labour Process Conference, 21st–23rd March, University of Strathclyde.

Grugulis, I. and S. Vincent (2004) 'Whose skill is it anyway? Soft skills and organisational politics', Presented at 22nd International Labour Process Conference, 5th–7th April, AIAS Amsterdam.

Grugulis, I. and A. Wilkinson (2002) 'Managing culture at British Airways: hype, hope and reality', *Long Range Planning* 35:179–94.

Grugulis, I., T. Dundon and A. Wilkinson (2000) 'Cultural control and the "culture manager": employment practices in a consultancy', *Work, Employment and Society* 14(1):97–116.

Grugulis, I., S. Vincent and G. Hebson (2003) 'The rise of the "network organisation" and the decline of discretion', *Human Resource Management Journal* 13(2):45–59.

Grugulis, I., C. Warhurst and E. Keep (2004) 'What's happening to skill', in *The Skills That Matter*, edited by C. Warhurst, I. Grugulis and E. Keep. Basingstoke: Palgrave Macmillan.

Guerrero, S. and B. Sire (2001) 'Motivation to train from the workers' perspective: example of French companies', *International Journal of Human Resource Management* 12(6):988–1004.

Guest, D. (1987) 'Human resource management and industrial relations', *Journal of Management Studies* 24(5):503–21.

Guest, D. (1992) 'Right enough to be dangerously wrong: an analysis of the "In Search of Excellence" phenomenon', in *Human Resource Strategies*, edited by G. Salaman. London and Milton Keynes: Sage and Open University Press.

Hackley, C. (2000) 'Silent running: tacit, discursive and psychological aspects of management in a top UK advertising agency', *British Journal of Management* 11(3):239–54.

Hales, C. (1999) 'Leading horses to water? The impact of decentralization on managerial behaviour.' *Journal of Management Studies* 36(6):831–51.

Hales, C. (2000) 'Management and empowerment programmes', *Work, Employment and Society* 14(3):501–519.

Hales, C. (2002) '"Bureaucracy-lite" and continuities in managerial work.' *British Journal of Management* 13(1):51–66.

Hales, C. (2005) 'Rooted in supervision, branching into management: continuity and change in the role of first-line manager.' *Journal of Management Studies* 42(3):471–506.

Hales, C.P. (1986) 'What do managers do? A critical review of the evidence.' *Journal of Management Studies* 23(1):88–115.

Hamermesh, D.S. and J.E. Biddle (1994) 'Beauty and the labour market', *The American Economic Review* 84(5):1174–94.

Hamper, B. (1992) *Rivethead: Tales from the Assembly Line*. London: Fourth Estate.

Hancock, P. and M. Tyler (2000) '"The look of love": gender and the organisation of aesthetics', in *Body and Organisation*, edited by J. Hassard, R. Holliday and H. Willmott. London: Sage.

Handy, C. (1990) *The Age of Unreason*. London: Arrow.

Hannerz, U. (1992) *Cultural Complexity: Studies in the Social Organisation of Meaning*. New York: Columbia University Press.

Hannon, E. (2005) 'Prospects for the upskilling of general workers in liberal market economies', presented at British Universities Industrial Relations Association, 7th–9th July, Northumbria University.

Harley, B. (1999) 'The myth of empowerment: work organisation, hierarchy and employee autonomy in contemporary Australian workplaces', *Work, Employment and Society* 13(1):41–66.

Harley, B. (2001) 'Team membership and the experience of work in Britain: an analysis of the WERS98 data', *Work, Employment and Society* 15(4):721–42.

Harley, B., J. Hyman and P. Thompson (2005) 'The paradoxes of participation', in *Participation and Democracy at Work: Essays in Honour of Harvie Ramsay*, edited by B. Harley, J. Hyman and P. Thompson. Basingstoke: Palgrave Macmillan.

Harrison, R.T. and C.M. Leitch (2000) 'Learning and organisation in the knowledge-based information economy: initial findings from a participatory action research case study', *British Journal of Management* 11(2):103–19.

Harvey, C. and S. Kanwal (2000) 'Self-employed IT knowledge workers and the experience of flexibility: evidence from the United Kingdom', in *Changing Boundaries in Employment*, edited by K. Purcell. Bristol: Bristol Academic Press.

Harvey-Jones, J. (1989) *Making it Happen: Reflections on Leadership*. London: Fontana.

Haskel, J. (1999) 'Small firms, contracting out, computers and wage inequality: evidence from UK manufacturing', *Economica* 66(1):1–21.

Haskel, J. and Y. Heden (1999) 'Computers and the demand for skilled labour: industry and establishment level panel evidence for the UK', *Economic Journal* 109:68–79.

Hasluck, C. (1999) 'Employment Prospects and Skill Needs in the Banking, Finance and Insurance Sector', in *Skills Task Force Research Paper*. Sudbury: DfEE.

Haworth, N. and S. Hughes (2003) 'International political economy and industrial relations', *British Journal of Industrial Relations* 41(4):665–82.

Hayes, N. and G. Walsham (2000) 'Self enclaves, political enclaves and knowledge working', in *Managing Knowledge: critical investigations of work and learning*, edited by C. Prichard, R. Hull, M. Chumer and H. Willmott. Basingstoke: Macmillan.

Hayward, G. and O. Sudnes (2000) 'Experimental learning and the work related curriculum: conceptual challenges and questions', *SKOPE Research Paper*. Universities of Oxford and Warwick.

Head, S. (2003) *The New Ruthless Economy: Work and Power in the Digital Age*. Oxford and New York: Oxford University Press.

Hebson, G. and I. Grugulis (2005) 'Gender and new organisational forms', in *Fragmenting Work: Blurring Organisational Boundaries and Disordering Hierarchies*, edited by M. Marchington, D. Grimshaw, J. Rubery and H. Willmott. Oxford University Press.

Heller, R. (1972) *The Naked Manager*. London: Barrie & Jenkins.

Heller, R. (1996) *The Naked Manager for the Nineties*. London: Warner.

Hencke, D. (2005) '700 Gate Gourmet workers ask for redundancy', *Guardian*, 12 September.

Hendry, C. (1993) 'Personnel leadership in technical and human resource change', in *Human Resource Management and Technical Change*, edited by J. Clark. London: Sage.

Heyes, J. (2001) 'Experiencing multi-skilling: evidence from the chemical industry', *Journal of Vocational Education and Training* 53(4):543–60.

Heyes, J. and A. Gray (2003) 'The implications of the national minimum wage for training in small firms', *Human Resource Management Journal*, 13(2): 76–86.

Heyes, J. and M. Stuart (1996) 'Does training matter? Employee experiences and attitudes', *Human Resource Management Journal* 6(3):7–21.

Heyes, J. and M. Stuart (1998) 'Bargaining for skills: trade unions and training at the workplace', *British Journal of Industrial Relations* 36(3):459–67.

Hill, S. (1995) 'From quality circles to total quality management', in *Making Quality Critical*, edited by A. Wilkinson and H. Willmott. London: Routledge.

Hillage, J. and J. Moralee (1996) 'The return on investors', in *Institute of Employment Studies Report*. Brighton: IES.

Hillage, J., J. Regan, J. Dickson and K. McLoughlin (2002) 'Employers Skill Survey 2002', in *Research Report*. Nottingham: DfES.

Hinings, C.R.B. and H. Leblebici (2003) 'Editorial introduction to the special issue: knowledge and professional organizations', *Organization Studies* (after 1 January 2003) 24(6):827–30.

Hirsch, W. (2004) 'Positive career development for leaders and managers', in *Leadership in Organizations: current issues and future trends*, edited by J. Storey. London and New York: Routledge.

Hirsch, W. and S. Bevan (1988) *What Makes a Manager?* Brighton: Institute of Manpower Studies, University of Sussex.

Hirschhorn, L. and J. Mokray (1992) 'Automation and competency requirements in manufacturing: a case study', in *Technology and the Future of Work*, edited by P. Adler. Oxford University Press.

Hochschild, A.R. (1979) 'Emotion work, feeling rules and social structure', *American Journal of Sociology* 85:551–75.

Hochschild, A.R. (1983) *The Managed Heart: Commercialization of Human Feeling*. Berkeley: University of California Press.

Hogarth, T. and R. Wilson (2002) 'The demand for skills in England: from product market strategies to skill deficiencies', in *SKOPE Monograph*. Universities of Oxford and Warwick.

Höpfl, H. (1992) 'The making of the corporate acolyte: some thoughts on charismatic leadership and the reality of organizational commitment', *Journal of Management Studies* 29(1):23–33.

Höpfl, H. (1993) 'Culture and commitment: British Airways', in *Case Studies in Organizational Behaviour*, edited by D. Gowler, K. Legge and C. Clegg. London: Chapman.

Höpfl, H. (2002) 'Playing the part: reflections on aspects of mere performance in the customer–client relationship', *Journal of Management Studies* 39(2):255–67.

Höpfl, H. and S. Linstead (1993) 'Passion and performance: suffering and the carrying of organisational roles', in *Emotion in Organisations*, edited by S. Fineman. London: Sage.

Hoque, K. (2003) 'All in all it's just another plaque on the wall: the incidence and impact of the Investors in People standard', *Journal of Management Studies* 40(2):543–71.

Hoque, K., S. Taylor and E. Bell (2005) 'Investors in People: market-led voluntarism in vocational education and training', *British Journal of Industrial Relations* 43(1):135–53.

Horrell, S., J. Rubery and B. Burchell (1994) 'Gender and skills', in *Skill and Occupational Change*, edited by R. Penn, M. Rose and J. Rubery. Oxford University Press.

Hull, R. (1999) 'Actor network and conduct: the discipline and practices of knowledge management', *Organization* 6(3):405–28.

Hull, R. (2000) 'Knowledge management and the conduct of expert labour', in *Managing Knowledge: Critical Investigations of Work and Learning*, edited by C. Prichard, R. Hull, M. Chumer and H. Willmott. Basingstoke: Macmillan.

Hunter, L., P. Beaumont and D. Sinclair (1996) 'A "partnership" route to human resource management', *Journal of Management Studies* 33(2):235–57.

Huselid, M. (1995)' The impact of HRM practices on turnover, productivity and corporate financial performance', *Academy of Management Journal*, 38, 635–72.

Huselid, M. and B. Becker (1996) 'Methodological issues in cross-sectional and panel estimates of the human resource-firm performance link', *Industrial Relations* 35:400–22.

Hyde, P., A. McBride, R. Young and K. Walshe (2004) 'Role redesign: introducing new ways of working in the NHS', Presented at SKOPE Workshop on Job Design, 4th May, Westwood Training Centre, Coventry.

Hyland, T. (1994) *Competence, Education and NVQs*. London: Cassell.

Hyland, T. and P. Weller (1994) *Implementing NVQs in Further Education Colleges*, Warwick University, Continuing Education Research Centre.

Hyman, J. and B. Mason (1995) *Managing Employee Involvement and Participation*. London: Sage.

Hyman, R. (1987) 'Strategy or structure: capital, labour and control.' *Work, Employment and Society* 1(1):25–55.

Ichniowski, C., K. Shaw and G. Prennushi (1997) 'The effects of human resource management practices on productivity: a study of steel finishing lines', *American Economic Review* 87:291–313.

IFF (2004) *National Employers Skills Survey 2003: Main Report*. Learning and Skills Council.

Independent (1999) 23 November.

Jackall, R. (1988) *Moral Mazes*. New York and Oxford University Press.

Jackson, P.R., C.A. Sprigg and S. Parker (2000) 'Interdependence as a key requirement for the successful introduction of teamworking: a case study', in *Teamworking*, edited by S. Procter and F. Mueller. Basingstoke: Macmillan.

James, N. (1993) 'Divisions of emotional labour: disclosure and cancer', in *Emotion in Organisations*, edited by S. Fineman. London: Sage.

James, S. and G. Hayward (2004) 'Becoming a chef', in *Balancing the Skills Equation: Key Issues and Challenges for Policy and Practice*, edited by G. Hayward and S. James. Bristol: Policy Press.

Jarvis, V., M. O'Mahoney and H. Wessels (2002) 'Product quality, productivity and competitiveness: a study of the British and German ceramic and tableware industries', in *Occasional Paper*. London: National Institute of Economic and Social Research.

Jeong, J. (1995) 'The failure of recent state vocational training policies in Korea from a comparative perspective', *British Journal of Industrial Relations* 33(3):237–52.

Jones, E.W.J. (1986) 'Black managers: the dream deferred', *Harvard Business Review* 64:84–93.

Kanter, R.M. (1977) *Men and Women of the Corporation*. London: Basic Books.

Kanter, R.M. (1985) *The Change Masters*. London and New York: Routledge.

Karreman, D. and M. Alvesson (2004) 'Cages in tandem: management control, social identity and identification in a knowledge-intensive firm', *Organization* 11(1):149–75.

Keenoy, T. and P. Anthony (1992) 'HRM: metaphor, meaning and morality', in *Reassessing Human Resource Management*, edited by P. Blyton and P. Turnbull. London: Sage.

Keep, E. (1987) 'Britain's Attempts to Create a National Vocational Educational and Training System: A Review of Progress', in *Warwick Papers in Industrial Relations*. Coventry: University of Warwick.

Keep, E. (1989) 'Corporate training strategies: the vital component?', in *New Perspectives on Human Resource Management*, edited by J. Storey. London: Routledge.

Keep, E. (1994) 'Vocational education and training for the young', in *Personnel Management*, edited by K. Sisson. Oxford: Blackwell.

Keep, E. (1999) 'UK's VET policy and the "third way": following a high skills trajectory or running up a dead end street?', *Journal of Education and Work,* 12(3), 323–46.

Keep, E. (2001) 'If it moves, it's a skill', presented at ESRC seminar on The Changing Nature of Skills and Knowledge, 3rd–4th September, Manchester.

Keep, E. and D. Ashton (2004) 'The state', Presented at SKOPE High Skills Vision Conference, 28th–29th October, Lumley Castle.

Keep, E. and K. Mayhew (1988) 'The assessment: education, training and economic performance', *Oxford Review of Economic Policy* 4(3):i–iv.

Keep, E. and K. Mayhew (1996) 'Evaluating the assumptions that underlie training policy', in *Acquiring Skills,* edited by A. Booth and D.J. Snower. Cambridge University Press.

Keep, E. and K. Mayhew (1999) 'The assessment: knowledge, skills and competitiveness', *Oxford Review of Economic Policy* 15(1):1–15.

Keep, E. and K. Mayhew (2001) 'Globalisation, models of competitive advantage and skills', in *SKOPE Research Paper.* Universities of Oxford and Warwick.

Keep, E. and J. Payne (2002) 'What can the UK learn from the Norwegian and Finnish experience of attempts at work re-organisation?' in *SKOPE Research Paper.* Universities of Oxford and Warwick.

Keep, E. and H. Rainbird (2000) 'Towards the learning organisation?' in *Personnel Management: A Comprehensive Guide to Theory and Practice,* edited by S. Bach and K. Sisson. Oxford: Blackwell.

Keep, E. and C. Stasz (2004) 'The employers', Presented at SKOPE High Skills Vision Conference, 28th–29th October, Lumley Castle.

Keep, E., K. Mayhew and M. Corney (2002) 'Review of the evidence on the rate of return to employers of investment in training and employer training measures', in *SKOPE Research Paper.* Universities of Oxford and Warwick.

Keizer, A.B. (2005) *The Changing Logic of Japanese Employment Practices: A Firm-Level Analysis of Four Industries.* Rotterdam: Erasmus Research Institute of Management.

Kenyon, R. (2005) 'Contribution to skills review', Presented at Lord Leitch Review of Skills, 28th June, London.

Kessler, I., P. Heron and S. Bach (2005) 'The modernisation of public services and workforce re-structuring: the rise of the assistant', Presented at British Universities Industrial Relations Association, 7th–9th July, University of Northumbria.

Kidder, T. (1981) *The Soul of a New Machine.* Boston, MA and Toronto: Little, Brown.

Kinnie, N., S. Hutchinson and J. Purcell (2000) 'Fun and surveillance: the paradox of high commitment management in call centres', *International Journal of Human Resource Management* 11(5):967–85.

Kirsch, J., M. Klein, S. Lehndorff and D. Voss-Dahm (2000) 'The organisation of working time in large German food retail firms', in *Flexible Working in Food Retailing: A Comparison Between France, Germany, the UK and Japan,* edited by C. Baret, S. Lehndorff and L. Sparks. London and New York: Routledge.

Kitchener, M., I. Kirkpatrick and R. Whipp (2000) 'Supervising professional work under New Public Management: evidence from an "invisible trade".' *British Journal of Management* 11:213–26.

Knights, D., F. Murray and H. Willmott (1993) 'Networking as knowledge work: a study of strategic interorganisational development in the financial services industry', *Journal of Management Studies* 30(6):975–95.

Kondo, D.K. (1990) *Crafting Selves: Power, Gender and Discourse of Identity in a Japanese Workplace*. University of Chicago Press.

Korczynski, M. (2001) 'The contradictions of service work: call centre as customer-oriented bureaucracy', in *Customer Service: Empowerment and Entrapment*, edited by A. Sturdy, I. Grugulis and H. Willmott. Basingstoke: Palgrave.

Korczynski, M. (2002) *Human Resource Management in Service Work*. Basingstoke: Palgrave.

Krueger, A. (1993) 'How computers have changed the wage structure: evidence from microdata 1984–1989', *Quarterly Journal of Economics* 108:33–60.

Kunda, G. (1992) *Engineering Culture: Control and Commitment in a High-Tech Corporation*. Philadelphia, PA: Temple University Press.

Kunda, G. and G. Ailon-Souday (2005) 'Managers, markets and ideologies: design and devotion revisited', in *Oxford Handbook of Work and Organization*, edited by S. Ackroyd, R. Batt, P. Thompson and P.S. Tolbert. Oxford and New York: Oxford University Press.

Kunda, G., S.R. Barley and J. Evans (2002) 'Why do contractors contract? The experience of highly skilled technical professionals in a contingent labour market', *Industrial and Labor Relations Review* 55(2):234–60.

Labour Force Survey (2005) *Historical Quarterly Supplement: Job-Related Training Received by Employees*. http://www.statistics.gov.uk

Lafer, G. (2004) 'What is skill?', in *The Skills That Matter*, edited by C. Warhurst, I. Grugulis and E. Keep. Basingstoke: Palgrave Macmillan.

Lam, A. (2000) 'Tacit knowledge, organisational learning and societal institutions: an integrated framework', *Organization Studies* 21(3):487–513.

Lampel, J. and J. Shamsie (2003) 'Capabilities in motion: new organisational forms and the reshaping of the Hollywood movie industry', *Journal of Management Studies* 40(8):2189–210.

Lane, C. (1987) 'Capitalism or culture? A comparative analysis of the position in the labour process and labour market of lower white-collar workers in the financial services sector of Britain and the Federal Republic of Germany', *Work, Employment and Society* 1(1):57–83.

Lane, C. (1989) *Management and Labour in Europe*. Aldershot: Edward Elgar.

Lauder, H. (2001) 'Innovation, skill diffusion and social exclusion', in *High Skills: Globalisation, Competitiveness and Skill Formation*, edited by P. Brown, A. Green and H. Lauder. Oxford University Press.

Lave, J. and E. Wenger (1991) *Situated Learning: Legitimate Peripheral Participation*. Cambridge University Press.

Leadbeater, C. (2001) 'How should knowledge be owned?', in *Managing Industrial Knowledge*, edited by I. Nonaka and D. Teece. London: Sage.

Lee, R.A. and J. Piper (1988) 'Dimensions of promotion culture in Midland Bank.' *Personnel Review* 17(6):15–24.

Legge, K. (1994) 'Managing culture: fact or fiction?' in *Personnel Management*, edited by K. Sisson. Oxford: Blackwell.

Legge, K. (1995) *Human Resource Management, Rhetorics and Realities*. London: Macmillan.

Leidner, R. (1993) *Fast Food, Fast Talk: Service Wwork and the Routinizations of Everyday Life*. Berkeley and Los Angeles: University of California Press.

Leidner, R. (1996) 'Rethinking questions of control: lessons from McDonald's', in *Working in the Service Society*, edited by C.L. Macdonald and C. Sirianni. Philadelphia, PA: Temple University Press.

Lewis, R. and R. Stewart (1958) *The Boss*. London: Phoenix House.

Littler, C.R. (1982) *The Development of the Labour Process in Capitalist Societies*. London: Heinemann.

Littler, C.R. and P. Innes (2003) 'Downsizing and de-knowledging the firm', *Work, Employment and Society* 17(1):73–100.

Littler, C.R. and P. Innes (2004) 'The Paradox of Managerial Downsizing.' *Organization Studies* (after 1 January 2003) 25(7):1159–84.

Littler, C.R., R. Wiesner and R. Dunford (2003) 'The dynamics of delayering: changing management structures in three countries.' *Journal of Management Studies* 40(2):225–56.

Lloyd, C. (1999) 'Regulating employment: implications for skill development in the Aerospace industry', *European Journal of Industrial Relations* 5(2):163–185.

Lloyd, C. and H. Newell (2000) 'Selling teams to the salesforce: teamworking in the UK pharmaceutical industry', in *Teamworking*, edited by S. Procter and F. Mueller. Basingstoke: Macmillan.

Lloyd, C. and J. Payne (2003) 'What is the "high skills society"? Some reflections on current academic and policy debates in the UK', *Policy Studies* 24(2/3):115–33.

Lloyd, C. and J. Payne (2005) 'A vision too far? mapping the space for a high skills project in the UK', *Journal of Education and Work* 18(2):165–85.

Lopez, S.H. (1996) 'The politics of service production – routine sales work in the potato chip industry', in *Working in the Service Society*, edited by C.L. Macdonald and C. Sirianni. Philadelphia, PA: Temple University Press.

Macdonald, C.L. (1996) 'Shadow mothers: nannies, au pairs, and invisible work', in *Working in the Service Society*, edited by C.L. Macdonald and C. Sirianni. Philadelphia, PA: Temple University Press.

Macdonald, C.L. and C. Sirianni (1996) *Working in the Service Society*, Philadelphia, PA: Temple University Press.

Machin, S. (2001) 'The changing nature of labour demand in the new economy and skill-biased technology change', *Oxford Bulletin of Economics and Statistics* 63:753–776.

Machin, S. and A. Vignoles (2001) *The Economic Benefits of Training to the Individual, the Firm and the Economy: The Key Issues*. London: Performance Innovation Unit.

Malinowski, B. (1922) *Argonauts of the Western Pacific: An Account of Native Enterprise and Adventure in the Archipelagoes of Melanesian New Guinea*. London: Routledge & Kegan Paul.

Mallon, M. and J. Duberley (2002) 'Managers and professionals in the contingent workforce', *Human Resource Management Journal* 10(1):33–47.

Mangham, I.L. (2004) 'Leadership and integrity', in *Leadership in Organizations: Current Issues and Key Trends*, edited by J. Storey. London and New York: Routledge.

Mangham, I.L. and M.S. Silver (1986) *Management training, context and practice*. Bath: University of Bath, School of Management.

Manley, J. (2001) 'The customer is always right? Customer satisfaction surveys as employee control mechanisms in professional service work', in *Customer Service: Empowerment and Entrapment*, edited by A. Sturdy, I. Grugulis and H. Willmott. Basingstoke: Palgrave.

Mann, S. (1999) *Hiding What We Feel, Faking What We Don't: Understanding the Role of Your Emotions at Work*. Shaftesbury: Element.

Mant, A. (1977) *The Rise and Fall of the British Manager*. London: Macmillan.

Marsden, D. (2004) 'The "network economy" and models of the employment contract', *British Journal of Industrial Relations* 42(4):659–84.

Marsden, D. and P. Ryan (1995) 'Work, labour markets and vocational preparation: Anglo-German comparisons of training in intermediate skills', in *Youth, Education and Work*, edited by L. Bash and A. Green. London: Kogan Page.

Marshall, J. (1984) *Women Managers Travellers in a Male World*. Chichester: Wiley.

Martin, G., J. Pate and P. Beaumont (2001) 'Company based education programmes: what's the pay-off for employers?' *Human Resource Management Journal* 11(4):55–73.

Martinez Lucio, M. and R. MacKenzie (1999) 'Quality management. A new form of control?' in *Employee Relations in the Public Sector: Themes and Issues*, edited by S. Corby and G. White. London and New York: Routledge and Cardiff University.

Martinez Lucio, M., S. Jenkins and M. Noon (2000) 'Management strategy, union identity and oppositionalism: teamwork in the Royal Mail', in *Teamworking*, edited by S. Procter and F. Mueller. Basingstoke: Macmillan.

Mason, G. and D. Finegold (1995) *Skills, Machinery and Productivity in Precision Metalworking and Food Processing: A Pilot Study of Matched Establishments in the US and Europe*. London: National Institute of Economic and Social Research.

Mason, G., B. Van Ark and K. Wagner (1996) 'Workforce skills, product quality and economic performance', in *Acquiring Skills*, edited by A. Booth and D.J. Snower. Cambridge University Press.

Matlay, H. (1998) 'The paradox of training in the small business sector of the British economy', *Journal of Vocational Education and Training*, 49(4), 573–89.

Matlay, H. (2002) 'Contemporary training initiatives in Britain: a small business perspective', *SKOPE Research Paper*. Universities of Oxford and Warwick.

Maume, D.J.J. (1999) 'Glass ceilings and glass escalators: occupational segregation and race and sex differences in managerial promotions', *Work and Occupations* 26(4):483–509.

Maurin, E. and F. Postel-Vinay (2005) 'The European job security gap', *Work and Occupations* 32(2):229–52.

May, T.Y.-M., M. Korczynski and S. Frenkel (2002) 'Organisational and occupational commitment: knowledge workers in large corporations', *Journal of Management Studies* 39(6):775–801.

McCabe, D. (2000) 'The team dream: the meaning and experience of teamworking for employees in an automobile manufacturing company', in *Teamworking*, edited by S. Procter and F. Mueller. Basingstoke: Macmillan.

McCartney, J. and P. Teague (2001) 'Private sector training and the organisation of the labour market: evidence from the Republic of Ireland in comparative perspective', *International Journal of Human Resource Management* 12(5):772–99.

McDowell, L. (1997) *Capital Culture: Gender at Work in the City*. Oxford: Blackwell.

McGauran, A.M. (2000) 'Vive la différence: the gendering of occupational structures in a case study of Irish and French retailing', *Women's Studies International Forum* 23(5):613–27.

McGauran, A.M. (2001) 'Masculine, feminine or neutral? In-company equal opportunities policies in Irish and French MNC retailing', *International Journal of Human Resource Management* 12(5):754–71.

McGuire, G. (2000) 'Gender, race, ethnicity and networks: the factors affecting the status of employees' network members', *Work and Occupations* 27(4):501–23.

McInerney, C. and D. LeFevre (2000) 'Knowledge management: history and challenges', in *Managing Knowledge: Critical Investigations of Work and Learning*, edited by C. Prichard, R. Hull, M. Chumer and H. Willmott. Basingstoke: Macmillan.

McKinlay, A. (2000) 'The bearable lightness of control: organisational reflexivity and the politics of knowledge management', in *Managing Knowledge: Critical Investigations of Work and Learning*, edited by C. Prichard, R. Hull, M. Chumer and H. Willmott. Basingstoke: Macmillan.

McKinlay, A. (2005) 'Knowledge management', in *Oxford Handbook of Work and Organization*, edited by S. Ackroyd, R. Batt, P. Thompson and P.S. Tolbert. Oxford and New York: Oxford University Press.

McMillan, C.J. (1996) *The Japanese Industrial System*. Berlin and New York: de Gruyter.

McNulty, T. (2002) 'Re-engineering as knowledge management: a case of change in UK healthcare', *Management Learning* 33(4):439–48.

Meek, V.L. (1988) 'Organizational culture: origins and weaknesses', *Organization Studies* 9(4):453–73.

Micklethwait, J. and A. Wooldridge (1996) *The Witch Doctors: What the Management Gurus Are Saying, Why It Matters and How to Make Sense of It*. London: Heinemann.

Miech, R.A., W. Eaton and K.Y. Liang (2003) 'Occupational stratification over the life course: a comparison of occupational trajectories across race and gender during the 1980s and 1990s', *Work and Occupations* 30(4):440–73.

Miles, R.E., C.C. Snow, J.A. Mathews, G. Miles and H.J. Coleman (2002) 'Organizing in the knowledge age: anticipating the cellular form', 280–98 in *Managing Knowledge*, edited by S. Little, P. Quintas and T. Ray. London: Sage Publications Ltd.

Mintzberg, H. (1973) *The Nature of Managerial Work*. London: Harper & Row.

Mintzberg, H. (1975) 'The manager's job: folklore and fact', *Harvard Business Review*:49–61.

Mitchell, T. (1985) 'In search of excellence versus the 100 best companies to work for in America: a question of perspectives and value', *Academy of Management Review* 10(2):350–55.

Mole, G. (1996) 'The management training industry in the UK: an HRD director's critique', *Human Resource Management Journal,* 6(1), 19–26.

Mole, G. (2004) 'Can leadership be taught?' in *Leadership in Organizations: Current Issues and Future Trends,* edited by J. Storey. London: Routledge.

Molloy, J.T. (1977) *The Woman's Dress for Success Book.* New York: Warner Bros.

Moore, W.E. (1951) *Industrial Relations and the Social Order.* London: Macmillan.

Morgan, G. (1988) *Riding the Waves of Change: Developing Managerial Competencies for a Turbulent World.* London: Sage.

Moss, P. and C. Tilly. (1996) 'Soft skills and race: an investigation into black men's employment problems', *Work and Occupations* 23(3):252–76.

Moss-Kanter, R. (1977) *Men and Women of the Corporation.* New York: Basic Books.

Mueller, F. (1994) 'Teams between hierarchy and commitment: change strategies and the "internal environment"', *Journal of Management Studies* 31(3):383–403.

Mumford, A., G. Robinson and D. Stradling (1987) *Developing Directors: The Learning Process.* Sheffield: Manpower Services Commission.

Munro, A. and H. Rainbird (2001) 'Access to workplace learning and trade union voice under different regulatory regimes: cleaning and care work', Presented at British Universities Industrial Relations Association conference, 7th–9th July, Manchester.

Murakami, T. (1997) 'The autonomy of teams in the car industry: a cross national comparison', *Work, Employment and Society* 11(4):749–58.

Murray, F.E. (2001) 'Following distinctive paths of knowledge: strategies for organisational knowledge building within science-based firms', in *Managing Industrial Knowledge,* edited by I. Nonaka and D. Teece. London: Sage.

Murray, G., J. Belanger, A. Giles and P.A. Lapointe (2002) *Work and Employment Relations in the High-Performance Workplace,* London and New York: Continuum.

National Statistics. (2005) *Labour Market Statistics,* London: National Statistics Office http://www.statistics.gov.uk

Newell, H. (2004) 'Who will follow the leader? Manager's perceptions of management development activities: an international comparison', *SKOPE Research Paper.* Oxford and Warwick: Universities of Oxford and Warwick.

Newell, S., M. Robertson, H. Scarbrough and J. Swan (2002) *Managing Knowledge Work.* Basingstoke: Palgrave.

Newell, S., H. Scarbrough and J. Swan (2000) 'Intranet and knowledge management: decentred technologies and the limits of technological discourse', in *Managing Knowledge: Critical Investigations of Work and Learning,* edited by C. Prichard, R. Hull, M. Chumer and H. Willmott. Basingstoke: Macmillan.

Newell, S., H. Scarbrough and J. Swan (2001) 'From global knowledge management to internal electronic fences: contradictory outcomes of intranet development', *British Journal of Management* 12(2):97–111.

Nickson, D., C. Warhurst, A. Witz and A.-M. Cullen (2001) 'The importance of being aesthetic: work, employment and service organisation', in *Customer Service: Empowerment and Entrapment,* edited by A. Sturdy, I. Grugulis and H. Willmott. Basingstoke: Palgrave.

Nolan, P. (2001) 'The future of work', presented at Work, Employment and Society Conference, 11th–13th September, Nottingham.

Nolan, P. and G. Slater (2003) 'The labour market: history, structure and prospects', in *Industrial Relations: Theory and Practice*, edited by P. Edwards. Oxford: Blackwell.

Nonaka, I. and H. Takeuchi (1995) *The Knowledge Creating Company: How Japanese Companies Create the Dynamics of Innovation*. New York and Oxford University Press.

Nonaka, I. and D. Teece (2001) 'Introduction', in *Managing Industrial Knowledge*, edited by I. Nonaka and D. Teece. London: Sage.

Nonaka, I., R. Toyama and N. Konno (2001) 'SECI, ba and leadership: a unified model of dynamic knowledge creation', in *Managing Industrial Knowledge*, edited by I. Nonaka and D. Teece. London: Sage.

Noon, M. (1992) 'HRM: a map, model or theory?' in *Reassessing Human Resource Management*, edited by P. Blyton and P. Turnbull. London: Sage.

Noon, M. and P. Blyton (1997) *The Realities of Work*. Basingstoke: Palgrave.

O'Dell, C. and C.J. Grayson (1998) 'If only we knew what we know: identification and transfer of internal best practices', *California Management Review* 40(3):154–74.

Ogbonna, E. (1992/1993) 'Managing organisational culture: fantasy or reality?' *Human Resource Management Journal* 3(2):42–54.

Ogbonna, E. and L.C. Harris (2002) 'Organisational culture: a ten year, two phase study of change in the UK food retailing sector', *Journal of Management Studies* 39(5):673–706.

Ogbonna, E. and L.C. Harris (2005) 'The adoption and use of information technology: a longitudinal study of a mature family firm', *New Technology, Work and Employment* 20(1):2–18.

Ogbonna, E. and B. Wilkinson (1988) 'Corporate strategy and corporate culture: the management of change in the UK supermarket industry', *Personnel Review* 17(6):10–14.

Ogbonna, E. and B. Wilkinson (1990) 'Corporate strategy and corporate culture: the view from the check-out', *Personnel Review* 19(4):9–15.

Ogbonna, E. and B. Wilkinson (2003) 'The false promise of organisational culture change: a case study of middle managers in grocery retailing', *Journal of Management Studies* 40(5):1151–78.

Oliver, J.M. and J.R. Turton (1982) 'Is there a shortage of skilled labour?' *British Journal of Industrial Relations* 20(2):195–200.

Orbach, S. (1978) *Fat Is a Feminist Issue*. Feltham: Hamlyn.

Orr, J. (1996) *Talking About Machines: An Ethnography of a Modern Job*. Ithaca, NY: IRL Press.

Ouchi, W.G. (1981) *Theory Z*. Reading, MA: Addison-Wesley.

Parker, M. (2000) *Organisational Culture and Identity*. London: Sage.

Parker, M. and J. Slaughter (1988) *Choosing Sides: Unions and the Team Concept*. Boston, MA: South End Press.

Paton, R., S. Taylor and J. Storey (2004) 'Corporate universities and leadership development', in *Leadership in Organisations: Current Issues and Key Trends*, edited by J. Storey. London and New York: Routledge.

Paules, G.F. (1991) *Dishing It Out: Power and Resistance Among Waitresses in a New Jersey Restaurant*. Philadelphia, PA: Temple University Press.

Paules, G.F. (1996) 'Resisting the symbolism of service among waitresses', in *Working in the Service Society*, edited by C.L. Macdonald and C. Sirianni. Philadelphia, PA: Temple University Press.

Payne, J. (1991) *Women, Training and the Skills Shortage*. London: Policy Studies Institute.

Payne, J. (1999) 'All Things to All People: changing perceptions of "skill" among Britain's policymakers since the 1950s and their implications', *SKOPE Research Paper*. Universities of Oxford and Warwick.

Payne, J. (2000) 'The unbearable lightness of skill: the changing meaning of skill in UK policy discourses and some implications for education and training', *Journal of Education Policy* 15(3):353–69.

Payne, J. (2004) 'What can the UK learn from the Finnish workplace development programme?' Presented at SKOPE workshop, 4th May, Westwood Training Centre.

Payne, J. (2005) 'What progress is Norway making with lifelong learning? A study of the Norwegian competence reform', *KOPE Working Papers*. Universities of Oxford and Warwick.

Peck, J. (1993) 'The trouble with TECs: a critique of the Training and Enterprise Councils initiative', *Policy and Politics* 21(4):289–305.

Penn, R. (1984) *Skilled Workers in the Class Structure*. Cambridge University Press.

Penn, R., M. Rose and J. Rubery (1994) *Skill and Occupational Change*. Oxford University Press.

People Management (2003) News, 6 September.

Performance and Innovation Unit (2001) *In Demand: Adult Skills for the 21st Century*. London: PIU, Cabinet Office.

Peters, R.S. (1973) *Philosophy of Education*, London: Oxford University Press.

Peters, T. (1987) *Thriving on Chaos*. London: Pan Books.

Peters, T. and N. Austin (1985) *A Passion for Excellence*. London: Fontana/Collins.

Peters, T. and R.H. Waterman (1982) *In Search of Excellence*. London: Harper & Row.

Pettigrew, A. (1973) *The Politics of Organisational Decision Making*. London: Tavistock.

Pettigrew, A. (1979) 'On studying organisational cultures', *Administrative Science Quarterly* 24:570–81.

Pettigrew, A. (1985) *Awakening Giant*. Oxford: Blackwell.

Pfann, G.A., J.E. Biddle, D.S. Hamermesh and C.M. Bosman (2000) 'Business success and businesses' beauty capital', *Economics Letters* 67:201–7.

Pfeffer, J. (1998) *The Human Equation; Building Profits by Putting People First*. Boston, MA: Harvard Business School Press.

Phillips, A. and B. Taylor (1986) 'Sex and skill', in *Waged Work: A Reader*, edited by Feminist Review. London: Virago.

Pierce, J.L. (1995) *Gender Trials: Emotional Lives in Contemporary Law Firms*. Berkeley: University of California Press.

Pierce, J.L. (1996) 'Reproducing gender relations in large law firms: the role of emotional labour in paralegal work', in *Working in the Service Society*, edited by C.L. Macdonald and C. Sirianni. Philadelphia, PA: Temple University Press.

Piore, M. and C. Sabel (1984) *The Second Industrial Divide: Possibilities for Prosperity*. New York: Basic Books.

Polanyi, M. (1962) *Personal Knowledge*. University of Chicago Press.

Polanyi, M. (1975) 'Personal knowledge', in *Meaning*, edited by M. Polanyi and H. Prosch. University of Chicago Press.

Pollard, S. (1965) *The Genesis of Modern Management*. London: Edward Arnold.

Pollert, A. (1981) *Girls, Wives, Factory Lives*. Basingstoke: Macmillan.

Popham, J. (1984) 'Specifying the domain of content or behaviours', in *A Guide to Criterion-Referenced Test Construction*, edited by R.A. Berk. Baltimore: Johns Hopkins Press.

Powell, W.W. (1998) 'Learning from collaboration: knowledge and networks in the biotechnology and pharmaceutical industries', *California Management Review* 40(3):228–40.

Power, M. (1997) *The Audit Society*. Oxford: Oxford University Press.

Prais, S. and K. Wagner (1985) 'Some practical aspects of human capital training: training standards in five occupations in Britain and Germany', *National Institute Economic Review* 105.

Prais, S. and K. Wagner (1988) 'Productivity and management: the training of foremen in Britain and Germany', *National Institute Economic Review* 123.

Prichard, C. (2000) 'Knowledge, learn and share! The knowledge phenomena and the construction of a consumptive-communicative body', in *Managing Knowledge: Critical Investigations of Work and Learning*, edited by C. Prichard, R. Hull, M. Chumer and H. Willmott. Basingstoke: Macmillan.

Pring, R. (2004) 'The skills revolution', *Oxford Review of Education* 30(1):105–16.

Protherough, R. and J. Pick (2002) *Managing Britannia*. Exeter: Imprint Academic.

Psoinois, A. and S. Smithson (2002) 'Employee empowerment in manufacturing: a study of organisations in the UK', *New Technology, Work and Employment* 17(2):132–48.

Purcell, J. (1979) 'A strategy for management control in industrial relations', in *The Control of Work*, edited by J. Purcell and R. Smith. London: Macmillan.

Purcell, K. (2000) 'Changing boundaries in employment and organisations', in *Changing Boundaries in Employment*, edited by K. Purcell. Bristol: Bristol Academic Press.

Purcell, K. and P. Elias (2004) 'Higher education and gendered career development', in *Researching Graduate Careers Seven Years On*. Bristol and Warwick: Employment Studies Research Unit, University of the West of England and Warwick Institute for Employment Research.

Purcell, K., P. Elias and N. Wilton (2004) 'Higher education, skills and employment: careers and jobs in the graduate labour market', in *Researching Graduate Careers Seven Years On*. Bristol and Warwick: Employment Studies Research Unit, University of the West of England and Warwick Institute for Employment Research.

Putnam, L. and D.K. Mumby (1993) 'Organisations, emotions and the myth of rationality', in *Emotion in Organisations*, edited by S. Fineman. London: Sage.

Pye, D. (1968) *The Nature and Art of Workmanship*. Cambridge University Press.

Quinn, J.B., P. Anderson and S. Finkelstein (2002) 'Managing professional intellect: making the most of the best', in *Managing Knowledge*, edited by S. Little, P. Quintas and T. Ray. London: Sage.

Raffe, D. (2004) 'Discussant', Presented at High Skills Vision Conference, 28th–29th October, Lumley Castle.

Raggatt, P. (1994) 'Implementing NVQs in colleges: progress, perceptions and issues', *Journal of Further and Higher Education* 18(1):59–74.

Raggatt, P. and S. Williams (1999) *Government, Markets and Vocational Qualifications: An Anatomy of Policy*. London: Falmer Press.

Rainbird, H. (1990) *Training Matters: Union Perspectives on Industrial Restructuring and Training*. Oxford: Blackwell.

Rainbird, H. and A. Munro (2003) 'Workplace learning and the employment relationship in the public sector', *Human Resource Management Journal* 13(2):30–44.

Rainbird, H., A. Munro and L. Holly (2004) 'Employer demand for skills and qualifications', in *The Skills That Matter*, edited by C. Warhurst, I. Grugulis and E. Keep. Basingstoke: Palgrave Macmillan.

Rainnie, A. (1988) *Employment Relations in the Small Firm*. London: Routledge & Kegan Paul.

Ram, M. (2000a) 'Investors in people in small firms: case study evidence from the business services sector', *Personnel Review* 29(1):69–91.

Ram, M. (2000b) 'Hustling, hassling and making it happen: researching consultants in a small firm context', *Organization* 7(4):657–77.

Ramanujam, V. and N. Venkatraman (1988) 'Excellence, planning and performance', *Interfaces* 18(3):23–31.

Ramsay, H. (1977a) 'Cycles of control: worker participation in sociological and historical perspective', *Sociology* 11(3):481–506.

Ramsay, H. (1977b) 'Participation: the shop floor view', *British Journal of Industrial Relations* 14:128–41.

Ramsay, H. (1997) 'Fool's gold? European works councils and democracy at the workplace', *Industrial Relations Journal* 28:314–22.

Randle, K. and A. Rainnie (1997) 'Managing creativity, maintaining control: a study in pharmaceutical research', *Human Resource Management Journal* 7(2):32–46.

Ray, T. (2002) 'Managing Japanese organizational knowledge creation: the difference', in *Managing Knowledge*, edited by S. Little, P. Quintas and T. Ray. London: Sage.

Ray, T., S. Clegg and R. Gordon (2004) 'A new look at dispersed leadership: power, knowledge and context', in *Leadership in Organizations: Current Issues and Future Trends*, edited by J. Storey. London and New York: Routledge.

Reed, M. (1984) 'Management as a social practice.' *Journal of Management Studies* 21(3).

Reed, M. (1989) *The Sociology of Management*. London: Harvester Wheatsheaf.

Reed, M. (1996) 'Expert power and control in late modernity: an empirical review and theoretical synthesis', *Organization Studies* 17(4):573–97.

Reed, M. and P. Anthony (1992) 'Professionalising management and managing professionalisation.' *Journal of Management Studies* 29(5):591–613.

Reeder, D. (1979) 'A recurring debate: education and industry', in *Schooling in Decline*, edited by G. Bernbaum. London: Macmillan.

Rees, B. and E. Garnsey (2003) 'Analysing competence: gender and identity at work', *Gender, Work and Organization* 10(5):551–78.

Reich, R. (1993) *The Work of Nations*. London: Simon & Schuster.

Reskin, B.F. and P.A. Roos (1990) *Job Queues, Gender Queues: Explaining Women's Inroads into Male Occupations*. Philadelphia, PA: Temple University Press.

Reskin, B.F., D.B. McBrier and J.A. Kmec (1999) 'The determinants and consequences of workplace sex and race composition', *Annual Review of Sociology* 25:335–56.

Rinehart, J., J. Huxley and D. Robertson (1997) *Just Another Car Factory? Lean Production and Its Discontents*. Ithaca, NY: Cornell University Press.

Ritzer, G. (1996) *The McDonalidization of Society*. Thousand Oaks, CA and London: Pine Forge Press.

Ritzer, G. and T. Stillman (2001) 'From person- to system-oriented service', in *Customer Service: Empowerment and Entrapment*, edited by A. Sturdy, I. Grugulis and H. Willmott. Basingstoke: Palgrave.

Robertson, M. and J. Swan (1998) 'Modes of organising in an expert consultancy: a case study of knowledge, power and egos', *Organization* 5(4):543–64.

Robertson, M. and J. Swan (2003) '"Control – what control?" Culture and ambiguity within a knowledge intensive firm', *Journal of Management Studies* 40(4):831–58.

Robertson, M. and J. Swan (2004) 'Going public: the emergence and effects of soft bureaucracy within a knowledge intensive firm', *Organization* 11(1):123–48.

Robertson, M., H. Scarbrough and J. Swan (2003) 'Knowledge creation in professional service firms: institutional effects', *Organization Studies* (after 1 January 2003) 24(6):831–57.

Roos, J. and G. von Krogh (1996) 'The epistemological challenge: managing knowledge and intellectual capital', *European Management Journal* 14(4):333–38.

Root, J. (1984) *Pictures of Women*. London: Pandora and Channel 4 Television.

Rose, M. (2000) 'Work attitudes in the expanding occupations', in *Changing Boundaries in Employment*, edited by K. Purcell. Bristol Academic Press.

Rose, M. (2003) 'Good deal, bad deal? Job satisfaction in occupations', *Work, Employment and Society* 17(3):503–30.

Rose, M. (2005) 'Do rising levels of qualification alter work ethic, work orientation and organizational commitment for the worse? Evidence from the UK 1985–2001', *Journal of Education and Work*, 18(2), 131–64.

Rose, M., R. Penn and J. Rubery (1994) 'Introduction, the SCELI skill findings', in *Skill and Occupational Change*, edited by R. Penn, M. Rose and J. Rubery. Oxford University Press.

Rosenthal, P., S. Hill and R. Peccei (1997) 'Checking out service: evaluating excellence, HRM and TQM in retailing', *Work, Employment and Society* 11(3):481–503.

Rothenberg, S. (2003) 'Knowledge content and worker participation in environmental management at NUMMI', *Journal of Management Studies* 40(7):1783–802.

Rowlinson, M. and S. Procter (1999) 'Organizational culture and business history', *Organization Studies* 20(3):369–96.

Roy, D. (1958) '"Banana time": job satisfaction and informal interaction', *Human Organization* 18:158–68.

Royle, T. (2000) *Working for McDonald's in Europe: The Unequal Struggle*. London: Routledge.

Rubery, J. and D. Grimshaw (2001) 'The employment changes associated with ICT: the problem of job quality', *International Labour Review* 140(2):165–92.

Rubery, J. and D. Grimshaw (2003) *The Organization of Employment*. Basingstoke: Palgrave Macmillan.

Rubery, J. and F. Wilkinson (1979) 'Notes on the nature of the labour process in the secondary sector', Presented at Low Pay and Labour Markets Segmentation Conference Papers, Cambridge.

Rubery, J., J. Earnshaw, M. Marchington, F.L. Cooke and S. Vincent (2002) 'Changing organisational forms and the employment relationship', *Journal of Management Studies* 39(5):645–72.

Rubery, J., M. Carroll, F.L. Cooke, I. Grugulis and J. Earnshaw (2004) 'Human resource management and the permeable organisation: the case of the multi-client call centre', *Journal of Management Studies* 41(7):1199–222.

Ryan, M.K. and S.A. Haslam (2005) 'The glass cliff: evidence that women are over-represented in precarious leadership positions.' *British Journal of Management* 16(1):81–90.

Sako, M. (1999) 'From individual skills to organisational capability in Japan', *Oxford Review of Economic Policy* 15(1):114–26.

Salaman, G. (1995) *Managing*. Buckingham: Open University Press.

Salaman, G. (2001) 'The management of corporate culture change', in *Human Resource Management: A Critical Text*, edited by J. Storey. London: Thomson Learning.

Salaman, G. (2004) 'Competences of managers, competences of leaders', in *Leadership in Organizations: Current Issues and Future Trends*, edited by J. Storey. London: Routledge.

Saundry, R., V. Antcliffe and M. Stuart (2005) 'Living with dinosaurs. Networks, trade unionism and 'collective' identity amongst freelance workers in the UK audio-visual sector', Presented at British Universities Industrial Relations Association, 7th–9th July, University of Northumbria.

Scarbrough, H. (1993) 'Problem-solutions in the management of information systems expertise', *Journal of Management Studies* 30(6):939–55.

Scarbrough, H. (1996a) 'Information systems for knowledge management', in *The Management of Expertise*, edited by H. Scarborough. Basingstoke: Macmillan.

Scarbrough, H. (1996b) 'Understanding and managing expertise', in *The Management of Expertise*, edited by H. Scarborough. Basingstoke: Macmillan.

Scarbrough, H. (2000) 'The HR implications of supply chain relationships', *Human Resource Management Journal* 10(1):5–17.

Scarbrough, H. and J. Swan (2001) 'Explaining the diffusion of knowledge management: the role of fashion', *British Journal of Management* 12(1):3–12.

Scase, R. and R. Goffee (1989) *Reluctant Managers their work and lifestyles*. London: Unwin Hyman.

Schein, E.H. (1985) *Organizational Culture and Leadership*. San-Francisco, CA: Jossey-Bass.

Scott, P. and A. Cockrill (1997) 'Multi-skilling in small- and medium sized engineering firms: evidence from Wales and Germany', *International Journal of Human Resource Management* 8(6):807–24.

Senker, P. (1996) 'The development and implementation of National Vocational Qualifications: an engineering case study', *New Technology, Work and Employment* 11(2):83–95.

Sennett, R. (1998) *The Corrosion of Character*. New York and London: Norton.

Sheldrake, J. and S. Vickerstaff (1987) *The History of Industrial Training in Britain*. Avebury: Gower.

Shibata, H. (2001) 'Productivity and skill at a Japanese transplant and its parent company', *Work and Occupations* 28(2):234–60.

Sisson, K. (1993) 'In search of HRM?' *British Journal of Industrial Relations* 31(2):201–10.

Sisson, K. and S. Timperley (1994) 'From manpower planning to strategic human resource management?' in *Personnel Management: A Comprehensive Guide to Theory and Practice*, edited by K. Sisson. Oxford: Blackwell.

Skills Task Force (1999) *The Second Report of the Skills Task Force*. Sheffield: DfEE.

Skuratowicz, E. and L.W. Hunter (2004) 'Where do women's jobs come from? Job resegregation in an American Bank', *Work and Occupations* 31(1):73–110.

Sloane, P. and H. Ertl (2003) 'Current challenges and reforms in German VET', Presented at Vocational Learning for the 21st Century: International Perspectives, 22nd–23rd July, Oxford.

Smircich, L. (1983) 'Studying organisations as cultures', in *Beyond Method*, edited by G. Morgan. Beverley Hills, CA and London: Sage.

Smith, A. ([1776]/1993) *The Wealth of Nations*. Oxford and New York: Oxford University Press.

Smith, A. and G. Hayton (1999) 'What drives enterprise training? Evidence from Australia', *International Journal of Human Resource Management* 10(2):251–72.

Smith, V. (1990) *Managing in the Corporate Interest: Control and Resistance in an American Bank*. Berkeley, Los Angeles and Oxford: University of California Press.

Smithers, A. (1993) *All Our Futures*. London: Channel 4 Television.

Spender, J.C. (1996) 'Making knowledge the basis of a dynamic theory of the firm', *Strategic Management Journal* 17 (Winter special issue):45–62.

Spender, J.C. and R.M. Grant (1996) 'Knowledge and the firm: overview', *Strategic Management Journal* 17 (Winter special issue):5–9.

Spenner, K.I. (1990) 'Skill: meanings, methods and measures', *Work and Occupations* 17(4):399–421.

Spilsbury, M. (2001) *Learning and Training at Work 2000* (No. 269) Nottingham: DfES.

Squires, G. (2001) 'Management as a professional discipline.' *Journal of Management Studies* 38(4):473–487.

Starbuck, W. (1993) 'Keeping a butterfly and an elephant in a house of cards: the elements of exceptional success', *Journal of Management Studies* 30(6):885–921.

Stasz, C., G. Hayward, S.-A. Oh and S. Wright (2004) *Outcomes and Processes in Vocational Learning: A Review of the Literature.* London: Learning and Skills Research Centre, RAND and SKOPE.

Stasz, C. and S. Wright (2004) *Emerging Policy for Vocational Learning in England,* London: Learning and Skills Research Centre, RAND and SKOPE.

Steedman, H. (2001) *Benchmarking Apprenticeship: UK and Continental Europe Compared.* London: Centre for Economic Performance, LSE.

Steedman, H., H. Gospel and P. Ryan (1998) *Apprenticeship: A Strategy for Growth.* London: Centre for Economic Performance, LSE.

Steedman, H., K. Wagner and J. Foreman (2003) *The Impact on Firms of ICT Skill-Supply Atrategies: An Anglo-German Comparison.* London: Centre for Economic Performance, LSE.

Steiger, T.L. (1993) 'Construction skill and skill construction', *Work, Employment and Society* 7(4):535–60.

Steinberg, R.J. (1990) 'Social construction of skill: gender, power and comparable worth', *Work and Occupations* 17(4):449–82.

Stevens, M. (1999) 'Human capital theory and UK vocational training policy', *Oxford Review of Economic Policy* 15(1):16–32.

Stewart, H. (2005) 'Bosses say school leavers can't read, write or count', *Observer,* 21 August.

Stewart, R. (1963) *The Reality of Management.* London: Heinemann.

Stewart, R. (1976) *Contrasts in Management.* Maidenhead: McGraw-Hill.

Stewart, R. (1988) *Managers and Their Jobs.* Basingstoke: Macmillan.

Stewart, T. (1997) *Intellectual Capital: The New Wealth of Organisations.* London: Nicholas Brealy.

Storey, J. (1980) *The Challenge to Management Control.* London: Kogan Page.

Storey, J. (1989) 'Management development: a literature review and implications for future research Part I: conceptualisations and practices.' *Personnel Review* 18(6):3–19.

Storey, J. (1990) 'Management development: a literature review and implications for future research Part II: profiles and contexts.' *Personnel Review* 19(1):3–11.

Storey, J. (1992) *Developments in the Management of Human Resources.* Oxford: Blackwell.

Storey, J. (2001) 'Human resource management today: an assessment', in *Human Resource Management: A Critical Text,* edited by J. Storey. London: Thomson Learning.

Storey, J. (2002) 'HR and organizational structures', in *Managing Knowledge,* edited by S. Little, P. Quintas and T. Ray. London: Sage.

Storey, J. (2004a) 'Changing theories of leadership and leadership development', in *Leadership in Organizations: Current Issues and Future Trends,* edited by J. Storey. London: Routledge.

Storey, J. (2004b) 'Signs of change: "damned rascals" and beyond', in *Leadership in Organizations: Current Issues and Key Trends,* edited by J. Storey. London: Routledge.

Storey, J. (2005) 'What next for strategic-level leadership research?' *Leadership* 1(1):89–104.

Storey, J. and E. Barnett (2000) 'Knowledge management initiatives: learning from failure', *Journal of Knowledge Management* 4(2):145–57.

Storey, J. and P. Quintas (2001) 'Knowledge management and HRM', in *Human Resource Management: A Critical Text*, edited by J. Storey. London: Thomson Learning.

Storey, J., P. Quintas, P. Taylor and W. Fowle (2002) 'Flexible employment contracts and their implications for product and process innovation', *International Journal of Human Resource Management* 13(1):1–18.

Storey, J. and G. Salaman (2004) *Managers of Innovation: Insights into Making Innovation Happen*. Oxford: Blackwell.

Strauss, A., L. Schatzman, D. Ehrlich, R. Bucher and M. Sabshin (1973) 'The hospital and its negotiated order', in *The Hospital in Modern Society*, edited by E. Friedson. New York: Free Press.

Streeck, W. (1987) 'The uncertainties of management in the management of uncertainty: employers, labour relations and industrial adjustment in the 1980s', *Work, Employment and Society* 1(3):281–308.

Streeck, W. (1992) *Social Institutions and Economic Performance: Studies of Industrial Relations in Advanced Capitalist Economies*. London: Sage.

Streeck, W. (1997) 'German capitalism: does it exist? Can It Survive?' in *Political Economy of Modern Capitalism*, edited by C. Crouch and W. Streeck. London: Sage.

Streeck, W., J. Hilber, K. van Kevalaer, F. Maier and H. Weber (1987) *The Role of the Social Partners in Vocational Education and Training in the FRG*. Berlin: CEDE-FOP The European Centre for the Development of Vocational Education and Training.

Sturdy, A. (1997) 'The consultancy process – an insecure business', *Journal of Management Studies* 34(3):389–414.

Sturdy, A. (1998) 'Customer care in a consumer society', *Organization* 5(1):27–53.

Sturdy, A. (2001) 'Servicing societies: colonisation, control, contradiction and contestation', in *Customer Service: Empowerment and Entrapment*, edited by A. Sturdy, I. Grugulis and H. Willmott. Basingstoke: Palgrave.

Sturdy, A. (2001) 'The global diffusion of customer service: a critique of cultural and institutional perspectives', *Asia Pacific Business Review* 7(3):73–87.

Sturdy, A. and Y. Gabriel (2000) 'Missionaries, mercenaries or car salesmen? MBA teaching in Malaysia.' *Journal of Management Studies* 37(7):979–1002.

Sturdy, A. and M. Korczynski (2005) 'In the name of the customer: service work and participation', in *Participation and Democracy at Work: Essays in Honour of Harvie Ramsay*, edited by B. Harley, J. Hyman and P. Thompson. Basingstoke: Palgrave Macmillan.

Swan, J. (1996) 'Professional associations and the management of expertise', in *The Management of Expertise*, edited by H. Scarborough. Basingstoke: Macmillan.

Swan, J., S. Newell and M. Robertson (1999) 'National differences in the diffusion and design of technological innovation: the role of inter-organisational networks', *British Journal of Management* 10:45–59.

Swan, J. and H. Scarbrough (2001) 'Knowledge management: concepts and controversies', *Journal of Management Studies* 38(7):913–21.

Swan, J., H. Scarbrough and M. Robertson (2002) 'The construction of "communities of practice" in the management of innovation', *Management Learning* 33(4):477–96.

Swart, J. and N. Kinnie (2003) 'Sharing knowledge in knowledge-intensive firms', *Human Resource Management Journal* 13(2):60–75.

Szulanski, G. (1996) 'Exploring internal stickiness: impediments to the transfer of best practice within the firm', *Strategic Management Journal* 17 (Winter special issue):27–43.

Tamkin, P. and J. Hillage (1997) 'Individual Commitment to Learning: Motivation and Rewards', DfEE Research Report RR11, December. Sheffield: DfEE.

Taylor, F.W. (1949) *Scientific Management*. London: Harper & Row.

Taylor, P. and P. Bain (1999) 'An assembly line in the head: work and employee relations in the call centre', *Industrial Relations Journal* 30(2):101–17.

Taylor, P. and P. Bain (2003) ''Subterranean worksick blues': humour as subversion in two call centres', *Organization Studies* 24(9):1487–509.

Taylor, P., G. Mulvey, J. Hyman and P. Bain (2002) 'Work organisation, control and the experience of work in call centres', *Work, Employment and Society* 16(1):133–50.

Taylor, S. and M. Tyler (2000) 'Emotional labour and sexual difference in the airline industry', *Work, Employment and Society* 14(1):77–96.

Teece, D. (1998) 'Capturing value from knowledge assets: the new economy, markets for know-how and intangible assets', *California Management Review* 40(3):55–79.

Teece, D. (2001) 'Strategies for managing knowledge assets: the role of firm structure and industrial context', in *Managing Industrial Knowledge*, edited by I. Nonaka and D. Teece. London: Sage.

Tengblad, S. (2004) 'Expectations of Alignment: Examining the Link Between Financial Markets and Managerial Work.' *Organization Studies* (after 1 January 2003) 25(4):583–606.

Thelen, K. (2004) *How Institutions Evolve: The Political Economy of Skills in Germany, Britain the United States and Japan*. Cambridge University Press.

Thomas, R. and D. Dunkerley (1999) 'Careering downwards? Middle managers' experiences in the downsized organisation.' *British Journal of Management* 10(2):157–69.

Thompson, G. (2005) 'Inter-firm relations as networks', in *Oxford Handbook of Work and Organization*, edited by S. Ackroyd, R. Batt, P. Thompson and P.S. Tolbert. Oxford and New York: Oxford University Press.

Thompson, M.P.A. and G. Walsham (2004) 'Placing knowledge management in context', *Journal of Management Studies* 41(5):725–47.

Thompson, P. (2003) 'Disconnected capitalism: or why employers can't keep their side of the bargain', *Work, Employment and Society* 17(2):359–78.

Thompson, P. (2004) *Skating on Thin Ice: The Knowledge Economy Myth*. Glasgow: University of Strathclyde/Big Thinking.

Thompson, P., C. Jones, D. Nickson and T. Wallace (1996) 'Internationalisation and integration: a comparison of manufacturing and service firms', Presented at The

Globalisation of Production and Regulation of Labour Conference, University of Warwick.

Thompson, P. and D. McHugh (2002) *Work Organisations: A Critical Introduction*. Basingstoke: Palgrave.

Thompson, P. and T. Wallace (1996) 'Redesigning production through teamworking', *International Journal of Operations and Production Management* 16(2):103–18.

Thompson, P., C. Warhurst and G. Callaghan (2000) 'Human capital or capitalising on humanity? Knowledge, skills and competencies in interactive service work', in *Managing Knowledge: Critical Investigations of Work and Learning*, edited by C. Prichard, R. Hull, M. Chumer and H. Willmott. Basingstoke: Macmillan.

Thompson, P., C. Warhurst and G. Callaghan (2001) 'Ignorant theory and knowledgeable workers: Interrogating the connections between knowledge, skills and services', *Journal of Management Studies* 38(7):923–42.

Thompson, P., T. Wallace, J. Flecker and R. Ahlstrand (1995) 'It ain't what you do, it's the way that you do it: production organisation and skill utilisation in commercial vehicles', *Work, Employment and Society* 9(4):719–42.

Tijdens, K. and B. Steijn (2005) 'The determinants of ICT competencies among employees', *New Technology, Work and Employment* 20(1):60–73.

Townsend, M. (2005) 'BA makes a meal of food fight', *Observer*, 14 August.

Toynbee, P. (2005a) 'Free-market buccaneers', *Guardian*, 19 August.

Toynbee, P. (2005b) 'Don't shrug off low pay', *Guardian*, 26 August.

Tran, M. (2005) 'Gate Gourmet to offer redundancy money', *Guardian*, 26 August.

Tregaskis, O. (2003) 'Learning networks: power and legitimacy in multinational subsidiaries', *International Journal of Human Resource Management* 14(3):431–47.

Trethewey, A. (1999) 'Disciplined bodies: women's embodied identities at work', *Organization Studies* 20(3):423–50.

Trist, E.L. (1974) 'The structural presence of post-industrial society', in *Man-Made Futures*, edited by N. Cross, D. Elliott and R. Roy. London: Hutchinson.

Tsoukas, H. (1996) 'The firm as a distributed knowledge system: a constructionist approach', *Strategic Management Journal* 17 (Winter special issue):11–25.

Tsoukas, H. (2002) 'Introduction: knowledge based perspectives on organisations, situated knowledge, novelty and communities of practice', *Management Learning* 33(4):419–26.

Tsoukas, H. and E. Vladimirou (2001) 'What is organisational knowledge?' *Journal of Management Studies* 38(7):973–93.

Turner, H.A. (1962) *Trade Union Growth, Structure and Policy*. London: George Allen & Unwin.

Un, C.A. and A. Cuervo-Cazurra (2004) 'Strategies for knowledge creation in firms', *British Journal of Management* 15(1):27–41.

Useem, M. and C. Gager (1996) 'Employee shareholders or institutional investors? When corporate managers replace their stockholders.' *Journal of Management Studies* 33(5):613–32.

Vallas, S.P. (1990) 'The concept of skill: a critical review', *Work and Occupations* 17(4):379–98.

Vallas, S.P. (2003) 'Rediscovering the colour line within work organisations: the 'knitting of racial groups' revisited', *Work and Occupations* 30(4):379–400.

van den Bosch, F.A.J. and H.W. Volberda (1999) 'Managing organisational knowledge integration in the emerging multimedia complex', *Journal of Management Studies* 36(3):379–98.

Van Maanen, J. (1991) 'The smile factory: work at Disneyland', in *Reframing Organisational Culture*, edited by P. Frost, L. Moore, M. Luis, C. Lundberg and J. Martin. California: Sage.

Vernon, G. and M. Rogers (2005) 'Joint regulation and productivity', Presented at British Universities Industrial Relations Association, 7th–9th July, Northumbria University.

Vincent, S. and I. Grugulis (2005) 'Strategy, contracts and control in the management of government IT Work', in *The Future of Work*, edited by P. Stewart. Oxford University Press.

Visser, J. (1998) 'Two cheers for corporatism, one for the market: industrial relations, wage moderation and job growth in the Netherlands', *British Journal of Industrial Relations* 36(2):269–92.

von Krogh, G. (1998) 'Care in knowledge creation', *California Management Review* 40(3):133–53.

Vroom, V.H. and A.G. Jago (1988) *The New Leadership: Managing Participation in Organizations*. Englewood Cliffs, NJ: Prentice-Hall.

Vroom, V.H. and P.W. Yetton (1973) *Leadership and Decision Making*. University of Pittsburgh Press.

Walker, R.M. (2004) 'Innovation and Organisational Performance: Evidence and a Research Agenda', in *AIM Research Working Paper Series*. London: AIM, London Business School.

Wallis, E. and M. Stuart (2005) 'Workplace training and the performance of low-skilled public sector employees', Presented at Second International Conference on Training, Employability and Employment, 21st–23rd September, Prato.

Walsh, C. (2005) 'Cheapside', *Observer*, 28 August.

Walton, R.E. (1985) 'From control to commitment in the workplace', *Harvard Business Review*:77–84.

Warhurst, C. and D. Nickson (2001) *Looking Good, Sounding Right*. London: Industrial Society.

Warhurst, C. and P. Thompson (1998) 'Hands, hearts and minds: changing work and workers at the end of the century', in *Workplaces of the Future*, edited by P. Thompson and C. Warhurst. London: Macmillan.

Watson, T.J. (1977) *The Personnel Managers*. London: Routledge & Kegan Paul.

Watson, T. J. (1994) *In Search of Management*. London: Routledge.

Webster, J. (1990) *Office Automation: The Labour Process and Women's Work in Britain*. New York and London: Harvester Wheatsheaf.

Weeks, J. (2004) *Unpopular Culture: The Ritual of Complaint in a British Bank*. Chicago and London: University of Chicago Press.

Weierter, S.J.M. (2001) 'The organization of charisma: promoting, creating, and idealizing self', *Organization Studies* 22(1):91–115.

Wellington, C.A. and J.R. Bryson (2001) 'At face value? Image consultancy, emotional labour and professional work', *Sociology* 35(4):933–46.

Wensley, R. (1999) 'Product strategies, managerial comprehension and organisational performance', *Oxford Review of Economic Policy,* 15(1), 33–42.

Werr, A. and T. Stjernberg (2003) 'Exploring management consulting firms as knowledge systems', *Organization Studies* (after 1 January 2003) 24(6):881–908.

Whalen, J. and E. Vinkhuyzen (2000) 'Expert systems in (inter)action: diagnosing document machine problems over the telephone', in *Workplace Studies: Recovering Work Practice and Information Systems Design*, edited by C. Heath, J. Hindmarsh and P. Luff. Cambridge University Press.

Wharton, A.S. (1996) 'Service with a smile: understanding the consequences of emotional labour', in *Working in the Service Society*, edited by C.L. Macdonald and C. Sirianni. Philadelphia, PA: Temple University Press.

Whitley, R. (1984) 'The fragmented nature of management studies: reasons and consequences.' *Journal of Management Studies* 21(3):331–48.

Whitley, R. (1989) 'On the nature of managerial tasks and skills: their distinguishing characteristics and organisation.' *Journal of Management Studies* 26(3):209–24.

Whitley, R. (2003) 'The institutional structuring of organizational capabilities: the role of authority sharing and organizational careers.' *Organization Studies* (after 1 January 2003) 24(5):667–95.

Whyte, W.H. (1963) *The Organisation Man*. Harmondsworth: Penguin.

Wickens, P. (1987) *The Road to Nissan: Flexibility, Quality, Teamwork*. London: Macmillan.

Wilkinson, A. (1998) 'Empowerment', in *International Encyclopaedia of Business and Management: The Handbook of Human Resource Management*, edited by M. Poole and M. Warner. London: International Thomson Publishing.

Wilkinson, A. (2001) 'Empowerment', in *Contemporary Human Resource Management*, edited by T. Redman and A. Wilkinson. London: Financial Times Prentice Hall.

Wilkinson, A. and H. Willmott (1995) *Making Quality Critical*, London: Routledge.

Williams, C.L. (1992) 'The glass escalator: hidden advantages for men in the 'female' professions', *Social Problems* 39:253–67.

Willmott, H.C. (1984) 'Images and ideals of managerial work: a critical examination of conceptual and empirical accounts.' *Journal of Management Studies* 21(3):349–68.

Willmott, H. (1993) 'Strength is ignorance; slavery is freedom: managing culture in modern organisations', *Journal of Management Studies* 30(4):515–52.

Winch, G. and E. Schneider (1993) 'Managing the knowledge-based organisation: the case of architectural practice', *Journal of Management Studies* 30(6):923–37.

Wolf, A. (1995) *Competence-Based Assessment*. Buckingham and Philadelphia, PA: Open University Press.

Wolf, A. and R. Silver (1986) 'Work based learning: trainee assessment by supervisors', in *Research and Development Series*. Sheffield: Manpower Services Commission.

Wood, M. (2005) 'The fallacy of misplaced leadership.' *Journal of Management Studies* 42(6):1101–21.

Wray-Bliss, E. (2001) 'Representing customer service: telephones and texts', in *Customer Service: Empowerment and Entrapment*, edited by A. Sturdy, I. Grugulis and H. Willmott. Basingstoke: Palgrave.

Wright, M. and P.K. Edwards (1998) 'Does teamworking work and, if so, why? A case study in the aluminium industry', *Economic and Industrial Democracy* 19:59–90.

Wright, S. and G. Hayward (2003) 'VET policy and participation: the English patient', Presented at Vocational Learning for the 21st Century: International Perspectives, 22nd–23rd July, Oxford.

Wright Mills, C. (1956) *White Collar: The American Middle Classes*. New York: Oxford University Press.

Young, M. (2001) 'Conceptualising vocational knowledge', presented at Joint Network/SKOPE/TLRP International Workshop, 8th–10th November, Sunley Management Centre, University College Northampton.

Zahra, S.A. and I. Filatotchev (2004) 'Governance of the entrepreneurial threshold firm: a knowledge-based perspective', *Journal of Management Studies* 41(5):885–97.

Zaleznik, A. (1992) 'Managers and leaders: are they different?' *Harvard Business Review*:126–35.

Zhou, J. and J.M. George (2001) 'When job satisfaction leads to creativity: encouraging the expression of voice', *Academy of Management Journal* 44(4):682–96.

Index

Notes: b = box, **bold** = extended discussion or heading emphasised in main text.

recruitment (*cont.*)
  'homosocial reproduction' (Moore)   119,
    141
  'players' versus 'purists'   76b
  triumph of style over substance   76b
Red Lobster restaurant chain   98
redundancy/redundancies   6, 11, 41, 52,
    57, 125, 147, 148
  France   40–1
Reed, M.   150, 158
  'entrepreneurial professions'   165
  management 'social and political activity'
    138
Reeder, D.S.   80
Rees, B.   82, 84
regional development associations   55
regional groupings   172
Registrar General's classification   25
regulated (educational) approach   36, 37,
    38, 40
regulation   36, 51–2, 116
  locus   103
  'supports skill development'   52
regulations
  resistance   21
Reich, R.   50, 167
repeat orders   30
replaceability   169
reputation   59, 88, 139b, 140
reputational capital   149
research and development   13, 44, 52, 157,
    178, 179
  Reading University   50
research institutes/laboratories   49, 181
researchers   158
resistance   99, 102, **108–11**, 114, 129–30
  debtors   104b
Reskin, B.F.   89
respect   95, 111, 139b
responsibility   16, 43, 91, 102, 124, 145,
    147, 152, 154
  devolved 43
restaurants   12, 22, 94, 97, 98, 153, 181
  down-market   79–80, 100, 111
  fast food   103, 142, 168
restrictive practices   66
restructuring   125, 146, 147, 148, 149
retail sector   6, 46, 49, 50, 64, 66, 68, 85,
    93b, 97, 98, 147

retraining   40, 86, 182
revenue targets
  personal and divisional   160
rewards and sanctions   116
rhetoric   ix, 123, 134, 138
  gulf with reality   x, 126, 127, 140, 158,
    165, 184, 185
  leadership   145
risk   2, 139b, 141, 146, 147, 152, 176
Robertson, M.   160
Robertson, M., *et al.* (2003)   74b, 158,
    160
Rogers, M.   51
Roos, J.   156
Roos, P.A.   89
Rosenthal, P., *et al.* (1997)   126
'Route' (down-market American restaurant
    chain)   100, 101, 111, 112, 114
routine operative jobs   178
routinisation   22, 24, 25, 165, 166, 168,
    184
Roy, D.   12, 130
Royle, T.   20b, 21
Rubery, J.   i, 27, 32, 44, 46
Rubery, J., *et al.* (2004)   29–30
rules   143, 151
rules of game   76b
Russia   45b

Sabel, C.   175
Sakamoto, A.   50, 51
Salaman, G.   73, 135
salaries   83
salary premia   45
sales   80–1, 90, 99, 100, 101, 106, 170
sales staff   83, 113, 127, 138
  contacts   159
sales targets   84, 105
salesmanship   80–1
samizdat   110
Sarajevo   153b
satisfaction surveys   100
Sayles, L.R.   140
Scarbrough, H.   i, 168, 169, 176
Scase, R.   137–8
Schneider, E.   158
school caretakers   27
school-leavers   47, 58, 75

work (*cont.*)
  'not organised on sectoral basis' 63–4
  old economy 182
  optimistic predictions (corrective) 185
  part-time 141
  petty subdivision 185
  professional 165
  real world 166
  realities 92
  regimented practices 19, 20b, 21
  rhetoric versus reality 185
  skilled 15
  social aspects 163
  status and content 'politically determined' 30b
  transformed into labour 103
  unskilled 24
work design 18, 28, 35, 70, 83, 154, 186
  interplay with skills possessed by workers, 23
work experience 48b
work intensification 78, 121, 126, 186
Work of Nations (Reich, 1993) 50
work organisation 42b, 92, 176
work processes 158, 170
work rates 19
work reorganisation 11
Work Skills in Britain (Felstead *et al.*, 2002) 23–4
work structures 187
work–effort bargain 13
work–life balance 180
workers ix, 1, 2, 3, 4, 8, 9, 18, 22b, 44, 45, 73b, 117, 118, 155, 170, 185, 187
  bargaining power 90
  clerical 8b
  commitment 10
  defence of 'skilled' status 25, 26, 71, 183
  dehumanised 21
  'empowerment' 125–6
  experienced/expert 7, 89
  full-time 28
  highly-skilled 52, 53
  knowledgeable 167, 181
  knowledgeable (risk of quitting organisation) 159
  low-paid 39, 46

  low-skilled/unskilled 27, 28, 39, 46, 178
  'maze bright' (Jackall) 82, 140
  minority ethnic 85–6
  moral character 181
  poorly paid 46, 51, 166, 178
  'rational' 92
  redefine the work that they do 109, 114
  semi-skilled 26, 27
  skilled 5, 11, 29, 31, 37, 73, 48, 95, 157, 181
  skilled replaced with unskilled (Taylorism) 19
  temporary 5
  well-paid 95
  well-trained 7
  young 5, 43, 51, 69
  see also employees
workforce 13, 31, 62, 160, 167, 171, 178, 179, 184
working conditions 81, 168, 180
working with emotions **94–6**
working from home 21
working hours 18, 21, 52, 83, 102, 119, 121, 161, 186
working life 27b, 49, 184, 187
workload 147
'workmanship of certainty' (Pye) 21
'workmanship of risk' 21
workplace 5, 8, 13, 14, 30, 31, 34, 38, 41b, 61, 62, 69, 72, 73b, 90, 103, 111, 130, 141, 143, 158, 168, 180, 181, 184, 185
  'contested terrain' 10
  multiple cultures 127
  segregated 28
  soft skills **76–9**
  unitarist versus pluralist perspectives **9**
workplace development 49
Workplace Employee Relations Survey 178
workplace governance 33
workplace life x
workplace organisation
  criteria (Lloyd and Payne) 187
works committee 40–1
works councils 40, 42, 47